MARVEL

GREATEST
COMICS

100 COMICS
THAT BUILT A UNIVERSE

Senior Editor Cefn Ridout
Senior Art Editor Clive Savage
Production Editor Marc Staples
Senior Production Controller Louise Minihane
Managing Editor Sarah Harland
Managing Art Editor Vicky Short
Publisher Julie Ferris
Art Director Lisa Lanzarini
Publishing Director Mark Searle

First published in Great Britain in 2020 by
Dorling Kindersley Limited One Embassy Gardens,
8 Viaduct Gardens, London SW11 7BW
A Penguin Random House Company

DK, a Division of Penguin Random House LLC
20 21 22 23 24 10 9 8 7 6 5 4 3 2
004–316463–Oct/2020

A CIP catalogue record for this book
is available from the British Library.
ISBN 978-0-24141-005-9

Printed in China

ACKNOWLEDGEMENTS

DK would like to thank Melanie Scott and Stephen "Win" Wiacek for
their text and expertise; Joe Quesada for his Foreword; Sana Amanat, Tom Breevort,
Dan Buckley, C. B. Cebulski, Peter David, Al Ewing, Wil Moss, Ryan Penagos,
Bill Rosemann, Kelly Thompson, Mark Waid, Jordan D. White and Chip Zdarsky for their
expert commentaries; Brian Overton, Caitlin O'Connell, Jeff Youngquist and Joe Hochstein
at Marvel, and Mike Siglain and Nachie Marsham at Disney for vital help and advice;
Mark Penfound for the cover design; David Fentiman for editorial assistance;
Stefan Georgiou, Chris Gould and Marc Staples for design assistance;
Jennette ElNaggar for proofreading; and Vanessa Bird for creating the index.

For the curious

www.dk.com

MARVEL

GREATEST COMICS

— ⊛ —

100 COMICS
THAT BUILT A UNIVERSE

Written by Melanie Scott and
Stephen "Win" Wiacek

Contents

Foreword

Joe Quesada

I work at Marvel.

Seriously, twenty plus years later and I still need to pinch myself every time I say that.

Over those years, I've had the great privilege of collaborating with some of the most imaginative minds on the planet, creating characters and stories that now live within the most unimaginable place on earth, The Marvel Universe.

This 100-issue marvelous, mystery tour, is going to take you careening from 1939's *Marvel Comics* #1 all the way to 2018's *Avengers* #6. Are you buckled up? You better be because you're about to read stories that have not only become the foundation of today's modern-day Marvel, but more importantly, the road map to its future

As much as The Marvel Universe has always faced forward, True Believer, it's never been without a keen sense of legacy, and those who laid the earliest foundations. A foundation that's been fortified by successive generations of writers and artists. Creators, whom themselves have become as legendary as our most hallowed hall of heroes. From Stan Lee to Roy Thomas, from Jack Kirby to John Buscema, all the way to today's modern Marvel masters, that lineage is clear. So clear that when I began my career at Marvel, I could feel the weight of its rich history, but found comfort knowing that I was standing on the shoulders of giants. Yes, giants, giants larger than the largest Celestial, giants who eat Galactus for dinner.

Don't believe me?

Look at some of these stories. Stan Lee and Jack Kirby dominate this book, as they should. When Lee and Kirby got together, they created an explosion of creativity that has never been equaled. Just look at how many issues of Fantastic Four alone are on this list. And then there are all those inspired firsts—the first appearances of the X-Men, the Avengers, and Iron Man, for instance. Personally, I am glad to see *Fantastic Four* #51 here. Some of the best

artwork of Kirby's life—aided and abetted by the magic of Lee's words—tells an emotional story about the Thing. And in the same issue, Reed Richards crosses dimensions to discover the Negative Zone in a crazy Kirby collage. I mean seriously, you can't make this stuff up!

A-ha! Gotcha, someone did, Stan and Jack!

And as if that's not enough, imagine this if you can: sharing space on the comic racks at the *same time* was Lee and Steve Ditko's work on *Amazing Spider-Man*. Has there ever been a character, more human, more relatable, and more important than Peter Parker? And has there ever been a sequence as perfect as Spidey's desperate, heroic bid to free himself from the wreckage of Doc Ock's lair in *Amazing Spider-Man* #33? You would be hard-pressed to find it.

These 1960s stories were just the beginning, the spark that ignited a gamma blast of future storytelling without rival. Tales of love, loss and heroism in the face of it as told in *Daredevil* #181 and *X-Men* #137. A gothic love affair for the ages between Thanos and Death in *Infinity Gauntlet* #1. And perhaps Marvel's most humanistic story of the modern era, *Marvels* #1, which through the painted lens of Alex Ross, and the words of Kurt Busiek, perfectly captures the heart and soul of the man on the street, watching as Marvel history unfolds around him.

And yes, I'll be honest, of course, this list won't be perfect for everyone... actually, I know it won't be perfect for anyone. Every tried and true Marvelite has their own list, and I'm sure we missed one or two (or a dozen) of your favorites. But that's all part of the fun, isn't it? So, let the debates begin!

Maybe we'll just have to publish a second, third and fourth volume of these bad boys until we get it right.

See ya in the funnybooks,

Joe Quesada, *Marvel Executive Vice President and Creative Director*

Introduction

One of the world's best known and beloved brands, Marvel now ranks alongside multimedia monoliths such as Disney, Apple, and Google. A modern entertainment powerhouse, it dominates film, TV, comics, toys, and games. Yet this wasn't always so. In 1957, after nearly 20 years as a comic publishing titan and innovator of early Super Hero sagas, tough economic conditions and the draconian Comics Code Authority—introduced after US Senate Hearings into the harmful effects of comics on young minds—reduced Timely/Atlas, Marvel's previous incarnations, to a shoestring operation. Constrained to a handful of titles, the company followed then popular genres such as humour, war, western,

and science fiction, all heavily influenced by movies and television trends. However, disruptive change was around the corner.

Although its history harks back to 1939, Marvel Comics really began in the Fall of 1961, when the diminished publisher tested a recently revived fad for Super Heroes with its own tentative entry. Thanks to sharp writing and captivating art, *Fantastic Four* #1 was an instant hit, sparking follow-up titles and characters sharing an increasingly interconnected and recognizable universe.

Thanks to editor-writer Stan Lee, innovation remained high, especially after securing one of the industry's greatest artists and conceptualizers—Jack Kirby. Success was confirmed with the addition

of Steve Ditko—a relative newcomer who would become a unique driving force in comics. Fronting an expanding bullpen of veteran creators and fresh young talent, they ushered in a Marvel Age of Comics.

Now a confident House of Ideas, the freedom that creators enjoyed translated into booming sales as Marvel transitioned from genre tales to predominantly Super Hero stories. Under the guiding lights of Lee, Kirby, and Ditko, collaboratively devised, complex heroes and villains, and interwoven stories changed the comics-reading experience, blazing a trail for the rest of the industry to follow.

In an era where Super Heroes bestride visual media, it's hard to believe that for much of the 20th century comic books

were considered an inferior, disposable medium. This was exacerbated by lingering concerns about the possible harm comics do to impressionable readers. Wiser, more tolerant, heads have prevailed since then, mostly thanks to the quality of the material once so earnestly denigrated. However, if you still have to convince skeptics about comics' merit, which stories could change their minds, especially with over eight decades of comic books to choose from? The obvious answer is the very best ones—Marvel's greatest comics!

An enduring age of Marvels
Marvel has been at the forefront of Super Hero storytelling, from their heyday in the 1940s (left) to dominating 21st-century entertainment (below).

Clearly, these comics must be engaging, well-crafted, and visually striking, but for a company that has always prided itself on high standards and innovative thinking that's simply not enough. To make their mark, these singular stories or pivotal moments within extended storylines must also be significant, marking crucial events that have changed Marvel history: key debuts, deaths, triumphs, and defeats. The stories may also serve to place an appropriate spotlight on a particular creator's or creative team's finest hour. Ultimately, these stories must be truly memorable, groundbreaking, and inspiring. The kind you return to time and again, and are eager to show your friends.

In this book you will find 100 chronologically organised "must-read" comics and a Directory of honorable mentions. These are the venerable pioneers, radical upstarts, and future classics. The selection is based on commonly agreed standards as well as personal taste, and is supported with expert, cogent commentary from a panel of Marvel insiders and eminent creators. Invariably, you may not agree with every inclusion or omission, and this selection is not wholly definitive, since every week sees new, potentially deserving comics join the canon. That said, future editions of *Marvel Greatest Comics* may well see your favorites included as the Marvel Universe unceasingly expands. ∎

Panelists

Sana Amanat

Marvel's Vice President of Content and Character Development, Sana Amanat is the co-creator and editor of Marvel's first comic book series to star a Muslim female Super Hero, the Hugo Award-winning *Ms. Marvel*. She has also edited other innovative titles including *All-New Hawkeye*, *Captain Marvel and The Carol Corps* and *Elektra*.

Tom Brevoort

A veteran editor and currently Marvel's Senior Vice President of Publishing, Tom Brevoort has overseen hit titles such as *New Avengers*, *Civil War*, *Fantastic Four*, and *Marvel #1000/#1001*, as well as inventive miniseries like *Deadline* and *The Daily Bugle*. In 1997, he won an Eisner Award for Best Editor and edited the Eisner Award-winning *Fantastic Four: Unstable Molecules*.

Dan Buckley

President of Marvel Entertainment, Dan Buckley is a longtime publisher of Marvel Comics, having previously headed up the print, animation, and digital divisions of Marvel Worldwide, and has also been president of TV, publishing, and brand.

C. B. Cebulski

Marvel Comics' Editor in Chief C. B. Cebulski is a seasoned comic book writer and editor, best known for his work on titles such as *Marvel Fairy Tales*, *Mystic Arcana: Fire*, *Legion of Monsters: Morbius, the Living Vampire*, *Runaways*, and the miniseries *Loners*, *X-Infernus*, and *War of Kings: Darkhawk*.

Peter David

A legendary writer of comic books, novels, TV, films, and video games, Peter David's most notable Marvel work includes an award-winning 12-year stint on *Incredible Hulk*, and acclaimed runs on *She-Hulk*, *X-Factor*, and *X-Force*, for which he won a GLAAD Media Award. He wrote the video game *Spider-Man: The Edge of Time*, and cowrote the *New York Times* bestseller *Amazing Fantastic Incredible*—Stan Lee's graphic novel memoir.

Al Ewing

British comic book writer Al Ewing's diverse array of Marvel titles includes the critically lauded *Immortal Hulk*, as well as *Guardians of the Galaxy*, *Rocket*, *Contest of Champions*, *Loki: Agent of Asgard*, *Mighty Avengers*, *New Avengers*, *Ultimates*, *Valkyrie: Jane Foster*, and *You Are Deadpool*. He also masterminded and contributed to the celebratory anthology *Marvel #1000*.

Wil Moss

Senior Editor at Marvel Comics, Wil Moss' recent work includes runs on *Thor*, *Black Panther*, *Immortal Hulk*, and *Valkyrie: Jane Foster*. He has also worked on the praised *Vision* miniseries, as well as *Howard the Duck*, *Astonishing Ant-Man* and *New Avengers*.

Ryan Penagos

Vice President and Creative Executive of Marvel's New Media Group, Ryan Penagos, aka Agent M, hosts the long-standing weekly podcast/vodcast *This Week in Marvel*, and co-hosts *The Pull List*, which previews Marvel Comic's upcoming weekly releases.

Bill Rosemann

Vice President and Head of Creative at Marvel Games, Bill Rosemann has spent more than two decades immersed in the Marvel Universe as a comics writer and editor. He helped to revive *The Guardians of the Galaxy* in 2008, and has worked across countless top tier Marvel titles including *Amazing Spider-Man* and *Avengers*.

Melanie Scott

British editor and writer of a wide range of non-fiction publications on comic books, Scott's work includes *Marvel Black Widow: Secrets of a Super-spy*, *Ultimate Marvel*, *Marvel Avengers Ultimate Guide*, *Marvel Movie Collection*, and the *Marvel Ultimate Fact Book*.

Kelly Thompson

Novelist and prolific comic book writer, Kelly Thompson has worked on numerous Marvel titles, the most prominent being the 2018 relaunch of *Captain Marvel*, and the Eisner Award nominated *Hawkeye*, not to mention well-received runs on *A-Force*, *Jessica Jones*, *Captain Marvel and the Carol Corps*, *Mr. & Mrs. X*, *Uncanny X-Men*, *Deadpool*, and *Black Widow*.

Mark Waid

A perennially popular comic book writer, Waid's many Marvel comics include celebrated runs on *The Amazing Spider-Man*, *Fantastic Four*, *X-Men*, *Captain America*, *S.H.I.E.L.D.*, *Daredevil*, *Avengers*, *Champions*, and *Doctor Strange*. In 2012, Waid won Eisner and Harvey Awards for Best Writer for the relaunched *Daredevil* series. He also garnered enormous praise for his "in-world" chronicling of Marvel's 80-year history in the *History of the Marvel Universe* miniseries.

Jordan D. White

Senior Editor Jordan D. White currently oversees Marvel Comics' line of *X-men* titles. His previous work includes stints on *Hulk* and *Hercules* (2008–2011), and he has managed Marvel's *Star Wars* comics since their relaunch in 2015.

Stephen "Win" Wiacek

Wiacek is a veteran British journalist, writer, and editor on several comic book related publications, such as *The Marvel Book*, *Marvel Year By Year*; *Ultimate Marvel*, *Marvel Black Panther Ultimate Guide*, and *Marvel Fact Files*. From 1997–2007, he was chairman of the UK Comics Creators Guild, and manages the graphic novel review blog *Now Read This*.

Chip Zdarsky

A pen-name for Canadian comic book writer-artist Steve Murray, whose expanding list of Marvel credits includes *Howard the Duck*, *Spider-Man: Life Story*, *Star-Lord*, *Peter Parker: The Spectacular Spider-Man*, *Marvel Two-in-One*, *Invaders*, *Daredevil*, and *X-Men/Fantastic Four*. In 2016, he won a Harvey Award for *Howard the Duck*, and an Eisner Award and a Shuster Award for *Peter Parker: The Spectacular Spider-Man*.

Marvel Comics #1
October 1939

> *"This is the book that started it all. The sophisticated anti-hero character that has so defined Marvel to this day was introduced in its very first issue with Namor."*
>
> **Dan Buckley**

Publisher	Martin Goodman
Cover artist	Frank R. Paul
Writers	Carl Burgos (The Human Torch), Bill Everett (The Sub-Mariner), Paul Gustavson (The Angel), Al Anders (The Masked Raider), Art Pinajian as Tomm Dixon (Jungle Terror), Raymond Gill (Burning Rubber), Bob Byrd and Ben Thompson (Adventures of Ka-Zar the Great)
Pencilers, inkers	Carl Burgos (The Human Torch), Bill Everett (The Sub-Mariner), Paul Gustavson (The Angel), Al Anders (The Masked Raider), Art Pinajian as Tomm Dixon (Jungle Terror), Sam Gilman (Burning Rubber), Ben Thompson (Adventures of Ka-Zar the Great)

After a shaky start, the fledgling comic book publishing industry had become a bona fide moneymaker, with many established and start-up companies seeking to grab a piece of the action. By 1939, dozens of publishers were striving to create and own the "Next Big Thing," including pulp fiction publisher Martin Goodman, whose newly launched Timely Publications scored big with its initial offering, the anthology title *Marvel Comics*. Released in October 1939, *Marvel Comics #1*'s initial 80,000 print run swiftly sold out, and Goodman rushed out a second printing. Unfamiliar with comics, Goodman hired Lloyd Jacquet's "comics shop" Funnies Inc., freelance packagers who produced comic book material for publishing companies. Goodman would begin hiring his own staff soon after the runaway success of Marvel Comics.

Goodman reportedly favored the heroes Ka-Zar and The Angel as breakout features, however, neither appealed to kids as much as the anarchic fire and water antiheroes Human Torch and Namor, the Sub-Mariner. The super-powered misfits stole the show in this landmark issue, which may have been a little rough around the edges and hastily thrown together, but still exploded with raw action and engaging drama.

The issue led with Carl Burgos' Human Torch, a humanoid who ignites into a blazing fireball when exposed to air. Entombed in concrete, he escapes to unwittingly imperil humanity and is exploited by a gang boss as a terror-weapon. When the crime lord's scheme backfires, the hapless and innocent Torch becomes a fugitive: a misunderstood, flaming Frankenstein's monster.

Bill Everett's Sub-Mariner details how Prince Namor comes from an aquatic race living under the South Pole, which had been decimated by American undersea exploration a generation ago. Dispatched to spy upon them, Sub-Mariner's mother, Fen, fell in love with and had a son by one of the surface-world interlopers. Now, 20 years later, Namor is hungry for revenge on the air-breathers—which he exacts by attacking New York City.

Crafted by Paul Gustavson, the Angel dressed in tights and cape, but in reality was just an athletic, smart, tough guy, albeit able to cast huge angelic shadows! Not the greatest aid to battling monsters and madmen, but Angel more than managed. In his debut adventure, as befits his pulp hero influences, he ruthlessly cleans up New York's crime syndicate the Six Big Men. The Angel would go on to become a Golden Age stalwart and decades later was revived and revitalized in Ed Brubaker and Steve Epting's 2009-2010 miniseries *The Marvels Project*.

More derivative, lesser lights patterned on popular comic strips and fiction filled out the rest of the issue. Framed cowboy Jim Gardley becomes The Masked Raider to dispense six-gun justice in Al Anders' competent western mystery, before gentleman adventurers Ken Masters and Tim Roberts make their only appearance

in Tomm Dixon's (aka Art Pinajian's) "Jungle Terror" as adventurers searching for cursed diamonds in the Amazon.

Ray Gill's prose piece—a staple of early comics—recounted racing car melodrama "Burning Rubber" preceding the jungle "Adventures of Ka-Zar the Great," which began Ben Thompson's comics adaptation of Bob Byrd's pulp novel *King of Fang and Claw*. John Rand and his wife crash in the Belgian Congo and their son, David, grows up in jungle splendor, as brother to Zar, King of Lions. Young David's idyllic life is shattered when an explorer murders his father, leaving young David yearning for vengeance.

The Human Torch and Sub-Mariner were instant favorites, but most of the remaining characters were gradually

replaced as super heroic alternatives were dreamed up. Most rival comics publishers managed only one superstar, if any, at the outset. Within a year, the fire and water wonders would historically clash in the skies above Manhattan. Despite its success, Goodman altered the title to *Marvel Mystery Comics* with the second issue, but the cosmetic change (possibly to align the comic book with the company's pulp titles) had no overall impact on the public, who avidly seized upon its elemental heroes because they offered something novel and exciting. The Human Torch and Sub-Mariner would become the foundations of Timely's early success, and when Captain America debuted, he completed an irresistible triumvirate dubbed "the Big Three." ▪

Marvel Mystery Comics #9
July 1940

> "It set the template for the eventual Marvel Universe, a world in which all of the assorted heroes and villains live together in the same shared space."
>
> **Tom Brevoort**

Editor in chief	Joe Simon
Cover artists	Bill Everett, Alex Schomburg
Writers	Bill Everett, Carl Burgos, John Compton, Ray Gill
Pencilers, inkers	Bill Everett, Carl Burgos
Letterer	Bill Everett
Editor	Joe Simon

…what's your solution?
At the dawn of the comic book industry, with narrative rules still being established, there was little thought for fiction's "fourth wall." The final page of *Marvel Mystery Comics* #9 appealed to readers to resolve the stalemate between the elemental foes.

The hybrid offspring of an Atlantean princess and an American explorer, Namor, the Sub-Mariner is a being of immense strength and near invulnerability, who is able to fly above and thrive below the waves. He was created by Bill Everett and became one of the comic book superstars of the Golden Age. His popularity was rivalled only by another extraordinary outsider, the Human Torch, an android who could burst into flame, fly, and wield fire. Created by Carl Burgos, the Torch was a Super Hero, when not working as a New York cop under the pseudonym Jim Hammond. Both Namor and the Torch debuted in *Marvel Comics* #1 (October 1939), which became *Marvel Mystery Comics* from its second issue. Yet their appeal was such that they soon gained solo titles and, in a deft marketing move, were positioned as instinctive, unflinching adversaries.

At the time, each Super Hero inhabited their own discrete world, but in *Marvel Mystery Comics* #8 (June 1940), Bill Everett had Namor attack New York City only to be driven away by its fiery defender. But the real surprise came as their duel continued in the Human Torch section of the same issue, crafted by Carl Burgos. The chapter closed on a cliff-hanger and a teaser for "The Battle of the Comic Century! Fire vs. Water—A Fight to the Finish!" in the next issue. *Marvel Comics* #9 would become the memorable main act of a classic three-issue clash that would set the standard for Super Hero showdowns.

The eagerly awaited rematch in *Marvel Mystery Comics* #9 was touted like a heavyweight title fight. The expanded 22-page clash was a team effort from Bill Everett, Carl Burgos, John Compton, and Raymond Gill. It picks up where the previous issue left off, with the Torch driving off Namor when he attempts to destroy the George Washington Bridge. Their battle rages across the city, from the Statue of Liberty to beneath the Hudson River, with no clear victor. The Torch even tries to incapacitate his foe with chlorine gas but fails, and once more the fight ends in deadlock. Fans had to wait another month for the somewhat anticlimactic single-page wrap-up in the subsequent issue. Manhattan policewoman Betty Dean—Jim Hammond's colleague and occasional romantic interest for Namor—remonstrates with them both, before brokering a truce of sorts.

Despite its inconclusive result, the battle electrified readers who could now look forward to any of their favorite characters appearing in adventures together. It also confirmed the publishers' belief that what kids really wanted were staggering battles between their leading stars. This all occurred in the months before the US became involved in World War II, and although Namor and the Torch became grudging allies against the Nazis, they still clashed in repeat bouts throughout the 1940s, as befitting their inimical elemental nature. ▪

MARVEL COMICS Presents

THE HUMAN TORCH VERSUS THE SUB-MARINER

IN THE BATTLE OF THE COMIC CENTURY!

22 PAGES OF SIZZLING BLAZING ACTION!

By Bill Everett and Carl Burgos with John Compton

START NOW ON THE NEXT PAGE →

Battle of the Century
The confrontation between Sub-Mariner and the Human Torch was nonstop, brutal, and deviously imaginative. As well as their own powers, the combatants employed chemical weapons, super-scientific technology, and military hardware. This clash became the template for all future Marvel star battles: arrogance leading to misunderstanding and violence but with neither side ever confirmed as victor or defeated.

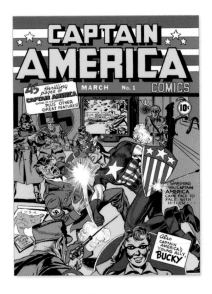

Cover artist	Jack Kirby
Writers	Joe Simon, Jack Kirby, Ed Herron
Pencilers	Jack Kirby, Joe Simon
Inkers	Al Liederman, Joe Simon, Jack Kirby
Letterer	Howard Ferguson
Editor	Joe Simon

Captain America Comics #1
March 1941

"Set squarely in the real world events of World War II, here we witnessed the birth of America's most patriotic Super Hero, with a classic cover that no one could ignore."

C. B. Cebulski

By the end of 1940, the Golden Age of comics was in full swing, with rival publishers trying to outdo each other to produce the next iconic hero of the medium. Also in full swing was the war in Europe, which Americans looked upon with increasing concern. Many favored isolationism and were unwilling to send their young people to fight and die in a conflict on the other side of the ocean. However, others saw involvement in the war as a moral imperative.

Two young Jewish men, Joe Simon and Jack Kirby, were at that time working for Timely Comics (later Marvel). Simon created a hero clad in the stars and stripes who could take the fight to the Nazis in the pages of a comic book and show America that war was the right thing to do. This hero carried a shield, also emblazoned with quintessentially American colors and symbols, and was named Captain America. In *Captain America Comics #1*, this shield was in the triangular "heater" style but, due to its similarity to a shield used by another hero called the Shield, was changed to the now iconic round version for Cap's second outing.

In the early '40s, patriotism was running high in America, and Simon and Kirby believed that a hero embodying that principle would sell comic books. Kirby brought Simon's hero to life on the page in an unforgettable way, with dynamic art that rendered action sequences more exciting than ever before. Motion lines imbued every punch and gunfight with drama. Publisher Martin Goodman liked what he saw and gave the go-ahead for Captain America to debut in his own title rather than as part of an anthology, which was more customary at the time.

The first issue introduced Captain America to the world, establishing parts of his origin that would remain canon even after his Silver Age revival. He was Steve Rogers, a wannabe soldier deemed too puny for active service but selected to be transformed into a Super-Soldier using a top-secret formula. The experiment's success was immediately followed by the killing of its key scientist by a foreign agent and the destruction of the serum. This made Cap the only one of his kind, rather than the first of many. The comic also depicted President Roosevelt, who was himself trying to make the case for involvement in the war, giving his blessing to the Super-Soldier project.

Steve Rogers' secret did not last long in the story, as his heroic identity was discovered by curious young army mascot James Buchanan "Bucky" Barnes. Not only did Cap decide to trust Bucky to keep his secret, but he even took him on as a crime-fighting partner. Also debuting in the issue was the villainous Red Skull, although this Red Skull was not the German Johan Shmidt but rather an unscrupulous American industrialist.

Star-spangled symbol
At a time when the US was not yet committed to entering WWII, portraying Captain America as the embodiment of the nation fighting Nazi villains was an overtly political act on the part of the comic's creators.

Captain America Comics #1 hit the stands in December 1940 and was simultaneously hugely popular and somewhat controversial. The cover famously featured Captain America punching Adolf Hitler in the face, openly casting a real-life political leader as a comic book villain. The memorable cover helped the issue sell around a million copies, but its message was not welcomed by isolationists. There were protests outside Timely's New York offices, and Simon and Kirby were reportedly even given police protection. The question of isolationism would be settled a year later when the Japanese attacked Pearl Harbor and Germany declared war on the US. Now the US was in the fight for real, and Captain America and Bucky could do their bit to raise morale as their stories were read by military personnel overseas and their anxious families back home.

Captain America took his place as one of Timely's "Big Three" alongside the android Human Torch and Namor, the Sub-Mariner. After Simon and Kirby's departure from Timely about a year after Cap's debut, young editor Stan Lee took over the reins of the star-spangled hero's comic. Although the title dipped in popularity after the war ended, Captain America's 1960s resurrection and membership of the Avengers superteam saw to it that he would become a fixture in the top echelons of Marvel's heroes. ∎

Super-Soldier

Steve Rogers was not born with super-powers—on the contrary, he was too weak to enlist in the army. This humble starting point made him hugely relatable to ordinary readers, who were able to daydream that one day they, too, might acquire super-strength through some miracle of science.

Editor in chief	Stan Lee
Cover artists	Jack Kirby, Steve Ditko
Writers	Stan Lee, Larry Lieber
Penciler	Jack Kirby
Inker	Dick Ayers
Colorist	Stan Goldberg
Letterer	Ray Holloway
Editor	Stan Lee

We can be heroes!
While some uncanny creatures returned—due to popular demand—the ordinary folk, decent kids, or noble citizen scientists who thwarted most pre-Marvel monsters seldom made a career out of defeating the unknown and vanished into obscurity.

Tales to Astonish #13
November 1960

"If you could have foreseen in 1961 that an alien tree monster named Groot would eventually become a household name, you should be buying more lottery tickets."

Mark Waid

Although rightly lauded with making comic book Super Heroes more realistic and accessible after the success of *Fantastic Four* in 1961, Marvel has also wisely maintained close ties with the outlandish sagas of cosmic calamity and alien invasion that immediately preceded and often informed them. In recent years, that relationship has paid big dividends, not only by enriching the Marvel Comics Universe, but also the Marvel Cinematic Universe.

As the 1950s closed, publisher Martin Goodman's Atlas Comics line was reduced to a shadow of its former self by a perfect storm of problems that contributed to a dramatic downturn in comic sales. These included a widespread public censorship crusade incited by the alarmist claims of child psychologist Dr. Frederic Wertham (and the subsequent Senate hearings), the unstoppable rise of "free" entertainment through the medium of television, and a severe new distribution deal limiting Atlas' comics output to eight titles a month.

Editor Stan Lee softened the blow by making the most of their small range of bimonthly anthology comics and by closely following genre trends in humor, romance, westerns, and science fiction, as enjoyed in movie theaters and drive-in screens and, ironically, television across America. His greatest asset was Jack Kirby, a visionary, immensely talented, and prolific artist, bursting with plenty of his own ideas. At the time, the world around them was gripped in a Cold War-fueled, atomic B-movie monster craze, so Lee, Kirby, and the equally imaginative and gifted artist Steve Ditko happily capitalized on the zeitgeist in titles such as *Strange Worlds*, *Journey into Mystery*, *Strange Tales*, *Tales of Suspense*, and *Tales to Astonish*.

In a near ceaseless procession of short, inspirational comic stories, dauntless, canny, or simply misfit human beings confronted and outsmarted a succession of bizarre aliens, mad scientists, the occasional ghost or sorcerer (since it was the early years of the Comics Code Authority, any depiction of the supernatural was frowned upon), and, of course, a bestiary of preposterous and monstrous beings.

These fantastical tales were hugely popular, immensely entertaining, and

strikingly illustrated. When Super Heroes began their sweeping takeover of comic books, many monsters became a valuable resource for recycling names and plots. Weird wonders like the stone man Thorr, the radioactive mutant known as Magneto, a (Molten) Man-Thing; and even a Hulk (later retrofitted as an actual Incredible Hulk foe, Xemnu the Titan) had their monikers transplanted to new characters. Some were even dropped wholesale into the Marvel Comics Universe as villains, such as the always-in-demand dragon Fin Fang Foom, the Abominable Snowman, shadowy warlord Kra, and missing link Gorgilla.

None, though, have had quite the success or evolutionary journey of would-be alien conqueror Groot. Predating the birth of the Marvel Age by exactly one year, and written by Stan Lee and his brother Larry Lieber, "I Challenged Groot! The Monster from Planet X" is the perfect example of a solid-gold formula. Leading off a quartet of terrific yarns in *Tales to Astonish* #13— the others being "I found the Abominable Snowman!," "My Friend is Not Quite

Human!," and "I found the Hidden World!")—"Groot" is rendered with moody, thrilling art from the pen and brush of Jack Kirby and Dick Ayers. The story details how a studious biologist in rural America saves humanity from a rapacious walking tree. The arrogant, floridly erudite alien can animate all forms of wood—living or dead—and is too hard for human weapons to harm. Intent on stealing Earth cities and their inhabitants to act as slaves on his own distant world, the imperious Groot is brought low by a cunning application of lowly termites!

Under a later generation of fans-turned-creators, Groot finally entered mainstream continuity: battling the Hulk (*Incredible Hulk Annual* #5, November 1976), joining Nick Fury's monster squad Howling Commandos, and ultimately teaming up with a new Guardians of the Galaxy during the "Annihilation Conquest" event. Now displaying a decidedly monosyllabic vocabulary, the former extraterrestrial villain has become a true champion and top drawer in movies, TV animation, games, toys, and, of course, wondrous comics stories. ∎

Roots of evil
The paranoid Cold War era of atomic stockpiles, space races, and flying saucer scares was a fertile environment for imaginative dramatists like Lee and Kirby. Readers were always apprehensive: primed for uncanny events and imminent invasions, eager to be enthralled or scared by a parade of horrors, but ultimately thrilled by the inevitable triumph of honest, smart men and women of honor.

YOU'VE TURNED INTO **MONSTERS**... BOTH OF YOU!! IT'S THOSE RAYS! THOSE TERRIBLE COSMIC RAYS!

NOW I KNOW WHY I'VE BEEN FEELING SO WARM! LOOK AT **ME**!! THEY'VE AFFECTED ME, TOO! WHEN I GET EXCITED I CAN FEEL MY BODY BEGIN TO BLAZE!

I'M LIGHTER THAN AIR!! I CAN **FLY**!! LOOK... I **CAN FLY**!!

MINUTES LATER, JOHNNY STORM'S FLAME SUBSIDED AND HE LANDED NEAR THE OTHER THREE! SILENTLY THEY WATCHED THE SMALL FIRE HE HAD STARTED IN THE UNDER BRUSH BURN ITSELF OUT!! SILENTLY THEY WERE EACH OCCUPIED WITH THEIR OWN STARTLING THOUGHTS!

WE'VE **CHANGED**! **ALL** OF US! WE'RE **MORE** THAN JUST HUMAN!

LISTEN TO ME, **ALL** OF YOU! THAT MEANS **YOU** TOO, BEN! TOGETHER WE HAVE MORE POWER THAN ANY HUMANS HAVE EVER POSSESSED!

YOU DON'T HAVE TO MAKE A SPEECH, BIG SHOT! WE UNDER-STAND! WE'VE GOTTA **USE** THAT POWER TO HELP MANKIND, RIGHT?

RIGHT, BEN, RIGHT!

I'M CALLING MYSELF **THE HUMAN TORCH**-- AND I'M WITH YOU ALL THE WAY!

SAME GOES FOR ME... **THE INVISIBLE GIRL**!

THERE'S ONLY **ONE** STILL MISSING... BEN!!

I AIN'T BEN ANYMORE-- I'M WHAT SUSAN CALLED ME--**THE THING**!!

AND I'LL CALL MYSELF... **MISTER FANTASTIC**!!

AND SO WAS BORN "THE FANTASTIC FOUR!!" AND FROM THAT MOMENT ON, THE WORLD WOULD NEVER AGAIN BE THE SAME!!

Fantastic Four #1
November 1961

" ...marks the turning point between the comic book industry that was and the one that was to come.... It's the first step on a larger journey that led to a wider and more colorful universe. "

Tom Brevoort

Editor in chief	Stan Lee
Cover artists	Jack Kirby, Dick Ayers
Writer	Stan Lee
Penciler	Jack Kirby
Inkers	George Klein, Christopher Rule
Colorist	Stan Goldberg
Letterer	Artie Simek
Editor	Stan Lee

◀ All four one
Although seemingly derivative in content, the style and tone of the Fantastic Four's first appearance instantly differentiates the team from previous Super Heroes. The emotional intensity is harsh and uncompromising, the men constantly squabble, even if Sue Storm's attempt to play peacemaker usually cools things down. And her brother, Johnny, the youngest team member, is no obedient boy scout, but a hot-headed kid with perhaps the greatest and certainly most flamboyant power, guaranteeing immediate reader identification and gratification.

As a general rule, "different" doesn't necessarily mean "better," but at the time of its launch, the *Fantastic Four* was like no other comic book on the market, and readers responded to it eagerly. After seeing the success of a rival company's new Super Hero team title, publisher Martin Goodman urged his nephew, Stan Lee, to develop a group of new super-powered characters for Marvel. The result took fans by storm. It wasn't the powers; they'd all been seen since the beginning of the medium. It wasn't the costumes; they didn't have any until the third issue. It was writer-editor Stan Lee's instantly relatable characters and sharp sense of drama, combined with artist Jack Kirby's bold visuals and compelling storytelling that connected. Quickly relocated from fictitious "Central City" to a recognizable real-world setting—Manhattan—four imperfect, prickly individuals banded together out of tragedy, disaster, and necessity to face the fantastic.

In June 1957, after a series of setbacks—including closing his own distribution arm to sell his titles through another company that went bust overnight—Goodman's vast comics enterprise, Atlas Comics, had been reduced to publishing a mere handful of titles. The comics division could afford to release only eight titles a month, which editor Stan Lee finessed by producing 16 bimonthly titles in a wide variety of genres. Although operating on a shoestring, Lee had two huge advantages over his competitors: Jack Kirby and Steve Ditko. Both were fan-favorite artists and phenomenal creative talents in their own right, adept at many genres and always seeking to push their artistic limits. From 1957, Kirby and Ditko had elevated science fiction, western, supernatural mystery, romance, and war titles with quality work, and both were ready for a change. So, in 1961, when Stan Lee restarted Super Heroes for Goodman's new company, Marvel, the stars aligned.

After tapping Kirby to draw the title, Lee felt they needed something to distinguish it from the run-of-the-mill costumed capers of the past. At first glance, *Fantastic Four* #1 appeared a little familiar, containing a trio of distinct tales featuring four fractious misfits battling weird beasts and a deranged madman— tried and tested scenarios used in the company's mainstay science fiction anthologies such as *Strange Tales* or *Journey into Mystery*. However, starring in the raw, thrilling, adventure romp for the whole issue were regular returning characters—a unifying, sales-boosting continuity was born.

Concocted by Lee and Kirby, with inks by George Klein and Christopher Rule, *Fantastic Four* #1 was passionate, vivid comic book excitement unlike anything young readers had seen before.

The all-too-human, constantly bickering group—before and after the team's incredible metamorphosis—and familiar locations struck a chord with readers, changing comic books forever.

From the outset, we are thrown into the middle of the action. There's no preamble or slow buildup, but a dramatic, fast-paced introduction to the main protagonists, responding to a strange flare exploding over the city. Capturing their, and most onlookers', attention is maverick scientist Reed Richards, who has summoned his fiancée, Susan Storm, their friend Ben Grimm, and Sue's teenaged brother Johnny. As they come together from different city locales, we see that the Fantastic Four are highly unusual people boasting uncanny powers. When they finally meet up, Richards gravely explains that a fearful task awaits them.

However, before we learn the nature of that task, an interleaved flashback reveals how these individuals gained their amazing abilities. Fearful that the Soviets might win the Space Race, Reed Richards convinces his friends to help commandeer a spaceship he'd designed, overruling Grimm's concerns that it had inadequate shielding against cosmic rays. The veteran test pilot is right, and radiation leaks into

Hidden depths
Even Marvel's first Super Villain, the Mole Man was complex. A twisted genius who conquered an incredible lost world, he was also a tragic figure warped by loneliness and persecution.

the ship, radically transforming the quartet and sending their craft crashing back to Earth. Freeing themselves from the wreckage, Reed discovers that his body has become elastic, Sue fades from sight, Johnny bursts into living flame, and Ben has been devolved into a leathery-

scaled brute. Shock and revulsion triggers an ill-tempered brawl between the four, but after coming to their senses, they vow to use their powers to benefit humankind. Prepared to live their heroic lives in public, Reed adopts the name Mr. Fantastic, Sue signs on as the Invisible Girl, Johnny calls himself the Human Torch, and Ben becomes the Thing.

The origin flashback concluded, the following tale returns to the main story. In "The Fantastic Four meet the Mole Man!," we discover the cause of Reed Richards' unease. He has deduced that the colossal horrors dragging atomic factories beneath the earth come from remote Monster Island. Here, the reluctant teammates uncover "The Mole Man's Secret!," confronting a human outcast ruling an astonishing underground realm of strange beasts, and thwart his plans for global conquest.

The bold storytelling shows Lee and Kirby were unafraid to flout dated Super Hero conventions. Yet, before long, the rest of the comic industry would take its cues from the innovations seen here. The action is gripping, the pacing relentless, and the characters wholly engaging. This landmark comic book achieves the aim of all great fiction: it leaves you wanting much more. ■

Where monsters dwell ▶
Throughout his career, Jack Kirby had proved himself a master of action and mood, inspired by the movies he watched during his infrequent downtime. The B-movie monster craze of the 1950s allowed him to transfer that inspiration to countless comics pages. With *Fantastic Four* #1, Kirby found the perfect opportunity to marry monstrous creatures and sensational Super Heroes with unforgettable verve and power.

Man or monster?
Stan Lee's modern-day interpretation of the Frankenstein story, a troubled monster made flesh, was brought to life by artist Jack Kirby, although the Hulk's signature green hue would not appear until the second issue. Kirby perfectly captured the contrast between mild-mannered, humane Bruce Banner and the mighty, brutish Hulk.

Incredible Hulk #1
May 1962

> ❝Lee and Kirby create the Hulk, and like Frankenstein, cannot control their creation. He'll last six chaotic issues—but the character refuses to die... and will never be tamed.❞
>
> **Al Ewing**

Editor in chief	Stan Lee
Cover artists	Jack Kirby, George Roussos
Writer	Stan Lee
Penciler	Jack Kirby
Inker	Paul Reinman
Letterer	Artie Simek
Editor	Stan Lee

In 1962, following the triumph of *Fantastic Four*, the pressure was on editor Stan Lee to come up with a new character for Marvel Comics. Lee had noticed from the fan mail rolling into Marvel HQ that the Thing was the most popular member of the Fantastic Four, and astutely surmised it was because fans identified with individuals who were less than perfect. He decided to create another character along similar lines, a super-strong being who could appear menacing but also carry an air of tragedy.

Lee would ultimately draw not only on his own creations for inspiration but also from classic literature. A longtime fan of Frankenstein, Lee believed that the monster created by Mary Shelley's eponymous scientist was not a villain but an unfortunate victim simply trying to make his way in the world. The Marvel editor also wanted his character to change back and forth between his monstrous and human identities, along the lines of Robert Louis Stevenson's Dr. Jekyll and Mr. Hyde. Lee tried to come up with a name that would capture the essence of a dangerous brute and settled on "the Hulk." He took his idea

to Jack Kirby, the artist he felt was best suited to create a singular look that would make the Hulk a fan favorite within the nascent Marvel pantheon.

By the early 1960s, Kirby had been in the comics business for decades, during which time he had demonstrated his talents across a wide range of genres. He had established himself as the go-to artist for science fiction and fantasy at Marvel and its predecessor, Atlas Comics: the artist who could bring monsters to life. However, unlike his previous creations Groot and Fin Fang Foom, Kirby's Hulk could not be just a monster—he had to make the creature inherently sympathetic to readers, with his humanity still clearly present.

The artist had shown in his trailblazing work on *Fantastic Four* that he was exceptional when it came to depicting relatable characters with real human emotions. *Incredible Hulk #1* exemplifies Kirby's ability to combine boundless imagination with a flair for creating intriguing characters in the unlikeliest scenarios. Hulk had an intimidating appearance and was enormously powerful, yet it was obvious that he was also at the mercy of his impulses.

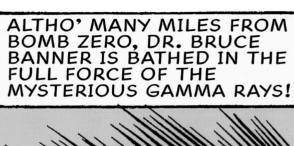

Adding to the challenge of making a hero out of a monster, Stan Lee added a teenage sidekick, a trope he had expressed some dislike for in the past, with the intention of proving that it could be done well. Rick Jones, pivotal to the Hulk's origin story, would stick around and provide an effective foil for the improbable hero without being "simpy." Jones would also go on to feature strongly in early *Avengers* comic books, and become a sidekick to Captains America and Mar-Vell.

Incredible Hulk #1 was published in May 1962. The first order of business in the issue was to reveal how the Hulk was created. In the desert, nuclear physicist Dr. Bruce Banner is preparing to test a gamma bomb, the inner workings of which only he knew. As the test is about to start, Banner sees teenager Rick Jones drive into the blast zone and rushes to save him before the bomb is detonated. Banner arrives on the scene in time to push Rick into a trench and stop the blast from harming him, but he is unable to jump in himself before he is overwhelmed by gamma rays. That night, with Rick as the solitary, horrified witness, Banner transforms into a hulking, immensely strong form—the Hulk is born.

Lee had wanted Hulk to have a distinctive skin tone that would distinguish him from ordinary humans and picked gray as a shade he hoped would bring drama to the character's appearance. However, as soon as he held the printed copy of *Incredible Hulk* #1 in his hands, Lee realized he had made a mistake. The four-colour printing process did not seem able to render gray consistently—in some panels it was pale, and in others almost black. Lee decided that he needed to forget about gray, and change Hulk's hue for the next issue. He finally settled on green as an eye-catching, easy-to-print color that was not commonly seen in other characters.

Although the initial series *Incredible Hulk* ended after six issues, the character found new life as a founding member of the Avengers. His solo stories also continued in the *Tales to Astonish* anthology title. Now he has become one of the most recognizable and popular Marvel heroes (or antiheroes), having reached a wider audience through a successful TV show and several cinematic outings. From a storytelling perspective, the enduring dramatic appeal of the Hulk, on the page and screen, is that while he can be heroic he often gets out of control causing more problems than he solves. And not even one of the smartest men on the planet, Bruce Banner, knows for sure what the Hulk will do when he's in the driver's seat. ■

THE WORLD SEEMS TO STAND STILL, TREMBLING ON THE BRINK OF INFINITY, AS HIS EAR-SPLITTING SCREAM FILLS THE AIR ...!

Atomic blast
The Hulk is born... Dr. Bruce Banner is struck by gamma rays, later discovering that they will trigger his continual, terrifying transformation into the superhumanly strong but volatile being known as the Hulk. Gamma radiation and experimental atomic bomb testing played on the real fears of an early 1960s readership, at a time when the Cold War was in its hottest phase. Over the years, gamma radiation would go on to spawn a host of Marvel heroes and villains, including the Abomination, the Leader, She-Hulk, and Amadeus Cho as the Totally Awesome Hulk.

Editor in chief	Stan Lee
Cover artists	Jack Kirby, Steve Ditko
Writer	Stan Lee
Penciler, inker	Steve Ditko
Colorist	Stan Goldberg
Letterer	Artie Simek
Editor	Stan Lee

Amazing Fantasy #15
August 1962

> **"** The famed "with great power, must also come great responsibility" is said by the narrator rather than a character. But it became the lesson Spidey carried with him forever, not to mention it gets 301 million hits on Google. **"**
>
> **Peter David**

The amazing Spider-Man was a long shot from the start. Publisher Martin Goodman wasn't sold on the character but was happy enough to feature him in a low-selling title such as *Amazing Fantasy*. Editor and lead writer Stan Lee, however, had other, bigger ideas. He decided to try something unique in comic books: an unglamorous, underappreciated young Super Hero, whose powers came from a creepy household pest. With Lee signing up to write the comic, he needed a sympathetic artist to create a distinctive visual style for his novel idea. His choice of artist—Steve Ditko—was inspired, and their collaboration brought to vivid life one of the most recognized and enduring comic book characters of all time.

Like the character he would help to create, Steve Ditko was quiet and unassuming, but his work was highly imaginative, subtle, and singular. His plots were innovative, meticulously polished, and often shaded with warmth and gentle humor. A feast of quirky and sometimes oddly disquieting detail, his stories and art explored the contrary qualities of human nature, where he found heroism and wickedness in equal measure. After years of crafting well-received mystery tales with Stan Lee, Ditko was rewarded with his own title. Converted from the generic monster magazine *Amazing Adventures*, *Amazing Adult Fantasy*

was an all-Ditko vehicle, featuring weird understated yarns, in contrast to Jack Kirby's grand epics with their devious aliens and rampaging monsters. Ditko's stories, often devised and plotted by him, increasingly featured sly, witty vignettes of magic, mystery and imagination.

Although never less than entertaining, *Amazing Adult Fantasy* had been slowly losing traction in the world of comics ever since the return of costumed heroes. Lee and Kirby had responded to the sea change with the Fantastic Four and the Incredible Hulk, but there was no indication of the renaissance to come when the soon-to-be-cancelled *Amazing Fantasy* #15 debuted a new, menacing Super Hero. Moreover, while Spider-Man grabbed the limelight—and the cover—which was penciled by Kirby and inked by Ditko, and occupied the first half of the comic book, it was business as usual for the rest of the issue. The subsequent pages boasted three short suspense tales by Lee and Ditko: "The Bell-Ringer!," "Man in the Mummy Case!," and "There Are Martians Among Us!"

The unheralded comics revolution came in just 11 captivating pages as "Spider-Man!" details the tragedy of brilliant high-school nerd Peter Parker. An orphan living with his aunt May and uncle Ben, Peter is unpopular at school, but his home life is filled with love even if money is tight.

Hyphenated hero
Lee and Ditko's creation was designed to be different, breaking every established rule of Super Hero storytelling. When the first issue of his own comic debuted, his title had gained a hyphen to distinguish "Spider-Man" from other costumed champions at the time.

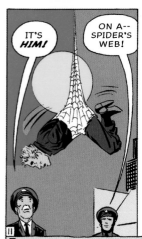

Action and reaction

Ditko's bold lines and stark composition allows room for dialogue, narration, and even editorializing without feeling overly cramped. *Amazing Fantasy* #15's final page delivers cathartic vengeance, Peter's realization of his own guilt, his resolution to forever atone, and promises more adventures—all in eight potent panels. It also delivers one of the most famous lines in comics.

Accidentally bitten by a radioactive spider at a science exhibit, Peter develops astonishing arachnid abilities: enhanced speed, strength, agility, and reflexes; an ability to sense danger; and the power to stick to walls.

Wearing a makeshift mask to conceal his identity, he tests himself against a professional wrestler. Easily defeating his opponent, Peter realizes he can be rich and famous. Devising a macabre costume and augmenting his powers with an adhesive system that mimics spiderwebs, he cashes in as a minor celebrity on television. Soon, fame and overconfidence turn his head, and Peter's vanity and self-importance keep him from catching a fleeing thief at the studio. But Peter's life changes forever when he returns home after a gig to find his uncle Ben has been shot dead by a burglar. Shocked and seeking revenge, he stalks the killer only to find it is the same felon he ignored weeks previously. Wracked with guilt, Peter decides that since his callous neglect led to uncle Ben's death, he must atone by using his abilities to help others: accepting that "with great power there must also come great responsibility."

The plot wasn't new, but the settings made it instantly accessible and familiar to everyone reading it. This wasn't the world of moon rockets, flying cars, giant monsters, or chisel-jawed heroes— it seemed this could happen to any kid. And the artwork was decidedly spooky yet completely engaging.

Cover-dated September 1962, *Amazing Fantasy* #15 came out the same month as *Journey into Mystery* #83, which featured the first appearance of The Mighty Thor and confirmed Marvel's commitment, as a new company, to establishing a Super Hero pantheon. It was Ditko's last issue of *Amazing Fantasy*, but the heartfelt tale of a teenager whose life is turned on its head struck a resounding chord with its young readership. By Christmas, a new superstar was ready to launch in his own title, with Lee and Ditko eager to show what Spider-Man could do. Keeping the "Amazing" title prefix to ensure at least some reader continuity, *Amazing Spider-Man* #1 hit the newsstands in March 1963 with two complete stories. The rest is history. ▪

Radioactive change
At a time of Cold War paranoia, nuclear proliferation was a symbol of anxiety and a favored narrative device for triggering terrifying change. Lee and Ditko utilized the great unknown— but always transformative—force of atomic mutation to imbue outcast teenager Peter Parker with the power to overcome his personal problems.

Journey into Mystery #83
August 1962

Editor in chief	Stan Lee
Cover artists	Jack Kirby, Joe Sinnott, Stan Goldberg
Writers	Stan Lee, Larry Lieber
Penciler	Jack Kirby
Inker	Joe Sinnott
Letterer	Artie Simek
Editor	Stan Lee

"Originally intended as a one-off story... even before it saw print, the decision was made to turn Thor, God of Thunder, into an ongoing concern [with] a greater emphasis on actual Norse mythology.**"**

Tom Brevoort

The early 1960s saw a creative explosion in the comic book industry as the popularity of Super Heroes snowballed. Following the successes of the *Fantastic Four* and *Incredible Hulk*, Marvel Comics wanted to keep the flow of new heroes coming. Editor Stan Lee was eager to push the boundaries even further, but in the Hulk he had created the strongest being it was possible to find on Earth. If he was to come up with an even stronger character, they would have to be something otherworldly.

During an interview at the time, Lee had been struck by a comment that Marvel was creating a new mythology for the 20th century. This idea chimed with something that had been playing on his mind for a while—how to use divine beings in his stories without offending any religious sensibilities, and so he turned to ancient mythology. Considering the Greco-Roman tradition to be too familiar, he lighted upon the Norse pantheon and chose Thor, the Asgardian God of Thunder, as the ideal subject for a new comic book hero. This would mean that the art team could play with Viking styles and weaponry to come up with a character design that would be visually exciting and indelible—and set apart from other contemporary characters.

Concerned that ordinary readers would not be able to relate to the God of Thunder, Lee came up with the alter ego of Dr. Donald Blake. This frail, all-too-human character provided the perfect contrast to the mighty Thor. The anthology title *Journey into Mystery* was chosen for the character's debut. The comic book had previously showcased horror and fantasy stories, but Lee had been phasing out horror in favor of science fiction. It is perhaps for this reason that the first enemies Thor faces are aliens trying to invade Earth. Although the extraterrestrials' advanced technology far outmatches Earth's regular military, Thor's strength and the power of his hammer easily defeats them, and they leave in a hurry, their plans in tatters.

The obvious choice to draw Thor's first appearance was longtime Marvel artist Jack Kirby. Thor would take Marvel in a new direction, to other dimensions and realms populated by strange and sometimes monstrous beings. Kirby's incredible imagination would take this challenge in its stride. *Journey into Mystery* #83 is one of his masterpieces. The emergence of Thor as one of the most powerful beings in the Marvel Universe is signaled with a plethora of action-packed panels. Kirby's signature

Stick shift
No sooner had Dr. Don Blake learned that striking the stick he had found in the cave could transform him into Thor than he was using his new power to save Earth from an alien invasion. Kirby was equally adept at creating convincing ordinary people as he was depicting godlike Super Heroes and monstrous extraterrestrials.

Power surge
The art by Jack "King" Kirby is packed with drama as the frail human becomes the mighty Thor. Later comics would reveal that Donald Blake had always unknowingly been Thor, sent to Earth by his father, Odin, to learn humility. It was Odin who had guided Blake to the remote cave on the Norwegian coast where he would meet his destiny.

flashes and dynamic motion show Donald Blake's memorable metamorphosis into a mighty god and how he subsequently sets about testing the limits of his new powers and the capabilities of his hammer.

Stan Lee realized that Marvel's continued success meant that his workload had simply become too great by this point for him to script the first story of the new character. Luckily, he had someone to turn to whom he trusted implicitly—his younger brother, Larry Lieber. It was Lieber who came up with the idea that Thor's hammer would be made out of the fictional metal Uru, lending it an even more mystical aura. Later, Lieber moved on and Stan Lee took over writing duties on Thor's stories, fashioning an antiquated, "Shakespearean" style of dialogue for the Asgardian, to underscore his differences from ordinary mortals and other Earthbound heroes. This dialogue is absent from *Journey into Mystery* #83, in which Thor speaks like Donald Blake, seized by wonderment as he processes his amazing transformation.

In the action-packed pages of the comic, readers saw Thor discover that his hammer would return to him if thrown, was virtually indestructible, and could be used to make him fly. It could even change the weather. The Asgardian quickly deployed these powers to find and rout the invasion force of rocklike aliens that was threatening Earth.

Thor proved to be another hit on Marvel's hands, and *Journey into Mystery* quickly evolved into a vehicle for ever more tales of Asgard, before being renamed *The Mighty Thor* in 1966. The stories of Thor and Asgard greatly broadened the scope of Marvel's cosmology and added new layers to the canon such as god-pantheons and interconnecting realms. Thor's great age and heritage also gave Marvel continuity a sudden injection of history, stretching back over many centuries.

Like the Hulk, Thor was a founding member of the Avengers superteam just two years after his debut. He went on to become one of the key characters in the Marvel Cinematic Universe, appearing in all the Avengers movies as well as several individual big-screen outings. ■

Thor soars
Journey into Mystery #83 introduces readers to Thor's incredible powers, including the magical properties of his hammer, later named Mjölnir. Thor co-creator Jack Kirby drew inspiration for the hammer straight from the tales of Norse mythology of which he and Stan Lee were big fans. Kirby's art conveys the immense speed of Thor's Mjölnir-driven flight, reducing the Thunder God to a silhouette of motion lines.

Editor in chief	Stan Lee
Cover artists	Jack Kirby, Dick Ayers
Writer	Stan Lee
Penciler	Jack Kirby
Inkers	Dick Ayers Joe Sinnott
Colorist	Stan Goldberg
Letterer	Artie Simek
Editor	Stan Lee

Fantastic Four #6
September 1962

" Still early in the series, Stan and Jack pitted the FF against not one, but two Super Villains in this issue, proving to fans they were firing on all cylinders right out of the gate. **"**

C. B. Cebulski

By the time of *Fantastic Four #6*, Stan Lee was satisfied that Super Heroes were back and a viable option for Marvel Comics. With their distributor accepting a maximum of only eight titles a month, writer-editor-publicist Lee had to carefully balance new ideas with proven sellers, and by the summer of 1962, he moved away from less popular genres such as romance, humor, and war stories.

The monthly stable of costumed stars with their own titles consisted of the Fantastic Four (FF), Thor, Ant-Man, and the Human Torch Johnny Storm in solo action in *Strange Tales*. The Hulk was released bimonthly and recent addition Spider-Man was set to return after a hugely successful tryout in *Amazing Fantasy #15* (August 1962). What Lee and Jack Kirby turned their attention to next, aside from creating more Super Heroes, were archenemies capable of giving them a riveting run for their money and worthy of return appearances.

After reviving Golden Age antihero Namor, the Sub-Mariner in *Fantastic Four #4*, a huge leap was made with the debut of hyper-scientific sorcerer Doctor Doom the following issue. Doom was an old college rival of Reed Richards who had, through sheer will, forged himself into the most dangerous man alive and the first new major league Super Villain of the budding Marvel Universe. The FF had met and defeated the monster-controlling Mole Man in their premiere appearance, but for all his dreams of global domination, he was a somewhat puny and tragic figure. Mole Man would not become a truly threatening

Super Villain until his second appearance in *Fantastic Four #22* (January 1964).

Rather than introduce another prime villain—and plenty of unique malcontents such as the Puppet Master, Red Ghost, and the Mad Thinker would debut in the months to come—Lee and Kirby again confounded expectations by pairing up two of their big hitters to take on the FF. And so a conflicted Atlantean ruler, Namor, bearing a justifiable grudge against humanity, joined forces with the devious armored mastermind Doom in Marvel's first ever team-up. Ultimately, assorted heroes would meet, clash, and bicker before uniting to defeat a common foe in what became a signature narrative device of the House of Ideas. However, "Captives of the Deadly Duo!," which established a fractious relationship between the menacing monarchs, depicted the overbearing villains coming together as wary allies only to devolve into sworn enemies after their true natures manifest.

Smarting from his recent defeat, Doom scours the oceans in search of the Sub-Mariner and, on finding him, slyly convinces the prince to renew his war of vengeance against the surface world by attacking the FF. Obsessed with Susan Storm, Namor agrees on condition that she is spared. He conceals a magnetic device in the Baxter Building that will propel the FF's HQ into space. His mission coincides with another family spat after Sue's brother, Johnny, destroys a photo of Namor that she's been hiding. The Sub-Mariner intervenes and becomes trapped when his partner-in-villainy

Divided loyalties
Susan Storm's affections for the tragic Namor dictated the shape of many early FF stories. Their mutual attraction continued even after she married Reed Richards, offering potential emotional conflict and adding a compelling sophistication to the dramas.

strikes, dragging the skyscraper out of the atmosphere and toward the sun. Where the superteam's efforts fail, Namor's hybrid powers succeed, defeating Doom and hurling him into space, seemingly forever.

As well as breaking new ground, this exciting action adventure cemented the nature and motivations of the colorful antagonists in ways even the youngest reader could understand. Namor was a noble antihero gripped by a grievance

that was understandable and even laudable. He knew right from wrong and would do the right thing when necessary, while brilliant, ruthless Doctor Doom worked only for his own benefit: lying and callously killing to get what he wants. *Fantastic Four* #6 was a dry run for many future alliances between the two, most notably the intriguing 1970s series *Super-Villain Team-Up*, which would invariably end in duplicity, disappointment, and usually much destruction. ▪

Love and pride
Devious Doctor Doom uses Namor's guilt and wounded pride to make the former Prince of Atlantis his temporary ally and unwitting pawn. By playing his attraction to Susan Storm against the shame of failing to protect his people from destructive human atomic testing, Doom inflames Sub-Mariner's passions to counter his natural distrust of all surface-men.

Fantastic Four Annual #1

July 1963

> " The first Golden Age hero to return to Marvel, this issue reintroduced major aspects of Namor's life, such as Atlantis, [while also] giving us long-time lover, the lady Dorma, and enemy Krang. A major boost for the sea king's legend. "

Peter David

Editor in chief	Stan Lee
Cover artists	Jack Kirby, Dick Ayers
Writer	Stan Lee
Penciler	Jack Kirby
Inker	Dick Ayers
Colorist	Stan Goldberg
Letterers	Artie Simek, Ray Holloway
Editor	Stan Lee

Take two
Enthusiastic reader reception to the first meeting of the Fantastic Four and Spider-Man confirmed one of Stan Lee's theories: fans enjoyed seeing their favorite heroes fighting each other as much as they did battling villains.

A bona fide hit from the outset, the *Fantastic Four* proved the commercial viability of Super Heroes. As the title grew in popularity, the summer of 1963 saw the quartet become Marvel's first adventure characters to star in an annual. These were higher-priced, square-bound, 80-page holiday specials with a longer shelf life than standard issues, which had to be sold or returned within three months. The company had released only two annuals before: *Millie the Model Annual* #1 (January 1962), which featured evergreen humor-fashion star Millie Collins, and a compilation of monster and science-fiction reprints curated to fill the pages of *Strange Tales Annual* #1 (September 1962).

Fantastic Four Annual #1 was a marked departure. It boasted a brand new story that was a clever revision of a recent classic, fan-pleasing bonus material, and even reprinted the team's debut. Since *Fantastic Four* #2 (January 1962), readers had enjoyed infographic pages explaining how their powers worked and bombastic pinups of heroes and villains. These extras created a strong sense of shared experience, and with the increased space available in annual specials, Lee and Kirby went to town with a wealth of stunning imagery and technical revelations.

Their awe-inspiring "Gallery of the Fantastic Four's Most Famous Foes!" feature depicted Mole Man, The Hulk, the Skrulls, Miracle Man, Prince Namor,

Doctor Doom, Kurrgo: Master of Planet X, Puppet Master, Impossible Man, Red Ghost (plus his "indescribable" super-apes), and The Mad Thinker with his "awesome android." In the same vein, Q&As about the Fantastic Four and a diagrammatic trip "Inside the Baxter Building" made kids instant experts on their favorite characters.

Although Marvel was growing in both status and readership, Stan Lee kept looking for ways to cross-sell his stars. In a time before dedicated comic shops, back-issue stores, or even organized fandom, comics were a fleeting enjoyment. If readers came in late, they had few ways to catch up on what they missed. At the time, that didn't matter for other comic publishers, but Marvel's heroes shared a single universe and were constantly changing and evolving. *Fantastic Four Annual* #1's graphic extras were fun and collectible, and also provided useful background info, but Lee went further. He included a revised and retouched reprint of the first half of *Fantastic Four* #1, retelling their origin for new readers. This policy became standard practice in similar giant-sized titles such as *Marvel Tales* and *Marvel Collector's Items Classics*, giving new fans as well as late converts a handy, economical means of quickly acclimating themselves to the Marvel Universe.

In *Amazing Spider-Man* #1 (March 1963), the wallcrawler attempted to join the team, only to change his mind when he learned it was not a salaried position.

Lee and Kirby revisited and expanded
that brief scene to six boisterous pages
in "The Fabulous Fantastic Four Meet
Spider-Man!": a dynamic duel between
fledgling Marvel's most popular brands,
graced by Steve Ditko's moody inking to
create an ingenious and compelling event.

All these supporting features affirmed
the celebrated success of the Fantastic
Four and the innovative approach of its
creators. But the backbone and real
highlight of the annual was a spectacular
37-page epic by Lee, Kirby, and Dick
Ayers, which reveals how—after months
wandering the oceans searching for his
scattered people—Prince Namor finally
reunites with his nomadic subjects. After
marshaling his forces, the aggrieved
monarch leads the Atlantean army in
an invasion of New York City in "The
Sub-Mariner versus the Human Race!"

A monumental tale even by today's
standards, the story sees the Fantastic
Four triumphantly repel the overwhelming
undersea incursion through valiant
struggle, brilliant strategy, and Reed
Richard's technological genius. As an
added treat, the saga also reveals the
secret history of the aquatic race *Homo
mermanus* and recaps Namor's origins.
Even though the clash settles nothing
and merely returns all participants to a
bellicose status quo, the sheer drama and
excitement of this "longest uninterrupted
super-epic of its kind" are unforgettable. ■

Avengers #1
September 1963

> **"** No one could have dreamed that a book hastily assembled to fill a sudden hole in Marvel's schedule would, decades later, become the centerpiece of the most successful cinema franchise of all time. **"**
>
> **Mark Waid**

Editor in chief	Stan Lee
Cover artists	Jack Kirby, Dick Ayers
Writer	Stan Lee
Penciler	Jack Kirby
Inker	Dick Ayers
Colorist	Stan Goldberg
Letterer	Sam Rosen
Editor	Stan Lee

No sooner had Stan Lee, Jack Kirby, Steve Ditko, and their fellow Marvel creators invented a handful of modern heroes than most of them were brought together in an all-star superteam. Nearly 18 months after the publication of *Fantastic Four* #1 (November 1961), Marvel boasted a stable of superstars who could be assembled into a force for justice and soaring sales. While harnessing the combined skills and abilities of established heroes was far from unique, seldom had it been done with such style and exuberance as in "The Coming of the Avengers!"

There had been superteams before. In June 1941, just prior to the US's entry into World War II, Marvel's predecessor Timely published *Young Allies*, a series that blended the popular trend for kid gangs (seen in movies like *Angels with Dirty Faces* and *Our Gang*) with Super Hero action. In these adventures, Captain America's partner, Bucky Barnes, and the Human Torch's sidekick, Toro, led a diverse band of all-American youngsters into battle against crooks and spies. In 1946, the All-Winners Squad united seven well-known costumed crusaders: Captain America and Bucky (or at least their replacements after Steve Rogers and James Barnes were lost at the end of the war), the Torch, Toro, Whizzer, Miss America, and the Sub-Mariner. Although the All-Winners enjoyed only two epic adventures as the public's taste for Super Heroes waned after the war, the team is now considered a prototype for today's Avengers.

Scripted by Lee and illustrated by Kirby and Dick Ayers, *Avengers* #1 launched in September 1963 with one of the cannier origin tales in comics. Instead of starting fresh and assuming readers knew nothing of the comic's cast, the story demanded some familiarity with Marvel's other titles and wasted little time or energy on introductions or unnecessary exposition.

As Lee hoped the cross-promotion of *Avengers* would boost sales for its members' own titles, he took great efforts choosing the right characters for the new team. Established heroes Ant-Man and the Wasp, Thor, and newly launched Iron Man were sureties: all sold well but could benefit from more exposure. The Hulk, whose own title had been canceled at the start of 1963, still had many fans who would welcome his return. And after careful consideration, Lee decided not to enlist teen sensation Spider-Man and the recently debuted, commercially untested Doctor Strange in the Avengers. Given these characters' quirky, outsider appeal, Lee may have felt they were more suited to solo adventures than being team players. In time, both Spidey and Strange, and a host of other heroes, would often team up with and even become card-carrying Avengers.

The "book-length" epic *Avengers* #1 starts in the mythic realm of Asgard where an imprisoned Loki craves vengeance on Thor. The God of Mischief sets out to bedevil his half brother, engineering a tense situation that appears to show the

"THE COMING OF THE AVENGERS!"

THE FIRST OF A STAR-STUDDED SERIES OF **BOOK-LENGTH SUPER-EPICS** FEATURING SOME OF **EARTH'S GREATEST SUPER-HEROES!**

THE MIGHTY THOR

IRON-MAN

ANT-MAN and the WASP

The Incredible HULK

THE PLACE: ASGARD, HOME OF THE NORSE GODS!

THE TIME: THE PRESENT!

THE MAN: LOKI, GOD OF EVIL! A PRISONER ON THE DREADED **ISLE OF SILENCE...** PLOTTING AWESOME REVENGE AGAINST HIS MIGHTY ENEMY, **THOR,** THE THUNDER GOD!

| WRITTEN BY: | DRAWN BY: | INKING BY: | LETTERING BY: |
| **STAN LEE** | **JACK KIRBY** | **DICK AYERS** | **S.ROSEN** |

Call to arms

Malevolent Loki broods, plotting to destroy noble Thor. Yet his heartless use of unpredictable, uncontrollable mortal pawns is always his undoing. In this case, it is also the reason a host of fiercely independent Super Heroes grudgingly unite into an irresistible team that will forever defend the world and the universe.

Incredible Hulk is on another terrifying rampage. If Thor intervenes to stop the mighty monster, he might, Loki hopes, perish in the attempt. Meanwhile, the Hulk's teen confidante Rick Jones contacts the Fantastic Four for assistance, however, Loki diverts the emergency transmission to Thor's radio receiver and gleefully awaits the inevitable result of his machinations. Unfortunately for Loki, Iron Man and Ant-Man also receive the redirected SOS, and as they converge on the Southwest, from where the distress call originated, the heroes realize something isn't right.

A frustrated Loki lures Thor away with a mirage of the emerald man-monster and into a confrontation in his hellish otherworldly prison, leaving the remaining champions to tackle the Hulk. They find him disguised as a super-strong circus robot and are soon in ferocious combat with a brute far smarter and faster than he looks. Eventually, the Hulk flees, but is cornered in Detroit. As the battle escalates, Thor and his defeated half brother appear, but as explanations are given, Loki attacks with deadly radiation. At his moment of triumph, the evil one is brought down by the smallest of his mortal foes. The victors realize how much good they can continue doing if they work together. All that remains is for the Wasp to give them a suitably imposing name....

With typical, albeit prophetic, hyperbole, Stan Lee, as editor, ends the story praising the birth of "one of the greatest Super Hero teams of all time! Powerful! Unpredictable!... a new dimension is added to the Marvel Galaxy of Stars!" He may as well as have said the "Marvel Universe." All these characters and countless more, even war and cowboy stars, would ultimately interact in the same vast, shared continuity that came to form the all-encompassing Marvel Multiverse. Lee's clever cross-promotional gambit was successfully transplanted four decades later to Marvel's movie franchise. Iron Man, Hulk, Thor, and Captain America all tested the cinematic waters before joining forces in the Avengers, perhaps the world's most famous Super Hero team. ■

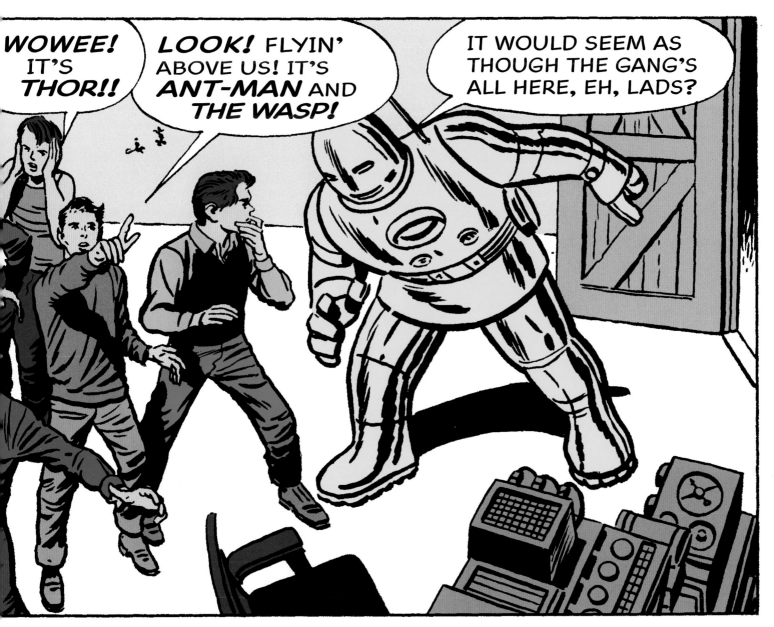

Chance meeting
Rick Jones and his Teen Brigade pals are overwhelmed by the surprise arrival of four new Super Heroes to stop the rampaging Hulk. These heroes initially join forces as a fractious, unstable union, choosing to battle the angry but innocent Hulk individually, in what could be construed as a rehearsal for the *Avengers* series. The first instance of actual teamwork would not be seen until the following issue.

School for mutants

Summoned by mental command, the group that Marvel presented in 1963 as the "strangest Super Heroes of all" assembles. Kirby and Lee's original X-Men lineup would lay the foundations for one of the company's most popular franchises. Key to the concept was the idea of outsiders joining together to find acceptance and a sense of family.

Editor in chief	Stan Lee
Cover artists	Jack Kirby, Sol Brodsky
Writer	Stan Lee
Penciler	Jack Kirby
Inker	Paul Reinman
Letterer	Sam Rosen
Editor	Stan Lee

New girl
The lineup is complete—for now—as Jean Grey joins the X-Men at Professor X's school. At first, Jean's new teammates have trouble seeing beyond her looks, but she quickly shows them that it is the power of her mind that defines her.

X-Men #1
September 1963

❝This book is a testament to the power of Stan Lee and Jack Kirby's collaboration, in that its relatively tepid launch still led to the creation of the most powerful Super Hero franchise ever.❞

Dan Buckley

It was 1963. The Fantastic Four was a breakaway success, comic book Super Heroes were enjoying a surge of popularity, and everything Marvel touched seemed to turn to gold. But readers wanted more, and Stan Lee and Jack Kirby were the men charged with coming up with new characters to match the fame of the Fantastic Four, Spider-Man, Hulk, and Thor.

Lee wanted to create another team, but he wasn't convinced about presenting a whole new slew of origin stories about how the characters acquired their powers. The solution he came up with may have made his life as a writer easier, but it was also a stroke of genius. The new team would be born with powers. This idea led naturally to a different narrative scenario than any that had gone before—how would ordinary people react to humans whose abilities were innate? How would a person born with a super-power learn to use it as they grew to adulthood? They would need a school, and a teacher, and so Lee and Kirby created Charles Xavier, aka Professor X, a man with extraordinary mental abilities. So that he would not seem too powerful, they decided to confine Xavier to a wheelchair.

When Marvel's publisher Martin Goodman rejected Stan Lee's name for the new team—The Mutants—Lee opted for the X-Men, after Professor X. The X-Men's status as mutants instantly set them apart as a group distinct from normal humans. The mistrust and fear that the nonmutant population might feel toward these misfits and outcasts had obvious parallels at the time with the civil rights struggle. Professor X's appearance may have been styled after actor Yul Brynner, but Stan Lee saw the X-Men's mentor—whose objective was to train mutants to protect humanity with their powers and foster greater understanding between the two communities—as a kind of Martin Luther King Jr. figure.

The "villain" that Kirby and Lee created for the X-Men's first comic book was also fighting for a worthy cause—the end of the oppression of mutantkind—but the way in which he went about it was very different. Magneto, revealed years later to be a Holocaust survivor, believed that humans and mutants could never really live together in harmony. He saw the natural position of mutants as being above normal people, ruling over them. Lee did not want Magneto to be a one-dimensional bad guy, and as the character developed, he would display shades of gray that meant that readers could empathize with him, even while rooting for the X-Men to stop his extreme plans. Jack Kirby's design for Magneto in *X-Men* #1 was an instant classic, and his distinctive helmet, in particular, was a mainstay of the character even into his 21st-century big-screen incarnations.

The original lineup of the X-Men, as presented to eager readers in the 1963 debut issue, was led by Cyclops, aka Scott "Slim" Summers, handpicked by Professor X as the mature leader of the group. There was also Beast (Hank McCoy), whose size, strength, and agility belied

a ferocious intellect, the winged Angel (Warren Worthington III), and Iceman (Bobby Drake), who at 16 was the youngest member of the team. Drake's appearance in these early issues was more snowman than Iceman, something that the creators even made an in-panel joke of in *X-Men* #1. Lee admitted that Iceman was at first just devised as an opposite to the already successful character of the Human Torch in the Fantastic Four. The opening pages of this issue show the X-Men meeting their new teammate, Jean Grey, who is revealed to have powerful telekinetic abilities. When Beast's attentions get a little annoying, Jean uses the power of her mind to lift him up, spin him around, and deposit him on the far side of the room.

Although the X-Men went on to become one of Marvel's most important and popular properties, in its early days, the book's sales did not hit the heights of its stablemates *Spider-Man* or the *Fantastic Four*. It would not be until their dramatic revamp in the following decade, when a diverse cast of new characters was sent to train at Professor X's school, that the X-Men really became a force to be reckoned with in comics. However, the iconic characters created in *X-Men* #1 by Stan Lee and Jack Kirby provided future lineups with a solid foundation and would themselves be involved in some of the most groundbreaking story lines in comic book history. They would also find fame outside comics fandom through a hugely successful movie franchise. ∎

Magnetic appeal

Magneto is established from the start as a formidable opponent, with his powers over magnetism enabling him to make short work of the rocket-launching site at Cape Citadel. It is in *The X-Men* #1 that Magneto first coins the term "*Homo superior*" for mutants, to set them apart as distinct from humanity. Jack Kirby's extreme close-up on Magneto in the panel above is often cited as the inspiration for Pop-Art maestro Roy Lichtenstein's famous 1963 print "Image Duplicator."

Editor in chief	Stan Lee
Cover artists	Jack Kirby, Sol Brodsky
Writer	Stan Lee
Penciler	Steve Ditko
Inker	Dick Ayers
Letterer	Sam Rosen
Editor	Stan Lee

Tales of Suspense #48
December 1963

" Featuring the first appearance of the forgettable Mr. Doll, this issue also debuted Iron Man's streamlined, aesthetically pleasing red-and-gold-armor. Tony's made many alterations since, but this design remained consistent. **"**

Peter David

The character of Tony Stark, the fabulously wealthy inventor and businessman, was created in 1963 by writer Stan Lee and artists Jack Kirby and Don Heck. In a counterintuitive move, Lee wanted to create a hero that was all the things his readers usually despised. Tony Stark would be a weapons manufacturer, a rich industrialist who profited from war. Lee's challenge to himself was to make Marvel Comics fans love Stark anyway, and he succeeded.

Iron Man's debut came in *Tales of Suspense* #39 (March 1963). It was the height of the Cold War, and Tony Stark was in Vietnam demonstrating to the army how his latest weapon could be used to fight the communists in the jungle. However, his life changed forever when he triggered a booby trap and was captured, a lethal piece of shrapnel lodging near his heart and inching ever closer to ending his life. Stark agreed to make weapons for his captors, while secretly planning to use them to defeat the terrorists. He was aided by fellow prisoner Professor Yinsen, a genius physicist. The result was the first Iron Man armor, which kept Stark alive and allowed him to escape, although Yinsen sacrificed his own life to help save "the Iron Man."

This Mark I armor, designed by Jack Kirby, was bulky and gray, which had the effect of making Iron Man appear more robotic than human. *Tales of Suspense* #48

would prove a milestone moment in the history of Iron Man, as it debuted a new look designed by another legendary artist—Steve Ditko. The new armor, known as the Mark II, was far more form-fitting than its predecessor and was realized in an eye-catching red-and-gold color scheme. The design was so effective that its basic shape and colors are still considered Iron Man's classic look more than half a century later.

Lee and Ditko clearly knew the significance this issue would come to hold, devoting three entire pages to a detailed breakdown of how Stark assembles and dons his newly built armor. Ditko used small close-up panels to build anticipation and painstakingly showing how each piece of the suit went on, saving the big reveal of the full armor until last. In-story, the Mark II armor is built in response to Iron Man's failure to beat the villain Mr. Doll, who uses a voodoo-style figure to inflict terrible pain on his victims—including the man inside the armor. A new suit and a smart upgrade to one of his transistorized devices enables Iron Man to finally turn the tables on Mr. Doll.

As first-time readers saw Stark in his now iconic armor, *Tales of Suspense* #48 is where the Armored Avenger as we know him today was born. Although Steve Ditko is perhaps better known for his pioneering work on *Spider-Man* and *Doctor Strange*, he also made a lasting contribution to the huge success that is Iron Man. ∎

Upgrade needed
Iron Man realizes that his Mark I armor leaves him painfully vulnerable to the new villain Mr. Doll. This leads him to design and build a new suit to counter the madman's schemes.

New look
Iron Man's red-and-gold armor is fully displayed for the first time. Steve Ditko's tantalizing slow reveal of the Mark II suit's component parts build toward a final large panel for maximum impact to debut the new look Iron Man.

Avengers #4
March 1964

Editor in chief	Stan Lee
Cover artists	Jack Kirby, Paul Reinman
Writer	Stan Lee
Penciler	Jack Kirby
Inker	George Roussos
Colorist	Stan Goldberg
Letterer	Artie Simek
Editor	Stan Lee

> **"** What makes Marvel so unique is that its publishing history is one enormous tapestry threaded with thousands of characters. That continuity gave Lee and Kirby the opportunity to reintroduce the most popular Marvel hero of the 1940s to a new audience. **"**
>
> **Mark Waid**

As Super Heroes became increasingly fashionable in comic books in the early 1960s, Marvel continued to mix new characters with revisions of its old Timely Comics costumed stars (last seen in the mid-1950s during a brief but unsuccessful revival attempt). The original Human Torch had already been reimagined in contemporary terms as a hot-headed teen rebel in *Fantastic Four #1* (November 1961), and Namor the Sub-Mariner resurfaced in *Fantastic Four #4* (May 1962) as an amnesiac enemy of humanity, blaming surface dwellers for the destruction of his kingdom, Atlantis. When the final member of the company's Golden Age "Big Three" returned to action in the modern era, he appeared little changed from his 1940s incarnation but was, in fact, the most radically reinvisioned.

Originally a fierce, flag-waving—and wearing—ultra-patriot during World War II and until the late 1940s, Captain America vanished for years before briefly resurfacing as a "commie-busting" militant for a short run of adventures starting with *Young Men #24* (December 1953). These tales were sidestepped in the landmark 1963 revival but ultimately incorporated into the Marvel canon by writers Roy Thomas and Steve Englehart in the 1970s.

The original Steve Rogers Captain America who reemerges in *Avengers #4* is a thoughtful, battle-scarred, guilt-ridden soldier who had been called forth when the US once more became embroiled in a foreign war. His rude reawakening in the 1960s as an emblematic force for justice during a time of immense change and turmoil is both telling and timely.

"Captain America joins the Avengers!" in *Avengers #4* follows a battle between the Avengers, Sub-Mariner, and Hulk on Gibraltar that ends inconclusively, with the combatants going their separate ways. As the heroes travel home, Namor travels north, terrorizing a group of superstitious Inuit and hurling their idol into the sea. The totem—a slab of ice enclosing a human body—hits fast-moving currents. Moving southward, the ice melts and the body drifts past the Avengers' submarine. They gaze upon a man clad in a familiar uniform, who the Wasp identifies as none other than the famed World War II hero Captain America. Suddenly, the red, white, and blue sleeper wakes and explosively topples the world's mightiest heroes.

Eventually, the thawed champion stops and reveals how he lost his partner, Bucky, in the closing days of the war. The Avengers plan to announce his resurrection in New York, but before a press conference begins, they are

Return to action
Roused from accidental hibernation, the world's first Super-Soldier does not realize decades have passed. Still lost in the terrible moment he failed to save Bucky, Captain America easily overwhelms his rescuers. This passionate determination will make him a worthy comrade and ultimately leader of Earth's greatest Super Hero team.

suddenly turned to stone. Cap, aided by Bucky lookalike Rick Jones, tracks the Avengers' assailant. They finally locate an alien who has been coerced by the Sub-Mariner into destroying the superteam. Cap compels the alien to restore the heroes, and when the Avengers salvage the extraterrestrial's spaceship, Namor and his Atlantean Guard attack. In the ensuing battle, Cap is pivotal to victory and subsequently sworn in as the newest Avenger.

Created by Stan Lee, Jack Kirby, and (then-uncredited) inker George Roussos, *Avengers* #4 was a milestone in Marvel's rapid growth in the 1960s. The fast-paced tale has everything that made the company's early stories so fresh and vital: the majesty of a legendary warrior returned; stark tragedy in the loss of his wartime boon companion; aliens, gangsters, and Super Villains; and even subtle social commentary wrapped up in kinetic, staggeringly well-crafted action courtesy of Jack Kirby. ■

Man of war

Cap's resurrection was powerful and deeply symbolic, but it was no surprise. Stan Lee and Jack Kirby had canvassed readers about it in *Strange Tales* #114 (November 1963). "The Human Torch meets… Captain America!" saw Johnny Storm battle an acrobat impersonating Cap. The last panel stated "You guessed it! This story was really a test! To see if you too would like Captain America to Return! Your letters will give us the answer!"

THOUGH SMALLER, THE THING IS MORE AGILE, FASTER-MOVING THAN THE LUMBERING HULK, AND SO HE LANDS THE FIRST BLOW... A THUNDEROUS HAYMAKER WHICH SENDS HIS HUGE FOE CRASHING THROUGH AN ABANDONED WAREHOUSE WALL!

THIS'LL SHOW YA, YOU'RE NOT PLAYIN' WITH KIDS NOW!!

BUT THE HULK MERELY SHRUGS OFF THE IMPACT AND CHARGES BACK INTO THE BATTLE, FILLED WITH A MAD, INSATIABLE RAGE!

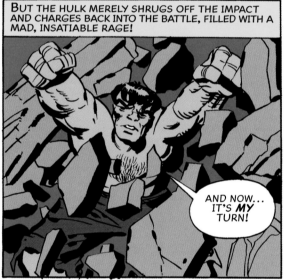

AND NOW... IT'S MY TURN!

MY BEST BET IS TRY TO TIRE HIM OUT BEFORE TANGLING WITH HIM AGAIN!

AIN'T YOU EMBARRASSED TO GO AROUND WITH THAT ANTI-SOCIAL ATTITUDE ALL THE TIME?

I'LL LET 'IM TAKE ONE MORE STEP, THEN DUCK OUT OF THE WAY! A SMART COOKIE LIKE ME OUGHTTA BE ABLE TO RATTLE HIM!

WHAT ARE YOU RUNNING AWAY FOR? I'LL GET YOU SOONER OR LATER...YOU CAN'T HIDE FROM ME BEHIND AN EMPTY BUS!

IT'S FOR YOUR OWN PROTECTION, JUNIOR! I'M AFRAID I MIGHT CLOBBER YOU TOO HARD AND SPOIL THOSE HANDSOME FEATURES!

TRY TO MAKE FUN OF THE HULK, WILL YOU??! YOU'LL SOON REGRET THAT!!

WHEW! ANEMIC HE AIN'T!

12.

Fantastic Four #25
April 1964

> **"**This is the greatest sustained fight scene in comics... and the fact that there's a clear winner and loser only adds to the experience... turning it into high drama.**"**
>
> **Tom Brevoort**

Editor in chief	Stan Lee
Cover artists	Jack Kirby, George Roussos
Writer	Stan Lee
Penciler	Jack Kirby
Inker	George Roussos (as "G. Bell")
Letterer	Sam Rosen
Editor	Stan Lee

◄ **None but the brave**
In early issues of the *Fantastic Four*, Ben Grimm was portrayed as tragic and embittered but gradually was fleshed out into a man of wit and rough charm. Here, facing a foe far more powerful and savage, the Thing proves that he is also immensely brave and unable to quit.

Fans and historians have always rightly celebrated how Marvel's early years reshaped the way Super Hero tales were told. Hugely innovative and imaginative, Stan Lee, Jack Kirby, Steve Ditko, and the small band of creatives in the "Marvel Bullpen" started a revolution in storytelling that delighted and inspired generations of fans, as well as artists and writers. However, it's important to remember that the stories they crafted were also exciting, funny, sad, and action-packed, to satisfy the readers' need for entertainment. Sometimes that meant complex plots with conflicted heroes and villains, at other times it meant pulse-pounding clashes where readers could root for their favorite champion.

In this matter, Marvel often addressed the question on many readers' minds: "who would win if...?" It was a sales ploy the company pioneered in the 1940s, through regular battles between the original Human Torch and Namor, the Sub-Mariner. In the 1960s, Marvel revived the idea, frequently using clashes between heroes to promote a new series. The strategy reached its pinnacle in *Fantastic Four #25*, the opening bout in a two-part yarn involving the Fantastic Four (FF), Hulk, and new superteam the Avengers. Billed as the "Battle of the Century," "The Hulk vs. the Thing" was actually a rematch. The two had first clashed in *Fantastic Four #12* (March 1963) when the Green Goliath was framed for sabotage, but in this raw, gritty, grudge bout, the Hulk was depicted as wholly monstrous, out of control, and determined to wreck New York City, with only Ben Grimm able to slow him down.

Hostilities begin after the Hulk—feeling teen confidante Rick Jones has abandoned him for recently revived Captain America—resolves to destroy the Avengers. Hulk storms into Manhattan, but his targets are still hunting him in the deserts of New Mexico, leaving only the FF to defend the city. The timing is awful: Reed Richards is stricken with a virus, and, without his tactical leadership, Invisible Girl and the Human Torch soon fall before the raging brute. With the city in peril, Grimm vows to stop the vastly stronger Hulk at all costs, leading to a staggering demonstration of raw power and guts. His defeat is inevitable, but even against impossible odds, the Thing keeps getting up and fighting on. His valor is rewarded when "The Avengers Take Over!" in *Fantastic Four #26* (May 1964), as the new group finally arrive on the scene. This initial meeting of Marvel's top teams results in the Hulk being driven off. With his own title canceled, Lee ensured the man-monster guest starred in many titles, pioneering a much used promotional gambit.

As well as one of the most momentous fight stories in comics history, this saga is also remembered for a classic error and deft backwriting of Marvel Continuity. For whatever reason, Bruce Banner is called "Bob" throughout, and nobody in the Marvel office caught it. When challenged on the gaffe in countless communiqués from fans, Stan Lee boldly replied in the letters page of *Fantastic Four #28* (July 1964) that the inventor of the Gamma Bomb's full name was Dr. Robert Bruce Banner—and it's been so ever since! ∎

Editor in chief	Stan Lee
Cover artists	Jack Kirby, George Roussos
Writers	Stan Lee, Don Rico
Penciler, inker	Don Heck
Letterer	Sam Rosen
Editor	Stan Lee

Tales of Suspense #52
April 1964

> **"In her first appearance, she seemed to step right out of a "Rocky and Bullwinkle" cartoon—she even had a partner named Boris! But Black Widow would go on to far greater—and more heroic—things."**
>
> **Tom Brevoort**

Starting out as a science-fiction anthology title in the late 1950s, *Tales of Suspense* became the home of Iron Man's adventures in 1963, featuring the debuts of Tony Stark and a cast of supporting characters and villains. However, some characters appearing in the title would grow far beyond being a bit-part player in an Iron Man story, and one of the outstanding examples was Natasha Romanoff, aka Black Widow.

Black Widow's first appearance came in *Tales of Suspense* #52. Having a hunch the character would prove popular with readers, the creative team of Stan Lee, Don Heck, and Don Rico had already planned for her to return in the very next issue. Natasha Romanoff was not the first character to bear the alias Black Widow—that honor belonged to the Timely Comics character Claire Voyant, debuting in 1940. Although the two were unrelated, Claire Voyant was among the first female costumed heroes in comic books, while her better-known namesake would go on to be the first female Marvel character to have her own comics series. Black Widows have had a habit of pushing at the limits of what was possible for female comic book characters.

Natasha Romanoff's opening story in *Tales of Suspense* #52 was, like her, a product of its time. The Cold War provided comic book creators with convenient go-to villains in the form of communist spies and saboteurs, and this was exactly the role Black Widow fulfilled. She had no super-powers or revealed particular skills in this issue, other than a expert talent for duplicity and manipulation. She did not wear a costume, but rather adopted the persona of a glamorous jet-setter, wearing the elegant clothes and accessories to match that identity.

The artist who cocreated Black Widow, Don Heck, was an ideal choice for her first outing. Heck was particularly skilled at drawing real people—he preferred drawing Tony Stark to drawing Iron Man, for example—and so he was well suited for this initial iteration of Natasha Romanoff, before her costumed career took off. He was also one of Marvel's best artists when it came to drawing beautiful female characters, a talent that was vital in creating a convincing femme fatale.

"Madame Natasha" proves irresistible to famous playboy Tony Stark in *Tales of Suspense* #52. He invites the mysterious Russian beauty to dinner, unwittingly giving her accomplice Boris the chance to break into the Stark factory where Soviet defector Ivan Vanko, aka the Crimson Dynamo, is using his expertise to help the Americans. Boris kidnaps Vanko and puts on the Crimson Dynamo suit himself, fighting Iron Man when he returns to investigate rumors of sabotage at the

Dramatic debut
Black Widow's very first panel in a Marvel comic book was drawn by Iron Man artist Don Heck. The character did not have a costume in her early appearances but was the epitome of glamour. This sophisticated look would prove useful in ensnaring Tony Stark in Black Widow's early missions.

factory. Black Widow plays no role in the fighting, only trying to distract Iron Man with a call for help at a crucial moment. When the American hero triumphs, Madame Natasha flees the scene, her cover blown.

Although she was ostensibly one of the main villains in this issue, the final panel of the comic nevertheless portrays Black Widow in a sympathetic light. The text on the panel describes her as lonely and abandoned, with fear of her constant companion. Eventually, Black Widow would leave the life of a Soviet spy behind her and, like Vanko, defect to the West. But her past would haunt her for the rest of her days, providing her with the motivation to keep trying to do the right thing to atone for her previous misdeeds.

The introduction of Black Widow was a key moment in Marvel history. The character would go on to be an agent of S.H.I.E.L.D., one of the key members of the Avengers, and have several self-titled comic book series. She would also become a pivotal character in the Marvel Cinematic Universe, with starring roles in the *Iron Man* and *Avengers* franchises, capped by her own solo movie. Natasha Romanoff is a much-loved and long-standing member of the Marvel Universe, yet in many ways she remains just as mysterious as she was on her debut in 1964. ■

Avengers #6
July 1964

Editor in chief	Stan Lee
Cover artists	Jack Kirby, Chic Stone
Writer	Stan Lee
Penciler	Jack Kirby
Inker	Chic Stone
Colorist	Stan Goldberg
Letterer	Artie Simek
Editor	Stan Lee

> 66 What purpose would there be for a team of Earth's mightiest heroes if there weren't a team of bad guys to take them on? Featuring the first major appearance of Baron Zemo, our intrepid heroes had their hands full. 99

Peter David

I WAS ADEPT AT EVERY FORM OF HAND-TO-HAND COMBAT KNOWN TO MAN WHILE YOU WERE STILL SAFE IN YOUR LABORATORY, SERVING YOUR NAZI MASTERS!

WHERE IS YOUR BRAGGADOCIO, *NOW*, MASTER OF EVIL?!!

Fighting words
Jack Kirby's flair for action sequences is clearly evident in the fight between Captain America and Baron Zemo. In just a few panels, this early example of a classic Captain America speech sums up the character for readers who did not know him before his 1960s revival.

After his surprise return to active duty in *Avengers* #4 (March 1964), not everyone was pleased that Captain America was alive and had joined Earth's mightiest heroes. Published in the summer of 1964, *Avengers* #6 introduced Marvel fans to an adversary of Cap's from his wartime days—Baron Heinrich Zemo. The story revealed that former Nazi scientist Zemo had caused the apparent death of Bucky Barnes, and that he believed he had killed Captain America, too. Zemo explained to a henchman that it was Cap who caused his mask to be permanently stuck to his head with the powerful Adhesive X. He thought he had got his revenge, but now it seemed he would have to kill the hero all over again.

Since Captain America now fought alongside the Avengers, Zemo decided it would be prudent to assemble a team of his own. This would be the earliest incarnation of the Masters of Evil, the first Marvel Super Villain team-up using separately created characters. It comprised Iron Man adversary the Melter, Thor's enemy Radioactive Man, and the Black Knight, then a foe of Giant-Man. Each villain had a particular ability that gave him an edge against one of the Avengers.

Avengers #6 gave readers a chance to see the continuing evolution of the Avengers as a fighting unit, one which had acquired a new skill set with Captain America emerging as the team's leader. Cap had a natural aptitude for tactics and strategy, honed on the battlefields of World War II, and it was he who suggests switching opponents so each Avenger could fight another's enemy, neutralizing their supposed advantages. For his part, Cap takes on the group's leader, Zemo, in a classic fight sequence penciled by Jack Kirby. As the fight rages, Captain America upbraids Zemo in a speech championing democracy over tyranny, capturing the essence of what the hero is about.

This issue was one of the very first to use the famous "Marvel Method." Writer Stan Lee would give artist Jack

THE FIRST TO SPRAY THE CONTENTS OF HIS CYLINDER IS THE HIGH-FLYING BLACK KNIGHT...TOTALLY UNAWARE THAT HE IS FREEING THE CITY RATHER THAN IMPRISONING IT!
SOMETHING IS WRONG! INSTEAD OF GLUING EVERYTHING TO THE SPOT...THE SPRAY IS FREEING THOSE WHO WERE TRAPPED BEFORE! BUT... HOW??

Knight error
This beautifully drawn splash panel shows the evil Black Knight riding high above New York City. Although the villain thinks he is covering the people below with a strong adhesive, he has actually been tricked into freeing them with a dissolving formula.

Kirby a rudimentary outline of the planned story, which Kirby used to sketch pencil roughs of all the pages. When these pages returned to Lee for dialogue, they also bore notes in the margin from Kirby, giving Lee pointers as to what he intended the art to show, as well as scripting suggestions. In July 1964, Kirby had been relieved of some of his considerable workload after passing penciling duties on *Sgt. Fury and His Howling Commandos* to Dick Ayers. Now Marvel's principal artist could devote more time to drawing *Avengers* #6. The Marvel Method gave artists far more creative freedom than they might have at other publishers, and, honed by Lee and Kirby, it would be adopted by writers and artists across Marvel's titles.

As well as being the debut of Zemo and the Masters of Evil, *Avengers* #6 strengthened the foundations of the Marvel Universe as a concept. Crucial to the Avengers' defeat of the bad guys is another bad guy, the much-maligned Paste-Pot Pete. Having been put in jail following a run-in with the Human Torch in a *Strange Tales* issue more than a year previously, Pete helps the Avengers by providing them with a "Super-Dissolver" to counteract Zemo's Adhesive X. His appearance reinforces the notion that all the Marvel stories of the time took place in the same continuity.

Avengers #6 is a classic of the Silver Age, a story with a colorful cast of heroes and villains and a plot that is irresistibly kooky. But in between the bad guys shooting glue guns and the heroes "water skiing" on a piece of a New York street, there is vital character development of Captain America. Readers saw his desire to get justice for his lost friend Bucky, and the love of liberty and compassion that is woven into his DNA. After resurrecting him for a new generation, Marvel writers and artists were doing their utmost to modernize the character and make the readers of the 1960s love Cap as much as their parents had. ■

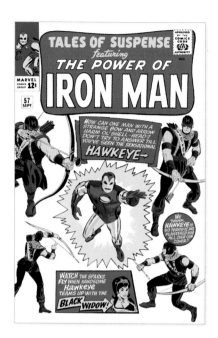

Tales of Suspense #57
September 1964

"While this issue debuted Hawkeye, it is equally noteable for introducing duality into the Marvel Universe... where a villain could change his or her stripes and become a hero."

C.B. Cebulski

Editor in chief	Stan Lee
Cover artist	Don Heck
Writer	Stan Lee
Penciler, inker	Don Heck
Letterer	Sam Rosen
Editor	Stan Lee

Glancing blow
Hawkeye's fledgling career as a bad guy starts badly as his arrow deflects off Iron Man's armor and inadvertently wounds his partner, Black Widow. However, even his love for Natasha Romanoff could not stop Barton from following his conscience, and he would later give up crime to fight with the Avengers.

It may not have been obvious at the time, but *Tales of Suspense #57*, published in 1964, laid the groundwork for characters and story lines that would become integral to the Avengers mythos both in the comics and on screen. The issue saw the debut of Hawkeye, a character who was completely unlike most other major players populating the Marvel landscape at the time. Most notably, he had no super-powers, just incredible skill with his bow and arrow. Starting out in a carnival sideshow, Clint Barton couldn't help but notice how his audience was much more interested in the amazing exploits of Iron Man than his sharpshooting act. Deciding to siphon off some of that public adulation for himself, Barton made a costume and went looking for heroic acts to perform.

Happening upon a jewelry store robbery, Barton, now calling himself Hawkeye, intervenes—but the police think he is the robber's accomplice. Fleeing the scene, Hawkeye is rescued by a mysterious beauty. Instantly smitten, he has no idea that the woman is a communist spy known as the Black Widow (Natasha Romanoff). She has a grudge against Iron Man, and Hawkeye agrees to help her take down Tony Stark's "bodyguard," as Iron Man was considered at the time. In the space of an afternoon, Hawkeye has gone from would-be costumed hero to fledgling villain—and traitor to his country.

Although Hawkeye may not have had super-powers, his uncanny talent for always hitting the target was further weaponized when his new ally, Natasha, uses her Soviet connections to supply him with an arsenal of trick arrows. Now he can take on far more powerful opponents, demonstrated in *Tales of Suspense #57* when he uses a modified arrow to stop Iron Man by rusting his armor. However, his new partner in crime also turns out to be Hawkeye's weakness—this issue shows him rushing to aid an injured Black Widow and letting Iron Man escape. This is the first of several such encounters as Hawkeye and Black Widow try to defeat Iron Man.

In time, Black Widow falls in love with Hawkeye, despite herself, and the bond between them would be crucial in turning her from enemy agent to hero. Hawkeye's own conscience wouldn't allow him to be a bad guy for long either. He would later be accepted into the ranks of the Avengers when some of the original lineup went on various leaves of absence. Clint and Natasha's relationship was not the only romantic subplot in this issue, which also saw the continuing love triangle saga between Tony Stark, Pepper Potts, and Happy Hogan. Although at first Stark is in denial about his feelings for Pepper, over the course of the issue he begins to realize that he loves her as much as Happy does. Writer Stan Lee highlights Stark's tragedy—that he cannot enjoy a normal

Trick shot

Artist Don Heck, inking his own pencils in this issue, illustrated an early example of Hawkeye's signature trick arrows using a cutaway. The archer hopes to impress the glamorous Black Widow by defeating Iron Man, but his shot strikes Natasha by accident, and, in the confusion, the Golden Avenger escapes.

relationship because he fears that the reactor in his chest could fail and cause him to die at any moment.

While *Tales of Suspense* #57's dialogue came from the prodigious pen of Stan Lee, the pencils were by artist Don Heck, a stalwart of the Marvel bullpen. Heck's naturalistic style grounded his characters in real life. He had worked on Iron Man since the start, being instrumental in creating the look of most of the main "human" protagonists, such as Pepper Potts, Happy Hogan, and, of course, Tony Stark. As such, he was the perfect choice to draw the relatively low-tech, down-to-earth Hawkeye. Heck also brought a convincing ordinariness to Pepper and Happy in deliberate contrast to the suave Tony Stark, the ruggedly handsome Hawkeye, or the glamorous Black Widow, to create a rounded, believable cast of characters. And, unlike many other Marvel Bullpen artists, he frequently did the inking duties for his own pencils to maintain his sketchy look.

Hawkeye, and Black Widow, are excellent examples of how Marvel loved to champion complex heroes. Readers could see how easy it was for someone to make a bad choice and fall into crime without being an evil megalomaniac. Watching characters like Hawkeye wrestle with moral dilemmas, and navigate a world in which many of his opponents significantly outpower him, made a telling distinction from Marvel's other mighty Avengers. ■

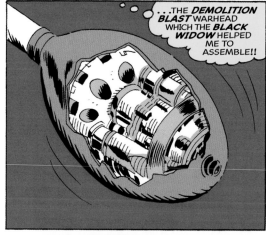

Editor in chief	Stan Lee
Cover artist	Steve Ditko
Writers	Stan Lee, Steve Ditko
Penciler, inker	Steve Ditko
Letterer	Sam Rosen
Editor	Stan Lee

Take six
Stan Lee and Steve Ditko used the first Spider-Man annual to celebrate the "greatest hits" of the hero's first years of existence. This led to the gathering of the Sinister Six, a rogues' gallery of Spidey's most significant foes to date.

Amazing Spider-Man Annual #1
October 1964

“Everything that made Marvel stand apart from its competition, rolled into one oversized comic—an underdog hero, formidable and terrifying villains, and a relatable emotional crisis for the hero's alter ego.”

Mark Waid

Following the runaway success of Spider-Man after his debut in 1962, Marvel Comics published the first of many annuals for the web-slinger in 1964. As well as being the first Spider-Man annual, the book was significant for featuring the earliest appearance of the Super Villain team-up the Sinister Six. The ad hoc, criminal group would reoccur in later comics, with a number of variations to the roster, but the 1964 originals were Doctor Octopus, Electro, Sandman, Kraven the Hunter, the Vulture, and Mysterio.

Even though Spidey's enemies were working as a team, the *Amazing Spider-Man Annual #1* story line allowed the creators to give each villain his time in the spotlight, as the wall-crawler was forced to fight each one at a time. Thanks to the extra space an annual afforded over a regular comic book, each time Spider-Man fought one of the Sinister Six, Steve Ditko was able to show the one-on-one battle in a special splash page. Each member of the Sinister Six had faced Spider-Man before, and each time they had failed, albeit sometimes narrowly. Doctor Octopus, the organizer and leader of the group, reasoned that, although they had been individually defeated, Spider-Man wouldn't be able to beat them when they combined their efforts.

Since his first outing in *Amazing Spider-Man #3* (July 1963), Doc Ock, aka Otto Octavius, had proved a popular villain, featuring in two Spider-Man stories before forming the Sinister Six. Octavius had even unmasked Spider-Man in *Amazing Spider-Man #12* (May 1964), but neither he nor anyone else could bring themselves to believe that "puny" Peter Parker was the real web-slinger.

Vulture is another recurring villain, who had made a strong impression in early Spidey stories, and is an obvious choice for the motley band of evildoers. The other Sinister Six recruits had made only a single appearance in Spider-Man's regular title, but they would go on to become classic members of his rogues' gallery. Mysterio is an out-of-work special effects artist who uses his skills to commit crimes and frame Spider-Man for them. Electro has even been wrongly accused of being Spider-Man by irascible *The Daily Bugle* editor J. Jonah Jameson. Sandman remains infuriated about being vacuumed up by Spider-Man and humiliatingly handed over to the police in a bag. And, for his part, Kraven the Hunter's pride is still smarting after he failed to live up to his reputation and capture the annoying arachnid.

Among the many highlights
of the *Amazing Spider-Man
Annual* #1 were Steve Ditko's
full-page "pinup" splashes
showing Spider-Man fighting
each of the Sinister Six in turn.
Here, Spidey confronts the Vulture
high above New York City.

All the villains agree on their common
enemy, but that is about all they agree on.
The Sinister Six is not a team that has ever
worked together, which is why Doc Ock's
plan to fight and weaken Spider-Man one
after the other appeals to the miscreants.
Their plans are further aided in *Amazing
Spider-Man Annual* #1 after the hero
apparently loses his powers as a result of
being overwhelmed by guilt over the death
of his uncle Ben. The annual would prove
to be a great primer for readers both new
and old, as it adroitly wove in all the key
parts of Spider-Man's mythos that had
emerged in the two years since his debut.
Additional features at the end profile all the
key villains Spidey has faced to date, how he
gained his powers and what they are, plus a
light-hearted but fascinating look at Stan
Lee and Steve Ditko's creative process.

Amazing Spider-Man Annual #1 also
reinforced the interconnectedness of the
fledgling Marvel Universe. The main story
featured all the other Marvel big hitters of
the time: the Fantastic Four, Thor, Doctor
Strange, Giant-Man, Wasp, Captain
America, Iron Man, and the X-Men.
They were not integral to the plot but just
going about their business in New York,
showing the sheer range of heroes the city
could now call on in times of trouble. ■

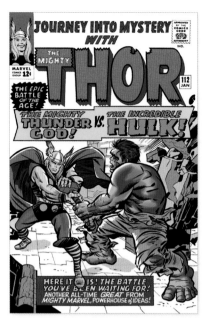

Journey into Mystery with THE MIGHTY THOR

THE EPIC BATTLE OF THE AGE!

THE MIGHTY THUNDER GOD! VS. THE INCREDIBLE HULK!

HERE IT IS! THE BATTLE YOU'VE BEEN WAITING FOR! ANOTHER ALL-TIME *GREAT* FROM MIGHTY MARVEL, POWERHOUSE of IDEAS!

Editor in chief	Stan Lee
Cover artists	Jack Kirby, Chic Stone
Writer	Stan Lee
Penciler	Jack Kirby
Inker	Chic Stone
Colorist	Stan Goldberg
Letterer	Sam Rosen
Editor	Stan Lee

Journey into Mystery #112
January 1965

> 66 Rather than telling a new story settling the question of whether the Hulk is stronger than Thor, Lee and Kirby recount an earlier unrevealed encounter in *Avengers* #3. It was this continuity that built the Marvel Universe brick by brick. 99

Tom Brevoort

In the space of two years, Stan Lee and Jack Kirby revolutionized the way Super Hero comics were told, and the rapidly growing Marvel Comics fan base rewarded them with high sales, fanatical devotion, and constant demands for more adventurous story lines. A large part of that success came from establishing and maintaining close links between their ever-expanding pantheon of heroes and villains—a relatively easy task with a small creative staff and a limited number of characters to keep track of. It also helped that Lee and Kirby were largely doing the kind of stories they wanted to, with scant regard for what had gone before or what rival companies were doing.

Part of that process was regularly testing, tweaking, and generally having fun with the fourth wall between fiction and fantasy. In 1963, *Fantastic Four* #11 had established that there was an "in-universe" comic book starring the Super Hero quartet and even depicted them directly answering questions from real-world fans—in a comics story! This official acknowledgment of their readership made them an integral part of their favorite comics: an inclusivity that broke down barriers and fostered lifelong loyalty.

With that as a starting point, Lee and Kirby went even further with *Journey into Mystery* #112, using bickering fans as a story catalyst and a way to revisit and

expand upon a key moment in early Marvel history, when Iron Man, Thor, Giant-Man, and the Wasp hunted their defecting teammate the Hulk. That desperate search led to a furious fight with their former comrade in deadly coalition with Prince Namor, the Sub-Mariner in *Avengers* #3 (January 1964).

Now as rival fan factions vigorously debate which hero is mightiest, Thor tries to settle the dispute by telling them of a secret moment in that earlier encounter when he and the Hulk truly tested each other's mettle. However, his furtive flashback was not simply an enjoyable battle romp. After years as a guest star in other comics after his solo title was canceled, the Hulk had recently been awarded his own series, in *Tales to Astonish* #60 (October 1964), and Lee was determined to keep the jade giant in the public eye. "The Mighty Thor Battles the Incredible Hulk!" in *Journey into Mystery* #112 was released to coincide with the man-monster's fourth appearance in *Tales to Astonish*, and he was also featured on the cover and inside three of Marvel's nine Super Hero releases that month.

Even the storytelling MacGuffin in this issue was smart and inventive. In *Avengers* #3, the climactic clash between the two Marvel powerhouses took up seven pages of somewhat cramped combat. However,

GOSH, THOR, MOST OF THAT WAS IN THE *PAPERS*... BUT IT'S MORE EXCITING TO HEAR IT FROM *YOU*!

BUT, WHAT HAPPENED *NEXT??* ACCORDING TO THE PAPERS, SUB-MARINER AND THE HULK JUST KINDA RAN OFF! I'LL BET THERE WAS MORE TO THE FIGHT THAN THAT!

Fan fiction
Marvel incorporated fans into stories, making them official Marvel Universe characters. Fans were often used to prompt answers to frequently asked questions, such as here where Thor and Hulk loyalists argue over what every reader wanted to know: who's strongest?

Fight without pity
The Incredible Hulk never looked more bestial and pitiless than in this brutal battle tale. Although fans still lacked a conclusive answer to who was strongest, after the dust settled, they were left in no doubt as to who was the most terrifying and unpredictable character of them all!

"SEEING ME LUNGE FORWARD AT HIM MADE THE HULK FORGET ABOUT SNAPPING THE HAMMER AS HE SWUNG IT AT ME INSTEAD!"

GIVE ME THAT HAMMER!!

THOUGH IT HAS NO POWER *NOW*... IT HAS BEEN AT MY SIDE THROUGH TOO MANY BATTLES FOR ME TO ALLOW IT TO BE DESTROYED!

when expanding here on what really happened for the benefit of fans, Lee allowed Kirby 13 pages for bigger, bolder panels that would amply demonstrate the sheer power of both combatants.

Arguably, Kirby and ideal inker Chic Stone's finest artistic moment, the action occurs after Thor begs All-Father Odin to temporarily suspend his magic hammer Mjölnir's enchantments. At this time, the Thunder God could manifest on Earth for only a minute unless he maintained physical contact with Mjölnir. Letting go of the hammer for any longer would return him to being frail Dr. Donald Blake. Now, with the Asgardian magic suspended by Odin, Thor relinquishes his wonder weapon to strive as the muscular equal of the gamma-powered goliath.

The private duel ultimately settled nothing, leaving fans of both contestants hungry for further rematches. Nor did it provide readers with a definitive answer to the perpetual question: "who is stronger?" What it did do was open up the story to Jack Kirby's visual artistry and gripping storytelling, and show what the "King" could produce when given full control of the pages he worked on. Gone would be Marvel's early reliance on dialogue-heavy adventures. From here on, stunning graphic virtuosity and spectacular action would play a greater part in the magic of Marvel Comics. ■

THERE IT IS! I'VE GOT TO GET IT OUT OF THE HULK'S REACH!

"BUT, I HAD NOT COUNTED ON THE HULK'S ALMOST-MIRACULOUS ABILITY TO BOUNCE BACK FROM A FALL ...!"

HOLD IT, THUNDER GOD! *YOU'RE* NOT GOIN' ANY-WHERE...!

...UNLESS *I* SEND YOU THERE!

KA-POW!

X-Men #9
January 1965

❝The X-Men go head-to-head with the Avengers for the first time, while we learn more about Lucifer, the man responsible for putting Professor X in a wheelchair. Years later the Beast will wind up joining the Avengers.❞

Peter David

Editor in chief	Stan Lee
Cover artists	Jack Kirby, Chic Stone
Writer	Stan Lee
Penciler	Jack Kirby
Inker	Chic Stone
Letterer	Sam Rosen
Editor	Stan Lee

◄ Team rivalry
Jack Kirby's riotous clash between the superteams perfectly captures the chaos of the moment in *X-Men* #9, which kickstarts the long history of the sometimes thorny relationship between the Avengers and the X-Men. Although there would be many more clashes over the years, several X-Men would also join the Avengers in a spirit of cooperation.

September 1963 was a milestone month in the history of Super Hero teams, as both *Avengers* and *X-Men* titles debuted. It was not long before the teams collided in *X-Men* #9, a comic book that marked the start of a rather testy relationship between the two super-groups.

The X-Men have traveled to Europe to help Professor X, who is being held there by a mysterious villain named Lucifer. However, the Avengers also arrive to investigate. Professor X knows that Lucifer must not be harmed, because his heartbeat is linked to a bomb that would detonate if it stopped. He mentally orders his young X-Men to hold off the Avengers while he deals with Lucifer. The X-Men at the time are all inexperienced teenagers, albeit ones who have been trained rigorously by their telepathic mentor.

Stopping the Avengers would be no small feat, but the young heroes manage to hold their own, possibly because the Avengers are holding back a little. Cyclops uses his optic beams to knock Thor's hammer from his hand, while Beast catches Captain America's shield in his outsized feet. Finally, Professor X makes mental contact with Thor and tells him why the Avengers cannot attack Lucifer. They duly leave the mission to the X-Men, and the teams part amicably.

The villain Lucifer had a surprising contribution to make to the history of the X-Men. Not a demonic entity as his name suggested but rather an alien from a race known as the Quists, Lucifer was revealed on his debut in *X-Men* #9 to have been the one responsible for earlier paralyzing Professor X. The full story would be seen the following year in *X-Men* #20 (May 1966).

X-Men #9 was produced by the exemplary creative team of Stan Lee and Jack Kirby, with Chic Stone and Sam Rosen on inking and lettering duties, respectively. The fracas that Lee and Kirby brought alive on the pages of *X-Men* #9 was the start of a long history of clashes between the teams. Although both the Avengers and the X-Men were fighting for good, their methods frequently differed, and conflict between them was often stirred up by third parties. Most commonly, that third party was Magneto, who brought a new dimension to the tensions when Scarlet Witch and Quicksilver left the Brotherhood of Evil Mutants—X-Men antagonists—to join the Avengers.

Confusion over Quicksilver and Scarlet Witch's true allegiance, and Magneto's mind-control powers, would lead to the next battle in *Avengers* #53 (June 1968). Later, in "X-Men vs. Avengers" (1987), Magneto was again at the center of the dispute when the two teams disagreed over how he should be brought to justice. In 1993, the "Bloodties" crossover celebrated the teams' 30th anniversary by embroiling them in a mutant-human civil war on the island of Genosha. In the "Heroic Age," the major crossover event "Avengers vs. X-Men" (2012) brought the two teams into epic battle over the fate of powerful mutant Hope Summers. But *X-Men* #9 was where it all began. ■

Daredevil #7
April 1965

> **“**The fact that Daredevil was so implacable and so dedicated, even though he doesn't stand a chance of [defeating Namor]... only makes him seem more heroic.**”**
>
> **Tom Brevoort**

Editor in chief	Stan Lee
Cover artist	Wally Wood
Writer	Stan Lee
Penciler, inker	Wally Wood
Letterer	Artie Simek
Editor	Stan Lee

As Marvel rapidly expanded in the mid-1960s, it began to suffer from its success, struggling to find enough experienced artists to handle its growing Super Hero pantheon. Steve Ditko and Jack Kirby were both fast and prolific, but even they couldn't handle the ever-increasing workload, and regular freelancers like Don Heck, Dick Ayers, Larry Lieber, and Joe Sinnott were already pushed to the limits of their capacities. Stan Lee's inspired solution was to recall veteran comic artists such as Bill Everett, Carl Burgos, and Bob Powell, who had worked for the company in its Atlas heyday, using Kirby and Ditko to smooth out any rough edges while they adapted to the modern Marvel style.

When Daredevil debuted in early 1964, he was illustrated by Bill Everett (with Ditko's input), before Joe Orlando took over for the subsequent three issues. They were seasoned, talented professionals, but not to the young kids who were their audience. Most importantly, they never quite gelled with the contemporary stylings Lee and Kirby were establishing. Everything changed when Wally Wood

stepped in. His solid figure composition, fluid storytelling, and sleek finishing had already made him a comics legend and one of America's most sought after commercial illustrators. And now he brought power, grace, and beauty to the pages of *Daredevil*. Thanks to Wood's deft handling of the Man Without Fear's exploits, the stories he illustrated became some of Marvel's most memorable. Wood's costumed crime fighter seemed to spring and dance across New York City's rooftops, and from panel to panel. Lee considered Wood's contribution such a coup for Marvel that the renowned artist got a glowing cover plug on his very first issue, *Daredevil* #5 (December 1964).

After wowing audiences with battles against the Matador and the Fellowship of Fear (Mr. Fear, the Eel, and the Ox), Daredevil ascended to the "heights of glory" predicted in *Daredevil* #5 only two issues later in *Daredevil* #7. Traditionally, Super Heroes were pitted against Super Villains of equivalent power and ranking. Nobody really expected Spider-Man to battle gods or the Fantastic Four to go after muggers, but "In Mortal Combat

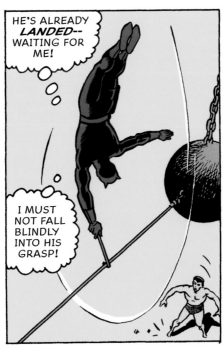

Punching up
Few comic artists could match Wally Wood for stark realism, graceful action, and technical illustration, especially in combat scenes. His careful staging of a brutal, unwinnable fight reinforces the sense of Daredevil's indomitable spirit and tireless ingenuity as the participants traverse New York devastating the streets and buildings around them.

with... Sub-Mariner!" depicted a truly momentous mismatch pitting one of Marvel's mightiest beings against a mere mortal, and a blind one at that.

Since his revival as a righteous foe of humanity in *Fantastic Four* #4 (May 1962), the Sub-Mariner's status had softened from villain to antihero in his various clashes with assorted heroes. Namor had gained a small supporting cast that included his frustrated consort Lady Dorma and the evil, ambitious warlord Krang, while readers saw him rebuild his scattered kingdom and mellow in his attitudes to the surface world. In *Daredevil* #7, the Prince of Atlantis travels to New York to have his day in UN courts and formalize his kingdom's relationship with mankind. After engaging attorneys Nelson and Murdock, he goes on a destructive rampage and easily defeats Daredevil in combat before cunningly surrendering to the authorities. However, his plan to force a legal hearing is

abandoned when he learns that Krang has seized the throne in his absence. Unable to languish in a cell when his kingdom is threatened, Namor breaks out, fighting his way to freedom and the sea. In his way are the army, countless residents of Manhattan, and a sightless hero resolved to stop him.

In this tale, Matt Murdock is first seen as a brilliant lawyer and passionate orator, while his one-sided second battle with one of the strongest creatures on Earth proves the courage and tenacity of his alter ego, even as it reinforces the aloof nobility of the Sub-Mariner. The clash was the final part in a sly buildup to awarding Namor his own series. The Sub-Mariner feature debuted four months later in *Tales to Astonish* #70 (August 1965). Most notably, but with no fanfare at all, Wood replaced the original yellow-and-black costume with the iconic signature all-red outfit we know today, confirming the solitary swashbuckler's elevation to the top tier of Marvel's Super Heroes. ■

Editor in chief	Stan Lee
Cover artists	Jack Kirby, Sol Brodsky
Writer	Stan Lee
Penciler	Jack Kirby (layouts)
Inker	Dick Ayers (artwork)
Colorist	Stan Goldberg
Letterer	Art Simek
Editor	Stan Lee

Recruitment drive
The search for new Avengers would become a semi-regular event. Many who made the grade would be former foes, such as Namor, Sub-Mariner—despite his initial refusal in *Avengers* #16— Wonder Man, Swordsman, Vision, Moondragon, Jocasta, and Firestar.

Avengers #16
May 1965

"Nothing like this had been done before... the new Avengers don't truly get along with one another, all [except Captain America] have something to prove to the world, and it casts the team as the eternal underdogs."

Tom Brevoort

When the Marvel Universe officially began, much of its success came from the inimitable ideas and artistic prowess of Jack Kirby. An artist both prolific and fast, his designs and covers were a crucial component of Marvel's early expansion, but even the "King" couldn't draw everything. To compensate for this, a pattern developed in which Kirby would illustrate most debut stories and follow-up issues before entrusting the title to another artist. This would most often be either inker Dick Ayers, who assumed art chores on *Sgt. Fury and His Howling Commandos*, *Human Torch*, and *Giant-Man*, or Don Heck, who also drew *Iron Man*, briefly took over *Thor*, and confirmed his star status with an epic run on the *Avengers*.

After handing over the reins, Kirby would return to draw only whenever a significant change occurred in a title, but often used to lay out and pace stories for other artists to finish. This occurred on the *Avengers* when writer-editor Stan Lee resolved to tackle a growing problem. The *Avengers* had originated as a series

for promoting other Marvel comic titles, building on the combined sales potential of popular characters who also had their own solo adventures. But as the lives of those individual heroes became more complex in a rapidly expanding shared universe, coordinating joint Avengers missions became concomitantly harder. Thor was away in Asgard, Iron Man had problems with the US government, and Giant-Man was soon to be replaced in *Tales to Astonish* by the Sub-Mariner.

The situation was tackled head on in *Avengers* #16, a continuation of the thrilling developments in the previous issue. In that issue, Captain America and Rick Jones confront and finally defeat Baron Zemo—Bucky's ruthless killer— in the Amazon rain forests, while the other Avengers tackle Zemo's Masters of Evil in New York City. The issue kicks off with a big battle and closes with a big announcement. "The Old Order Changeth!," visually broken down by Kirby and finished by Ayers, proclaimed a dramatic conceptual change for the series. After the World's Mightiest Heroes

bring a swift end to their confrontation with the Masters of Evil, thanks to the teleportation powers of Thor's enchanted hammer, they languish in concern for their missing comrades. As Cap and Rick Jones fight their way back to the US over weeks, Thor returns to Asgard, and the weary Avengers contemplate the unthinkable—disbanding the team. However, they soon modify their thinking after former villain Hawkeye breaks into their mansion and asks to join them. A display of his extraordinary archery talents convinces them of his valuable skills and sincerity. Fired up by the notion of replacing themselves, the heroes begin a very public search for new Avengers.

After being firmly but graciously refused by Namor, the Sub-Mariner, the Avengers accept heartfelt applications from reformed mutant villains Quicksilver and his sister, the Scarlet Witch. Just as Captain America and Rick Jones conclude their epic voyage home, the founders take leaves of absence, and the Star-Spangled Avenger agrees to carry on in their name, training a new generation of heroes.

The very concept of changing the roster of an entire superteam was groundbreaking enough, but to replace true heroes with wanted criminals was a huge gamble, even for a company who had always favored intriguing outsiders, antiheroes, and sympathetic villains. Their unorthodox decision also began a long-standing tradition of rehabilitating villains who had proved to be popular with the readership. Later members and future stars with cleaned-up records and reputations would include Black Widow, USAgent (formerly the Super-Patriot), second Ant-Man Scott Lang, and the Red Hulk.

At a time when rulebreaking and innovation were becoming commonplace—and tremendously successful—this radical reboot of the Avengers would prove to be the most significant of all. It freed the title from the accidental tyranny of shared continuity and allowed the team to grow into a vital, unique, and ever-changing force with its own narrative vision. It also consolidated the Avengers as Marvel's preeminent superteam. ▪

Media frenzy
The press had always played a large and important role in Marvel stories, usually as gadflies. Here, Lee uses the Fourth Estate to express opinions and concerns he wants the reader to consider. It built suspense and shaped expectations for future issues of the *Avengers* that could no longer rely solely on fan favoritism.

Strange Tales #135
August 1965

*"*Spurred by the James Bond spy-craze of the era and its acronymed agencies like U.N.C.L.E., SPECTRE, and CONTROL, Lee and Kirby created S.H.I.E.L.D., a name today recognized by millions of pop culture fans.*"*

Mark Waid

Editor in chief	Stan Lee
Cover artist	Jack Kirby
Writer	Stan Lee
Penciler	Jack Kirby
Inker	Dick Ayers
Letterer	Artie Simek
Editor	Stan Lee

*S*trange Tales #135 is a true landmark in the history of Marvel Comics. In the space of a mere 12 pages, Stan Lee and Jack Kirby introduced readers to a wealth of concepts that would become pillars of the Marvel Universe for decades to come. The issue saw the first appearances of not only S.H.I.E.L.D. but also Hydra, LMDs (Life Model Decoys), the flying car, and the awe-inspiring helicarrier.

Capitalizing on the popularity of spies in the mid-1960s in the wake of hits such as *James Bond* and *The Man from U.N.C.L.E.*, Stan Lee decided to repurpose the lead character in *Sgt. Fury and His Howling Commandos*. Nick Fury was a gruff army man who, in his Sgt. Fury iteration, was still fighting in World War II in his own title. For a new segment in the anthology title *Strange Tales*, Stan Lee brought Fury into the 1960s, promoted him to the rank of colonel, and added a CIA career to his valorous postwar backstory. Fury, though, was no suave and sophisticated Bond but still a rough-around-the-edges three-striper at heart. His no-nonsense demeanor and appearance was later said to closely resemble Jack Kirby, the artist who co-created him, with Kirby's son Neal commenting that Nick Fury was his father with an eyepatch.

In *Strange Tales #135*, Fury is introduced to a covert yet powerful organization called S.H.I.E.L.D., then an acronym for Supreme Headquarters International Espionage Law-Enforcement Division. From the start, it is portrayed as an international body, headquartered on a vast flying aircraft carrier. The look of the helicarrier was created by Kirby, who used S.H.I.E.L.D. as the perfect opportunity to put his prodigious imagination to work inventing cool gadgets and vehicles for the agents to use. His son Neal helped him design another classic S.H.I.E.L.D. vehicle, the flying car, which was based on a Porsche 904 with added missiles. Another example of a Kirby-created innovation appears in the very first panel of the issue, in which Fury is being measured for his "master mold," which can then be used to create hyper-real android clones of him called LMDs. The usefulness of the LMDs is shown soon afterward, when various assassins mistakenly target the androids, leaving the real Fury safe to fight another day.

In this inaugural issue, Tony Stark, moonlighting as head of S.H.I.E.L.D.'s special weaponry section, informs Fury that he has been chosen to lead the entire organization. At first, Fury is reluctant,

Command and control
Strange Tales #135 displays to excited readers the kind of firepower that S.H.I.E.L.D. had at its disposal, with Jack Kirby's full-page splash showing the first appearance of the organization's iconic, legendary helicarrier.

AND THEN, NICK FURY *SEES* WHERE HE IS--THOUSANDS OF FEET ABOVE EARTH, RIDING ALOFT IN A GIGANTIC HELI-CARRIER WHICH SERVES AS THE MOBILE COMMAND HEADQUARTERS FOR SHIELD'S SUPREME INTER-NATIONAL COUNCIL--AS EVER-VIGILANT MILITARY JETS MAINTAIN A 24-HOUR PATROL AROUND THE INCREDIBLE SKY CRAFT...!

WHOOOM!

but inadvertently proves his credentials when his instinct tells him that the helicarrier has been rigged with a bomb. His natural leadership abilities kick in as he saves the day and roots out the Hydra mole who planted the explosives. Seeing the risk posed by Hydra to the free world, Fury accepts the role of S.H.I.E.L.D. Director—and history is made.

Hydra was created as a natural nemesis for S.H.I.E.L.D., the comic book equivalent of SPECTRE, the global crime association in James Bond. It was named after the mythical beast fought by Heracles, giving rise to the Hydra motto "Cut off a limb and two more will take its place." This chilling credo also debuts in this issue, when a Hydra agent is killed and swiftly replaced by another for the unforgivable crime of failing the leader.

Strange Tales #135 is packed with classic Jack Kirby art, and the cover is no exception. It uses simple, bold imagery and split-screen framing to convey the looming threat of Hydra, the action hero status of Nick Fury, the up-to-the-minute spy-surveillance gadgetry, and suspenseful drama that readers could expect to find inside. The design was later strikingly homaged by artist Marko Djurdjevic for *Mighty Avengers* #18 (November 2008). ■

Editor in chief	Stan Lee
Cover artists	Jack Kirby, Joe Sinnott
Writer	Stan Lee
Penciler	Jack Kirby
Inker	Joe Sinnott
Colorist	Stan Goldberg
Letterer	Artie Simek
Editor	Stan Lee

Sound of silence

Black Bolt is one of the most powerful beings on Earth, and another intriguingly mighty yet impaired hero from Lee and Kirby. Afflicted with an uncontrollable vocal condition, his softest whisper can create a planet-shattering sonic explosion. But while he must stay silent, his actions always speak volumes.

Fantastic Four #45
December 1965

" Inspired in part by the 1960s TV show *The Munsters*, the Inhumans became one of the most eclectic groups in comics. Lee talked about giving them their own series for months, but the opportunity didn't arise [until a decade later]. "

Tom Brevoort

Stan Lee and Jack Kirby's collaboration on the *Fantastic Four* generated a host of characters and concepts comprising the basis of the Marvel Universe: astounding heroes and villains, alien civilizations, otherworldly dimensions and universes, and even cultures hidden on Earth. Among the latter, perhaps the most crucial was the Inhumans, a race who had shunned contact with mankind since primordial prehistory.

The first hints of their existence come in *Fantastic Four* #44 (November 1965) when a trio of Fantastic Four (FF) villains form the Frightful Four by recruiting a fierce female warrior with flowing, super-strong, and psychically controlled hair. Madame Medusa quits the gang when Gorgon, a mysterious powerhouse with metal hooves shows up. In desperation, she turns to Human Torch Johnny Storm for help against Gorgon, whose New York rampage embroils the FF, just as the monstrous android Dragon Man also attacks. It was all merely prelude: in the next issue readers encounter enigmatic super-beings who have secretly shared the Earth with humans for millennia.

"Among us hide... the Inhumans," in *Fantastic Four* #45 reveals Medusa as a member of the Royal Family of Attilan but now a fugitive after the true king, Black Bolt, was deposed in a coup organized by his brother, Maximus. She had joined the Frightful Four as a cover but was now being arrested by her own cousin Gorgon, reluctantly working for the triumphant usurper. The revelation comes after Gorgon drops a building on the FF and escapes while they are distracted by a renewed attack from Dragon Man. In the aftermath, young Johnny wanders the city and meets a bewitching girl named Crystal. She's scared but trusts him because of his flaming powers. She also has incredible abilities and a loyal giant teleporting dog dubbed Lockjaw. When Crystal innocently introduces the suspicious but smitten Johnny to her unusual family—Triton, Karnak, Gorgon, and Medusa—a fight breaks out. By the time the rest of the FF arrive, the battle is going badly and only gets worse when Black Bolt explosively steps in.

The House of Agon or Royal Family of Attilan are hereditary aristocracy, comprising King Black Bolt; his wife Medusa; her sister, Crystal; and their cousins aquatic Triton, bellicose Gorgon, and problem-solving martial arts master Karnak. They rule over and represent a nation of weirdly wonderful beings. Successive issues would see the FF unite with the Royals as Black Bolt regains his throne from Maximus the Mad. The usurper's plan to eradicate humanity is foiled, but the Inhumans become helplessly imprisoned inside their own city, separating young lovers Crystal and Johnny for months.

Black Bolt and his family would quickly become mainstays of the Marvel Universe and star in many short-run series, but the young Crystal and Lockjaw were the real stars in these debut issues. She would join the FF and the Avengers, while Lockjaw would go on to become a beloved icon of the Pet Avengers. Later stories revealed the Inhumans were genetically altered by Kree Empire scientists in Earth's distant past

and subsequently evolved into a technologically advanced civilization far ahead of emergent *Homo sapiens*. They isolated themselves from barbarous dawn-age humans, first on an island and latterly in a hidden valley in the Himalayas, and resided in a wondrous Shangri-La-like city called Attilan.

The mark of citizenship is immersion in the mutative Terrigen Mists, which enhance and transform individuals into unique and generally super-powered beings. The Inhumans are necessarily obsessed with genetic structure and heritage, worshipping the ruling Royal Family as the rationalist equivalent of mortal gods. In the 21st century, as the Inhumans gained their own TV series in the real world, a global escape of Terrigen in the comic book universe would create another subspecies of super-beings and almost eradicate Earth's mutant population.

Meet the family
Johnny Storm's instant attraction to Princess Crystal was passionately reciprocated, and despite initial difficulties, they become a celebrated power couple of early Marvel Comics. The Human Torch's first dramatic encounter with the rest of Crystal's Inhuman family—Gorgon, Medusa, Triton, and Karnak— saw him literally swept off his feet.

Amazing Spider-Man #33
February 1966

> **"** Spidey gets to prove his mettle here as never before (and never equaled since)... as he struggles to save Aunt May. A true classic in every sense of the word. **"**

Tom Brevoort

Editor in chief	Stan Lee
Cover artist	Steve Ditko
Writer	Stan Lee
Penciler, inker	Steve Ditko
Letterer	Artie Simek
Editor	Stan Lee

When nerdy high-school kid Peter Parker gains astonishing abilities after being bitten by a radioactive spider, his greed, arrogance, and complacency prevent him from saving the life of his beloved uncle Ben. Traumatized, the boy becomes determined to always use his powers to help those in need. For years the brilliant young hero suffers privation and anxiety at home, even as his alter ego Spider-Man endures public condemnation and distrust whenever he tries to do good. His only consolation is the abiding love of his last surviving relative, Aunt May. That tenuous scenario takes a drastic, life-altering turn when she falls desperately ill and is diagnosed with radiation poisoning. With horror, Peter Parker realizes it must have been a result of the blood transfusion he had once given her.

Since 1962, Stan Lee and Steve Ditko had collaborated on some of the most compelling and remarkable Super Hero sagas ever created, but now with the artist planning to move on, their efforts went into overdrive, generating a string of evocative and gripping tales, and setting new standards for years to come. Ditko's offbeat plots, quirky yet dynamic art, and gift for devising unconventional villains and story lines had been honed to a fine edge on *Amazing Spider-Man,* and the best was yet to come. He had perfected a clean, polished Super Hero style that

complemented the one developed by fellow conceptualizer, Jack Kirby, as a visual template for other artists to follow. For Spider-Man, Ditko eschewed his signature line-feathering and moody backgrounds, for a slicker, more streamlined approach, and deployed a dazzling array of camera angles to engage the reader's interest.

All these factors coalesced into an unmissable epic in the extended "Master Planner" story arc that also allowed Ditko to display his talent for intriguing plots, while Lee handled the scripting. Starting with *Amazing Spider-Man* #30 (December 1965), each successive issue piled on unbearable suspense that culminated in a cathartic finale in *Amazing Spider-Man* #33. The climax crackles with tension while also creating an inescapable sense of doom and overwhelming pressure as Peter battles impossible odds to save his dying aunt.

Spidey's dilemma stems from a series of high-tech robberies orchestrated by an enigmatic new crime lord. The hunt for the diabolically shrewd Master Planner leads the web-slinger into frustrating, time-consuming combat as the mysterious villain is eventually exposed as his old enemy Doctor Octopus. The thefts become all the more personal when the Master Planner's gang steal an experimental serum that was Aunt May's only hope of surviving her radiation poisoning. With time running out,

Spider-Man—pushed to the edge of
desperation—rips the town apart to find
the thieves. After tracking the serum
to a base beneath the Hudson River,
Spidey's dramatic battle with Doc Ock
leaves the exhausted hero trapped beneath
tons of fallen machinery. The serum is
agonizingly just out of reach and river
water is flooding the room....

The nail-biting conclusion of
"The Final Chapter!" is Ditko's (and
perhaps Spidey's) finest moment.
Trapped, injured, and seemingly helpless,
Spider-Man faces his greatest and most
intolerable failure as the clock inexorably
ticks down the seconds to Aunt May's
death. After initially giving in to
hopelessness, the hero at last responds
and digs deep to find the strength he needs
to burst free—the relief is palpable.

The most iconic sequence in Spider-
Man's long and storied history indulges
in five excruciatingly tense moment-by-
moment pages that revel in the sheer
power of will over circumstance. Freeing
himself from the fallen debris, Spider-
Man gives his absolute all—which also
sees him dispatch the entire Master
Planner gang as they foolishly try to
obstruct the hero's exit—to deliver the
vital medicine his aunt needs. For all his
extraordinary efforts, Peter Parker is,
for once, rewarded with a rare and truly
deserving happy ending. ◼

Fantastic Four #48
March 1966

> **"**One of the greatest comics in comic book history, introducing Galactus and his herald, the Silver Surfer, (and) beautifully blending Kirby cosmic craziness with touching moments.**"**

C.B. Cebulski

Editor in chief	Stan Lee
Cover artists	Jack Kirby, Joe Sinnott
Writer	Stan Lee
Penciler	Jack Kirby
Inker	Joe Sinnott
Letterer	Artie Simek
Editor	Stan Lee

Light in the sky
The Silver Surfer seems a coldly dispassionate force dreaded by many alien civilizations, but Kirby adds emotional depth by depicting him exultant in the joy of cosmic flight. His subsequent defection from Galactus, will be a watershed moment in Earth's history and the evolution of Marvel Comics.

At a time when America was ever more divided by generational unrest and social upheaval, ideas just seemed to explode from Jack Kirby. With scripter and editor Stan Lee, he began mixing and layering all his innovations in the pages of *Fantastic Four*. Despite being partway through one story line, *Fantastic Four #48* proclaimed "The Coming of Galactus!" and daringly put on hold the ongoing and swiftly developing Inhumans epic as the Fantastic Four (FF) head home, fearing an even greater, more immediate threat. This novel approach to storytelling approximated TV dramas and soap operas, where life doesn't always come with a beginning, middle, and end. Lee and Kirby frequently foreshadowed upcoming perils as a way to keep readers glued to the series, and it paid off.

After leaving the land of the Inhumans, with their foe Maximus the Mad seemingly triumphant, the FF fly back to the US, unaware of a cosmic entity nearing Earth, preceded by a gleaming herald on a board of pure energy. On arriving in New York, the FF encounter bizarre phenomena in the sky—blazing flames and floating rocks covering the planet—for which panicked New Yorkers blame them. In an atmosphere of mounting global terror, Reed Richards struggles to find answers, which come after immortal, and supposedly neutral, observer Uatu the Watcher appears. He admits to creating the sky effects to hide Earth from an approaching cosmic predator. However, the shining stranger easily penetrates the screens and sends a message to his master. Before long, colossal cosmic devourer Galactus walks the Earth.

In successive issues, we learn that the emotionless herald exists only to search out planets with abundant life energies for his voracious master and creator to consume. It is a mission he has carried out without qualm for countless years. Yet on this primitive world, the simple compassion of the Thing's companion Alicia Masters and the inherent nobility of humanity reawakens his own long-suppressed morality. Wracked with shame, the shining scout rebels against Galactus and helps save Earth, only to be imprisoned here, making him the ultimate outsider on a planet remarkably ungrateful for his sacrifice.

Breathtaking in scope and execution, the story line feels deliberately apocalyptic and reminiscent of a biblical blockbuster movie. Although a last-minute addition, Kirby's scintillating Silver Surfer became another overnight sensation. The Surfer became a byword for depth and subtext in the Marvel Universe and was a character whose stories Stan Lee would exclusively write for the next decade. Complex and captivating, and occurring in the middle of other crises, *Fantastic Four #48* and the ensuing "Galactus Trilogy" is a watershed moment in Marvel history. It introduced not only one of Marvel's most significant cosmic beings but also his best-known herald, a deeply philosophical and innocent stranger in a strange land. The Silver Surfer became a commentator on whatever topic Lee felt readers might respond to. His guest appearances and eventual solo stories further advanced the notion that comic books were not "just for kids." ▪

New visions
Every month *Fantastic Four* readers encountered dazzling new concepts and characters from artist Jack Kirby. Constantly challenging himself in an age before computer-assisted design, Kirby explored new ways of depicting unusual events, such as this surreal photo collage of Galactus' alien ship arriving over Manhattan.

Fantastic Four #51
June 1966

> **"**What's not to love about this comic? It features my favorite character! The title "This Man....This Monster!" sucks you in, and Kirby's classic cover is arguably one of his best.**"**

Dan Buckley

Editor in chief	Stan Lee
Cover artists	Jack Kirby, Joe Sinnott
Writer	Stan Lee
Penciler	Jack Kirby
Inker	Joe Sinnott
Letterer	Artie Simek
Editor	Stan Lee

Judgment call
In the 1960s, editorial restrictions tightly controlled the portrayal of death. In the story's moving finale, the stranger's imminent demise is subtly hinted at, leaving his final moments to the imagination of the reader.

During the 1960s, *Fantastic Four*— as crafted by Stan Lee, Jack Kirby, and Joe Sinnott—was the most inventive, action-packed title on the newsstands. In a monthly stream of interlinked, extended exploits, the "World's Greatest Comics Magazine" constantly lived up to its own hype with an astonishing surge of new characters who would enrich the Marvel Universe for decades to come. Curiously, though, one of their most memorable creations was a man with no name who, aside from a tantalizing cameo in *Fantastic Four* #48 (March 1966), featured only once in a brief interlude in a procession of cosmic sagas.

Under Lee and Kirby's inspired direction, the *Fantastic Four* became a must-read mix of astounding adventure, mind-boggling concepts, romantic melodrama, and frequently raucous humor, especially whenever rock-star everyman Benjamin J. Grimm was in the spotlight. Down-to-earth, valiant, and kind, Grimm's nature and origins reflected Kirby's own life and temperament. He was a child reared in New York's tenements, who endured Depression-era poverty, a harsh home life, and combat overseas before transcending his tough upbringing through sheer talent and dogged gumption. An irascible, funny, and big-hearted man, who always came through for his loved ones and people in need.

Those characteristics were a crucial counterpoint to the underlying appeal of the Thing: a noble hero trapped inside a monster's powerful body. In a world where even his fellow cosmic ray victims could pass for normal, the Thing was a

being of innate tragedy, always struggling against the urge to run away or hide. This contrast allowed Lee and Kirby to lace their audacious tales with an emotional resonance and maturity rare in comics.

Even when Grimm finally finds romance, it is with a blind woman, which fed his conviction that what Alicia Masters felt for him was pity, not love. "This Man… This Monster!" begins in the wake of the team's recent victory over Galactus. Alien ally Silver Surfer has been exiled on Earth, and Grimm misinterprets Alicia's compassion for the stranger as affection. Despairing of Reed Richards' constant yet futile attempts to restore his humanity, Grimm roams the streets weary and heartsick, until he is given shelter by a sullen stranger who then uses technology to usurp Grimm's form. His benefactor is an anonymous, petty-minded scientist with a grudge against Reed Richards, who has stolen the Thing's shape and power to infiltrate the Baxter Building and attack Mister Fantastic. However, he changes his mind after observing the true measure of his unsuspecting rival. When a subspace experiment threatens Richards' life, the stranger sacrifices himself to save the embattled super-genius.

Known for its exciting, imaginative adventures, the *Fantastic Four* always explored human relationships in extraordinary circumstances, and this poignant stand-alone parable is a landmark story. Ben Grimm's revulsion of his physical condition is sharply brought into perspective by the self-destructive behavior and redemptive response of a brilliant individual who had cut himself off from humanity and paid the price for it. ◼

THE FABULOUS **F.F.** MUST SOLVE THE TERRIBLE RIDDLE OF...

"THIS MAN... THIS MONSTER!"

QUITE POSSIBLY, THIS MAY BE ONE OF THE GREATEST ILLUSTRATED EPICS YET PRODUCED BY...

STAN LEE
WRITER

JACK KIRBY
PENCILLER

JOE SINNOTT
INKER

ARTIE SIMEK
LETTERER

Solitary hero
Kirby's drawing skill and affinity for the Thing allowed him to imbue the rock "monster" with a highly distinctive range of expressions and body language. Whether playing pranks on his partners, bursting into action, or, as in this evocative splash page, being paralyzed with loneliness and sadness, readers always knew what Ben Grimm was feeling.

Editor in chief	Stan Lee
Cover artist	Steve Ditko
Writer	Dennis O'Neil
Penciler, inker	Steve Ditko
Letterer	Artie Simek
Editor	Stan Lee

◀ **Here to Eternity**
Doctor Strange can only look on helplessly as Dormammu, lost in his own hubris, attacks the powerful being Eternity. The character of Eternity is a classic example of Steve Ditko's trailblazing work in the 1960s, when he saw comic books not as a lesser medium but rather the perfect place to explore themes of reality and existence.

Strange Tales #146
July 1966

" Long before the term "graphic novel" became commonplace, Ditko and Lee's 17-chapter epic pitted Doctor Strange against his greatest foes in a race to find the embodiment of all reality. **"**

Mark Waid

Strange Tales #146 begins with Nick Fury leading a mission against the evil A.I.M. organization, but it's the book's second story that makes it a true classic. It marks the culmination of a Doctor Strange story arc that began 16 issues previously, and, more importantly, it was the last time the legendary Steve Ditko drew a character he helped define.

Ditko had also been working hard on *Spider-Man* for several years by 1966, but the surprise popularity of Doctor Strange meant that he had to fit two books into his schedule. *Strange Tales*, in particular, gave Ditko's uncanny imagination and creativity free rein. Doctor Strange, Master of the Mystic Arts, was a creation unlike anything else in the Marvel stable. The stories had taken readers on a wild journey through alternate dimensions and realities, challenging the norms of traditional comic book material. And nearly everything that made the character and his milieu so unique came from the mind of Ditko. His art, reminiscent of Salvador Dali's, was lavished with psychedelic detail, while his characters inhabited stunningly surreal worlds where the normal rules of physics didn't apply.

Doctor Strange's stories anticipated the rise in popularity of Eastern mysticism and were perfectly attuned to the era's growing counterculture trends. The books found a receptive audience among college students, many believing the storytellers must have been taking hallucinogenic drugs to conjure such outlandish tales and artwork. However, none of the creators took any drugs—the imaginations of Steve Ditko, Dennis O'Neil, and Stan Lee were mind-expanding enough.

Although Ditko could also make the mundane seem magical, bringing to life the New York streets that were home to Stephen Strange, *Strange Tales #146* is almost entirely set within otherworldly dimensions. It concludes the battle between Strange and the dread Dormammu, which ends badly for the villain when he also tries to conquer the all-powerful being known as Eternity. Eternity was another typically Ditkoesque creation, an entity beyond the comprehension of the human mind, realized in the comic as a huge figure containing the vast reaches of space. Dialogue was provided by up-and-coming writer Dennis O'Neil in one of his very first jobs at Marvel Comics.

Entitled "The End—at Last!," the book ties up many loose plot threads in a single issue. Dormammu is apparently vaporized, the evil Baron Mordo is taken into the custody of the Ancient One, and Doctor Strange returns to Greenwich Village after freeing everyone in Dormammu's thrall, including a bewitching woman named Clea. She would later become romantically involved with Strange and a powerful sorcerer in her own right. The defeat of Dormammu cemented Doctor Strange's position as Master of the Mystic Arts.

The title and the conclusive nature of the comic seemed to put a full stop on Steve Ditko's time with Marvel. Although Doctor Strange was not among the bigger stars of the Marvel firmament, Ditko's extraordinary, peerless run on the character, which finished with a flourish in *Strange Tales #146*, earned him a legion of devoted and discerning fans and inspired future generations of comic creators. ▪

Editor in chief	Stan Lee
Cover artists	Jack Kirby, Joe Sinnott
Writer	Stan Lee
Penciler	Jack Kirby
Inker	Joe Sinnott
Colorist	Stan Goldberg
Letterer	Sam Rosen
Editor	Stan Lee

Fantastic Four #52
July 1966

"It took courage to introduce Black Panther in 1966—and the road wasn't smooth. Jack Kirby's "Coal Tiger" [had his] name changed and his costume redesigned to turn him into the Black Panther—and his cowl became a full face mask... to avoid alienating retailers in the South."

Tom Brevoort

By 1966, Stan Lee and Jack Kirby's *Fantastic Four* was firmly established as Marvel's signature title. The ongoing dramas had also been a forge for daring new concepts and characters. However, *Fantastic Four* #52 definitively broke the mold—and most comic book conventions. In a period when civil rights for African Americans were a contentious and frequently dangerous issue, Marvel had been slowly and cautiously introducing black characters into their books—despite the potential loss of sales in some US states. The first was Gabe Jones in 1963's *Sgt. Fury and His Howling Commandos* #1, but when Kirby devised an imposing black Super Hero called Coal Tiger, Lee agreed it was time for a bold move.

Trailblazing and unforgettable, *Fantastic Four* #52's "The Black Panther!" story heralded a powerful, highly educated, and wealthy black champion: an enigmatic African chieftain who lures the Fantastic Four to his previously unknown nation Wakanda. Boasting advanced, highly crafted technical devices, it's an offer arch-technologist

Reed Richards simply cannot ignore. Inviting Johnny Storm's college roommate Wyatt Wingfoot along, the heroes travel in a magnetically powered sky-craft to participate in a ceremonial hunt. However, it's only at the end of the phenomenally fast flight that Mister Fantastic suspects something isn't right. After clearing the expected abundant verdant foliage, the visitors are deposited in a vast electronic jungle of huge cables and colossal computer banks, where they are ambushed by a man in black cat costume.

Instantly, they counterattack but are quickly defeated by the ingenious traps and astounding combat abilities of their mysterious opponent, who later identifies himself as the Black Panther. Taking them out one by one, the Panther is ultimately frustrated by the surprisingly capable Wingfoot, who overcomes a unit of Wakandan soldiers and frees the captive quartet. In a stunning turnabout, the feline foe then reveals his intentions are noble. He attacked the Fantastic Four only to test himself before pursuing his true enemy in search of revenge.

After such a bombastic, intense, and action-packed introduction, which still found space to keep fans apprised of developing subplots involving the uncanny Inhumans, the subsequent issue would reveal that Wakanda was a secretive kingdom concealing enormous wealth but under constant threat. As the only known source of the vibration-absorbing wonder metal Vibranium, its mineral riches had enabled King T'Challa, aka the Black Panther, to turn his country into a technological wonderland. Now, after years of preparation, he had enticed the famous American Super Heroes into his futuristic homeland as the last stage of an extended plan to visit vengeance on a man named Klaw.

Long ago, Ulysses Klaw, a ruthless researcher, had murdered T'Challa's father, T'Chaka, and enslaved the Wakandans to secure supplies of Vibranium as a power source for his sound-based weaponry. A young T'Challa wrecked his plans, and now that he had proved himself against the world's greatest Super Heroes, the Panther was bent on finishing the job he had begun as a child.

A revolutionary breakthrough and welcome addition to Marvel's ranks of unique characters, the Black Panther was used only sparingly at first, as real-world politics collided with comic book exploits. Although unrelated, the coincidentally named activist group The Black Panther Party (formerly the Lowndes County Freedom Organization) became an increasingly militant presence in the headlines, prompting caution in the publisher. At least African American readers now had a hero they could claim as their own. However, it would be eight years before T'Challa graduated from guest starring in *Captain America* and the *Fantastic Four*, and membership in the Avengers, to gaining his own series in *Jungle Action* #6 (September 1973).

Since then, the Black Panther has become a vibrant and permanent fixture in the Marvel firmament, on the page and the big screen. His hugely successful cinematic debut in 2018 echoed his groundbreaking comic book origins, shattering box-office records and earning unprecedented critical acclaim for its primarily black cast and crew. ▪

Ritual combat
Jack Kirby and his embellisher Joe Sinnott were masters of dynamic action. Their fight scenes never fail to take the breath away, and here, despite the readers believing the Black Panther to be a villain, his body language reveals the poise and attitude of an embattled hero outnumbered but never outmatched.

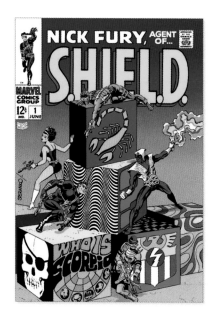

Nick Fury, Agent of S.H.I.E.L.D. #1
June 1968

"Nick Fury... was reinvented for the modern day as the eye-patched head of S.H.I.E.L.D. Steranko's trippy art gave the series a unique, psychedelic look that was pure 1960s and fit right in with the Bondian spy genre."

Peter David

Editor in chief	Stan Lee
Cover artist	Jim Steranko
Writer, penciler	Jim Steranko
Inker	Joe Sinnott
Letterer	Sam Rosen
Editor	Stan Lee

The success of Nick Fury, Agent of S.H.I.E.L.D., and Doctor Strange as the two features in the *Strange Tales* title led to it being canceled and each character being given his own title in 1968. The growing popularity of Fury's stories owed much to creative control having been handed to the multitalented Jim Steranko the previous year.

At age 28, Steranko came to comics after having more careers than many people fit into a lifetime. He had worked in advertising, and been a magician and escape artist. When Steranko showed Stan Lee samples of his art, Lee was so impressed that he gave him a job at Marvel on the spot. He started out following the style of Jack "King" Kirby but was soon creating his own pages and was even given writing and coloring duties, something that was very rare in the industry.

In an era of huge cultural change, Steranko's art took comics to a whole new level. His work was not aimed at children, but at young people and adults who appreciated realistic action and mature plotlines. Steranko's approach to graphic storytelling was revolutionary and cinematic. He frequently employed double-page spreads for maximum impact and even pioneered the four-page spread in *Strange Tales* #167 (April 1968). Readers had to buy two copies so that they could put them together to see the art as it was intended!

By this time, Fury had evolved from a military man to a super-spy, to capitalize on the fashion for espionage in books and films like the James Bond series and *The Man from U.N.C.L.E.* Steranko's work perfectly encapsulated the world of rugged spies, glamorous women, and eccentric villains, enlivened with flourishes of Pop Art and psychedelia. The cover of *Nick Fury, Agent of S.H.I.E.L.D.* #1 exemplifies this with its stylish imagery reminiscent of a movie poster. The filmic motifs continued within the comic. The first three pages of the issue were entirely "silent," with no captions or speech, as Nick Fury attempted to infiltrate a hostile installation.

Within the pages of this issue, readers didn't learn the answer to the question in its title: "Who is Scorpio?" The villain's getaway vehicle crashes in flames after being hit by a random bullet, and it is assumed that he has not survived the blaze. However, the head of the shadowy Zodiac cartel would return in future issues to plague Fury, and it is later revealed that Scorpio is in fact an LMD (Life Model Decoy) of Jacob Fury, Nick's younger brother.

The effort put in by Steranko on the art, script, and storytelling made it hard for him to meet the title's punishing monthly schedule, and the fifth issue of *Nick Fury, Agent of S.H.I.E.L.D.* was his last. He continued to work at Marvel as a cover artist and drew a memorable three-issue run of *Captain America*. However, the brief time he spent on Nick Fury saw him produce some of the most celebrated examples of the comic book medium ever. ◾

Cinematic storytelling
The opening three pages of *Nick Fury, Agent of S.H.I.E.L.D.* #1 exemplify its cinematic aesthetic. The story is told entirely in images, in narrow, wordless panels to add tension and convey the stealth of the super-spy. Steranko later revealed that this section was a homage to the classic French film noir *Rififi* (1955), the middle act of which depicts a heist in complete silence.

Avengers #57
October 1968

"The Vision is considered a quintessential Avenger... and his heroic conviction, all-too-human self-doubt, emotional complexity, and deep ties to the team—is here in his debut. Behold... an A+ character introduction!"

Wil Moss

Editor in chief	Stan Lee
Cover artists	John Buscema, George Klein
Writer	Roy Thomas
Penciler	John Buscema
Inker	George Klein
Letterer	Sam Rosen
Editor	Stan Lee

Look on my works... and despair!
The final, poetic page of *Avengers* #57 elevates it from an average comic book to a true classic. Percy Bysshe Shelley's famous sonnet "Ozymandias" captions the panels, emphasizing Ultron's hubris and the scale of his downfall.

*A*vengers #57 saw the debut of one of the team's most enduringly popular members—the Vision. Editor Stan Lee and writer Roy Thomas both felt that the title needed new blood, since the "A-listers" Iron Man, Captain America, Thor, and Hulk were no longer active. Rather than create a new character, Thomas was eager to repurpose a Golden Age hero named Aarkus, aka Vision—an otherdimensional being who wore a green suit with a flowing cape and upturned collar. However, Lee wanted the new Avenger to be an android, and so Thomas compromised, creating a robotic character whose appearance was based on Vision and shared his name.

John Buscema, the co-creator of the new Vision, designed his look accordingly. He changed the face from green to red but kept the style of the costume. He also added a gem on the Vision's forehead, which would become a significant part of the Avengers' mythos, both on the comic book page and in screen adaptations.

The concept of Vision as a sympathetic robot, with human emotions, came to Roy Thomas through his friendship with the science fiction author Otto Binder. In the "Adam Link" series of short stories (1939-1942) by Eando Binder (Earl and Otto Binder), the robot Adam becomes self-aware but faces prejudice from fearful humans. Adam understands more about itself and the human race after reading Mary Shelley's *Frankenstein*. For his creation, Roy Thomas used the word "synthezoid" rather than robot or android. Vision's synthetic body also contained an implanted

human consciousness, later revealed as that of Wonder Man (Simon Williams).

The villain of the story was Ultron-5, an evil robot also created by Thomas and Buscema, first introduced in *Avengers* #54 (July 1968). Ultron was conceived from the idea of a robot enacting its own will rather than being a mere automaton commanded by a human master. It represented the polar opposite of Vision for the potential of technology. Thomas wanted Ultron's face to wear a permanent wicked smile, an idea inspired by a character called Makino from the 1951 comic book *Captain Video*.

Ultron had programmed Vision to attack the Avengers and lure the heroes to his hideout so that he could destroy them himself. But Ultron hadn't anticipated Vision breaking from his control and helping the heroes. Ultron compounded his failure by giving the synthezoid the power to adjust his density so that he is intangible or super-solid. Vision provokes Ultron into attacking him when he is intangible, and the robot plummets into an energy vat and is destroyed. The end of the issue sees Ultron's disembodied head abandoned on a piece of wasteland, where it is played with by a passing child. The mighty had fallen.

It wasn't until the next issue that readers learned the truth about Ultron and Vision. Ultron had been the creation of Avenger Hank Pym, aka Goliath, whom the robot regarded as its father. From the start, Ultron had been unstable, attacking its creator and then wiping his memory before escaping to make its own plans. It was Ultron who created Vision to do its bidding. ■

THEN, SILENTLY, EFFORTLESSLY ...LIKE SOME GREAT, VENGEFUL *BIRD OF PREY*...HE SWOOPS INTO THE MOONLESS, CLOUD-DRAPED SKY...TOWARDS A TOWERING STRUCTURE NEARBY...

"BEHOLD...THE VISION!"

AN EERIE EXPEDITION INTO UNEXPLORED REALMS, CONDUCTED BY:
STAN LEE, EDITOR!
ROY THOMAS, WRITER!
JOHN BUSCEMA, ARTIST!

GEORGE KLEIN, INKER!
SAM ROSEN, LETTERER!

A Vision splendid
John Buscema and George Klein's moody, elegant art for *Avengers #57* perfectly captures Vision's inherent melancholy as he struggles to understand and accept his identity and the nature of his being. Buscema's striking duo-chromatic cover for this issue is one of Marvel's most iconic and homaged images.

Editor in chief	Stan Lee
Cover artists	John Buscema, Joe Sinnott
Writer	Stan Lee
Penciler	John Buscema
Inker	Joe Sinnott
Letterer	Artie Simek
Editor	Stan Lee

Hellfire and brimstone
The demonic Mephisto delighted in everything about Earth that made the Silver Surfer despair—the greed, belligerence, and prejudice. John Buscema's brooding splash page reveals the character at his malevolent, manipulative worst.

Silver Surfer #3
December 1968

66 If Stan Lee's Surfer was a fallen angel, lamenting man's inhumanity to man, then it was only natural to have him up against the literal devil in the form of Mephisto. **99**

Tom Brevoort

The Silver Surfer swept into public consciousness directly from the mind of Jack Kirby, who added him to the Fantastic Four story in which Galactus first appeared. Kirby reasoned that a mighty world-devourer such as Galactus would need a herald who could scout for planets he could consume. Although Stan Lee was initially surprised to see this bald spacefarer and his interstellar board when Kirby sent him the pencils for the issue, he quickly grew to love this iconic character, and so did the readers.

After guest spots in the pages of *Fantastic Four* following his first outing in 1966, the Silver Surfer was given his own title in August 1968. Stan Lee would be the writer, and John Buscema took on the art duties. At 72 pages, the first seven issues were twice the length of regular comics and, at 25 cents, were more than double the usual price. As compensation, the Silver Surfer lead feature was backed up by a Watcher story—a truly cosmic double bill.

Lee used the Silver Surfer to expound much of his own philosophy. The Surfer had been stranded on Earth after defying Galactus in *Fantastic Four*, which gave him time to observe the planet and the beings who inhabited it. The first two issues of *Silver Surfer* were devoted to his mysterious origins and his defense of Earth against an invasion by the evil aliens known as the Badoon. However, even as the Silver Surfer fought to protect Earth, the humans he encountered feared and mistrusted him, and he was attacked several times. Although his power made him virtually invulnerable to Earth weaponry, the Surfer was emotionally bruised by the rejection.

In *Silver Surfer #3*, the Surfer is once again fired upon by Earthlings as he tries to help a young woman wounded in the Badoon attack. This sent him into a vengeful anger, and he decided to demonstrate the power that he could unleash upon the world if he saw fit. However, he soon regretted giving way to rage. Stan Lee used the Surfer to comment on the absurdity of human behavior, as beings who seemingly have it all but still find reasons to fight each other over often spurious causes. Lee was a humanist by nature, believing, in essence, that people should get along with one another.

The Surfer soon had something far worse to worry about as he was attacked again—this time by the demon Mephisto. *Silver Surfer #3* was the first appearance of Mephisto, a demonic character created by Stan Lee and John Buscema. He provided a counterpoint to the noble purity of the Silver Surfer, as he reveled in the crime and conflict that ravaged humanity—it meant more souls sent to his dread domain for eternity. Buscema did some of his best work in *Silver Surfer*, and in this issue he amply displayed his talents by creating the fiery hellscape in which Mephisto resided, as well as a multitude of Earthly landscapes and outer-space vistas.

Although *Silver Surfer* would run for only 18 issues in this, its first volume, the series remains one of the all-time classics of Marvel's Silver Age. The iconic status of the character, coupled with the mature themes of morality and philosophy the title explores, make it a comic book that is as absorbing and thought-provoking now as it was when it was created in the 1960s. ■

Righteous rage
Provoked to fury by the constant displays of suspicion and outright violence toward him by humans on Earth, the Silver Surfer contemplated showing the planet a fraction of what his Power Cosmic could do. However, his innate goodness made him stop, regretting that he had sunk to such a level.

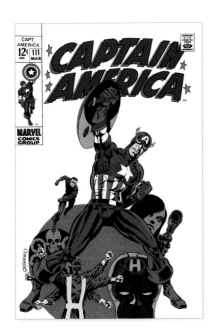

Captain America #111
March 1969

" Steranko was a revolutionary writer-artist who opened Marvel up to psychedelia and op-art influences, combining comics and film media to create storytelling techniques still imitated but never surpassed. "

Mark Waid

Editor in chief	Stan Lee
Cover artist	Jim Steranko
Writer	Stan Lee
Penciler	Jim Steranko
Inker	Joe Sinnott
Letterer	Sam Rosen
Editor	Stan Lee

◀ **Show and tell**
A signature Steranko technique for impart information and setting mood is a montage of small, tight images emulating cinematic cuts and close-ups. "For Tomorrow You Live, Tonight I Die!" the artist ratchets up tension at an amusement park arcade through rapid transitions that simultaneously establish location, deliver credits, and create an air of menace. The sequence presages the approaching threat as much as the ominous fortune-telling card that delivers the issue's title.

After reviving from frozen hibernation, Captain America swiftly evolved into one of Marvel's hottest, most recognizable properties, both as leader of the mighty Avengers and also in spectacular solo action. Cap initially shared *Tales of Suspense* with Iron Man before taking over and converting the title to *Captain America* with the 100th issue in 1968.

For a year or so, *Captain America* was illustrated by major artists, primarily Jack Kirby, but also by such luminaries as John Romita Snr. and Gil Kane, among others. None, however, arrived on the comics scene with the cachet or graphic sophistication of media sensation Jim Steranko, who united with scripter Stan Lee for a three-part epic in *Captain America* #110–113. The saga was actually paused at its most dramatic juncture for a Kirby-delineated *Captain America* #112 (April 1969), which commemorated the career of the Star-Spangled Avenger, supposedly slain at the end of the previous issue in a shocking cliff-hanger.

The pivotal moment of Lee and Steranko's sadly short run occurred in *Captain America* #111. The issue judiciously pulled together a number of loose plot threads while delivering a bravura action romp laced with contemporary Pop Art and surrealist psychedelia, as well as introducing Marvel's most seductive villain to date.

Since Cap's revival, perennial Super Hero aspirant and former Incredible Hulk sidekick Rick Jones had lobbied to become the Sentinel of Liberty's costumed partner, replacing fallen World War II warrior Bucky Barnes, who Jones coincidentally and disturbingly resembled. The turning point for guilt-plagued Steve Rogers comes following a brief but terrifying clash with the Hulk. After the Green Goliath rampages through Manhattan, Captain America at last accedes to Rick's requests. Jones suits up in patriotic red and blue just in time to clash with a splinter group of Hydra and its psychotic femme fatale leader Madame Hydra, and passes his combat graduation with distinction.

In "Tomorrow You Live, Tonight I Die!" a clandestine meeting with S.H.I.E.L.D. director Nick Fury at a Penny Arcade turns into a Hydra ambush that Cap barely survives, and he admits at last that he has made a grave mistake in going public with his secret identity. As Steve Rogers is systematically hunted by assassins, Rick Jones intercepts a drugged letter intended for his partner. His mind reeling with horrific images, Jones is dragged away by Hydra operatives after they break into Avengers Headquarters. Captain America chases the abductors, but despite his utmost efforts, the Hydra goons get away with their prize. With no other options, Captain America retraces his steps, searching the city, and ends up back at the amusement arcade where the ambush occurred. Entering what he knows is a lethal trap, Cap has no idea Rick has already escaped and is racing back to warn him. The distraught teen arrives just in time to see his mentor's bullet-riddled body drop into the East River. Mystery then compounds tragedy as the police trawl the waters and recover a shredded costume and plastic face mask. The conclusion is inescapable: Steve Rogers must have been a fake persona and the world can now only mourn a fallen hero whose real identity may never be known.

Scripted by Stan Lee, who had been the hero's primary writer since his revival, these episodes mark a high point in Steranko's artistic quest to unify the sequential narrative of the comics medium with the visual techniques of filmmaking. However, no one involved in crafting this epic ever forgets that this is a comic series built on breakneck action and heart-stopping derring-do. With his illustrative style of the period amplifying Jack Kirby's dynamism, inked to a sleek sheen by the crisp brushwork of Joe Sinnott, Steranko's artwork is intoxicating. The backgrounds are carefully detailed, while the idealized heroes are the epitome of All-American decency, just as the sinister villain is coldly alluring and her thuggish henchmen are satisfyingly grotesque.

Most importantly, Steranko acutely understands the impact of a cathartic moment. Often utilizing seven or more panels to a page to marry mood and tone while driving the plot forward, the artist always ensures he delivers well-placed, evocative full-body shots or a sizzling, poster-worthy, double-page spread. Steranko's figures are always in motion: tumbling and falling in training sequences when not evading hot pursuit or dispensing harsh justice to colorful villains. It's not often that the middle act of a comic book series hits all the sweet spots at once, but *Captain America* #111 triumphantly succeeds in standing on its own as a gloriously drawn and told Super Hero extravaganza—one that's impossible to ignore or forget. ◼

Cut to the chase
As a near comatose Rick Jones is hauled out of Avengers Mansion and bundled into a waiting car, Captain America hits the kidnappers like a guided missile, in a perfect example of the sinuous illustrative style and hyper-dynamic composition at which Steranko excelled.

X-Men #56
May 1969

Editor in chief	Stan Lee
Cover artist	Neal Adams
Writer	Roy Thomas
Penciler	Neal Adams
Inker	Tom Palmer
Letterer	Herb Cooper
Editor	Stan Lee

> **"**Although an action-filled tale [that premiered] the Living Monolith, this issue was particularly memorable for the X-debut of Neal Adams, who went on to become an acclaimed penciler.**"**
>
> **Peter David**

In 1969, Neal Adams was one of the top comic book artists, receiving the Alley Award for Best Penciler that year. He had been working at National Comics (later DC Comics) but was also freelancing for Marvel. *X-Men* #56 was his first Marvel comic, for which he teamed up with stalwart scribe Roy Thomas. The title's sales lagged behind Marvel bestsellers such as *Fantastic Four* and *Amazing Spider-Man*, and so Adams and Thomas had a simple mission— save the X-Men. The two, along with inker Tom Palmer, would prove to be an inspired creative team, producing work that is now considered among the finest examples of Silver Age comics.

X-Men #56 showcases the best of what Neal Adams would bring to the medium, starting with the high-impact cover showing the towering Living Monolith, the book's villain, holding the comic's title in his hands. More than a decade later, Adams' cover was homaged by artist John Byrne in *X-Men* #135 (July 1980), part of the Dark Phoenix saga—both comics now considered classics. In fact, Adams had to redraw the cover after the first version was rejected because X-Men team members obscured the title. Mastheads were very important at this time, as they were often the only part of a comic book visible on crowded newsstand racks.

Neal Adams was prepared to push the envelope and look at comic book art in a completely new way. This is evident throughout the issue, which contains a variety of perspectives and panel shapes rarely seen in comics of the time. Adams brought across stylistic approaches from his other work in advertising and newspaper strips, enabling him to visualize pages in a more aesthetic way than had been traditional in comic books. *X-Men* #56 reveals the artist's love of diagonal lines and irregularly shaped panels that place the reader at the center of the action as the X-Men take on the maniacal Living Monolith. This issue saw the creation of this flamboyant villain, who absorbs his power from Alex Summers, the younger brother of Scott Summers (Cyclops). Alex was a recently introduced character at this time, but would go on to be a regular in the X-Men's stories as the mutant Havok. At the end of the tale, Alex harnesses his powers to break free of the Living Monolith's prison and cause the villain's own powers to fade. However, the young hero can't control the energy coursing through him and is forced to deter the X-Men's involvement for their own safety.

As well as adopting a radical approach to structuring his pages and panels, Adams modernized comic book coloring. Before *X-Men* #56, artists had to choose from a more restrictive color palette for inside pages than for covers, largely for cost savings and convenience. However, Adams insisted on a greater range of colors for his interior art, and *X-Men* #56 became a testament to his maverick vision. Readers were now rewarded with the same level of quality throughout the story as they found on the cover. Although Adams and Thomas were unable to keep *X-Men* going for long as a new title, their trailblazing work over the next year saved the book from cancellation. After *X-Men* #66 (March 1970), new stories were replaced with reprints until the title's landmark revival in the 1970s. ◾

Flying colors
From the very first page of *X-Men #56*, fans knew that a new era had begun. Neal Adams' photorealistic style was used to full effect on this meticulous recreation of the famous temple at Abu Simbel, Egypt, while the X-Men sweep into the scene. The perspective used by the artist makes readers feel like they are flying in right behind the team.

Thor #169
October 1969

"The world gets what it demanded... the origin of Galactus as told by Stan and Jack. One of the things I love about this is that they told this story in Thor and not in the more obvious choice of Fantastic Four."

Dan Buckley

Editor in chief	Stan Lee
Cover artists	Jack Kirby, George Klein
Writer	Stan Lee
Penciler	Jack Kirby
Inker	George Klein
Letterer	Artie Simek
Editor	Stan Lee

BUT SOON ITS *HUNGER* WILL BE SO GREAT -- NAUGHT BUT A *WORLD* CAN APPEASE IT!

Fateful decision
Immeasurably powerful, all-knowing, and wise, Ecce the Watcher struggles with his conscience. He realizes the unique creature evolving before his eyes would shake the universe, causing inconceivable death and destruction unless he destroys it now. Ultimately, Ecce resolves to let destiny unfold as it will.

One of the most enticing aspects of the ever-unfolding Marvel Comics Universe was its brilliant combination of distinctly human characters with mind-boggling concepts and spectacular visuals. No creative team better conveyed this than Stan Lee and Jack Kirby. In *Fantastic Four*, they embedded then cutting-edge science fiction such as parallel dimensions, human cloning, and subatomic universes into a familial Super Hero soap opera. In *Thor*, they could really expand their horizons, exploring the outer reaches of the cosmos, wedding godlike power to human foibles, and blending action, adventure, and mythology into a dazzling unified whole.

The improbably powerful Galactus was introduced in *Fantastic Four* #48 (March 1966): an unstoppable threat to humankind dependent on vast amounts of life energy to survive and intent on consuming planet Earth. Jack Kirby envisioned him as an inverted allegory of the biblical Christian god: a destroyer rather than a life giver, seeking worlds to absorb with the help of his herald, the Silver Surfer. In a timely epiphany, the Surfer rebels against his creator to save humanity as a modern-day fallen angel.

Galactus was intended as a one-time threat, but vociferous reader reaction brought him back, initially as a brooding omnipotent menace and eventually as a fully realized character interacting with others, which often meant other "gods." Following a three-way war between Galactus, Ego, the Living Planet, and Thor, the Thunder God's father, Odin, decreed that his son should search for the world-devourer to see whether he posed a threat to Asgard. That quest reached its end in a two-part tale concluding in *Thor* #169.

Fans undoubtedly expected another stupendous fight, and while they may have been frustrated on that score, they were rewarded with a remarkable, stunningly rendered insight into the almighty extraterrestrial. After a minor skirmish, Galactus unexpectedly presented a startlingly human aspect to his character, sharing his origins in the last chapter "The Awesome Answer!"

Expanding and cementing Marvel's cosmology by incorporating another established alien race into an ever-growing tapestry, Lee and Kirby reveal how, eons ago, the highly advanced civilization of Taa was eradicated by a devastating plague. With no hope of a cure, the last dying beings flung themselves into the universe's largest sun as a final glorious act of defiance, only to have the explorer Galan survive, mutating into a wholly unique being. Weak but rapidly evolving, Galan and his crashed ship are found by a Watcher.

Introduced in *Fantastic Four* #13 (April 1963), Watchers are immortal super-beings stemming from the earliest days of creation. Deeply philosophical, curious, and almost godlike, the Watchers opt to share their advancements with other, lesser races. Traveling in small groups across the

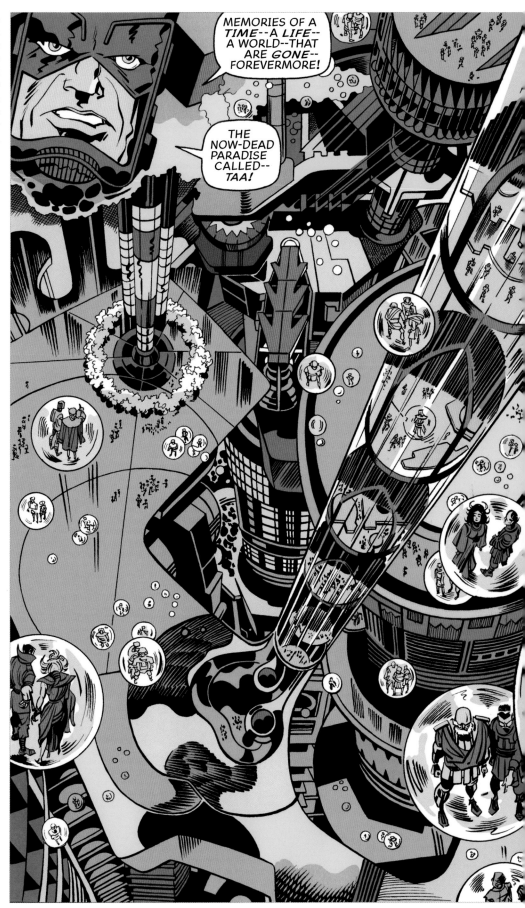

Strange worlds
Kirby's fertile visual imagination built and furnished incredible yet believable civilizations evoking awe and wonder. His monumental imagery perfectly captured power and grandeur, captivating readers who would nevertheless come to expect that no matter how magnificent, these edifices would soon be spectacularly destroyed.

universe, their well-intentioned teachings are perverted on planet Prosilicus, resulting in atomic war. On discovering what their actions have spawned, they vow that, from this time forward, they would simply observe all that occurs, but never again would a Watcher interfere with any other species or culture. Here, the Watcher later dubbed Ecce foresees the catastrophe the new entity will cause but resolutely honors his pledge and Galactus is born.

The origin of Galactus was a milestone in Marvel history, and greatly revised as decades passed. In *Super-Villain Classics: Galactus the Origin* #1 (May 1983), writer Mark Gruenwald revealed that Galan was actually a survivor of the death of a previous reality. As the Big Bang created the current Marvel Universe, Galan merged with the dying sentient essence of that previous reality. Creators John Byrne, Jim Starlin, and Louise Simonson would later elaborate on the premise, making Galactus a fundamental force among the higher powers of the modern Marvel Multiverse.

Thor and the Fantastic Four would clash with Galactus many times in the years to come, but this epic was the first to put a tragic, human face to the impassive, relentless cosmic horror first envisioned by Lee and Kirby. It laid the groundwork for a mind-boggling expansion of Marvel's continuity into a hierarchy of spiritual and metaphysical realms that would affect all later stories and become the basis of many cosmic crossover events. ■

Amazing
Spider-Man #86
July 1970

> 66 John Romita Sr. did more for Black Widow than Russia and Scarlet Johannsen combined, by replacing her drab fishnets-and-domino-mask outfit with a sleek, sexy look that became instantly iconic. 99

Mark Waid

Editor in chief	Stan Lee
Cover artist	John Romita Sr.
Writer	Stan Lee
Penciler	John Romita Sr.
Inker	Jim Mooney
Letterer	Sam Rosen
Editor	Stan Lee

The Black Widow (Natasha Romanoff) debuted in 1964, and for the rest of the decade made appearances in *Tales of Suspense* and *Avengers*, first as a villain and then defecting from her Soviet masters to become a hero. Her story contained a great deal of tragedy, not least when her husband Alexi Shostakov (Red Guardian) had apparently been killed. Natasha tried to adopt the safer life of an international jet-setter, but in *Amazing Spider-Man #86*, she returned to the world of Super Heroes with a bang. She could not find happiness as one of the idle rich; only by being Black Widow could she truly be herself.

Black Widow was a popular character, due partly to her exotic glamour and partly to her questionable past and the shades of gray in her ethics. Even while fighting beside the Avengers, she had broken their code by threatening to kill a foe. Believing that there was a lot of storytelling potential in such an intriguingly nuanced character, editor in chief Stan Lee commissioned a new title—*Amazing Adventures*—to showcase Black Widow's stories alongside another regular segment that featured the Inhumans. He also turned to one of Marvel's most talented artists, John Romita Sr., to completely refashion Natasha's look for the new decade.

In order to boost interest in Black Widow ahead of her new solo series, the character was included in *Amazing Spider-Man #86*. It was quite common

to use one of Marvel's more successful properties to highlight a less well-known character and create a buzz to drive readers to their title. Since this issue came out a month before the first *Amazing Adventures*, *Amazing Spider-Man #86* tantalized readers with a first look at Black Widow's soon-to-be iconic new costume.

Although Black Widow's new catsuit seemed to be influenced by the popularity of spies in franchises like James Bond, it was in fact inspired by something much older. John Romita Sr. had been a big fan of a syndicated newspaper strip called *Miss Fury*, published in the 1940s. Miss Fury held the honor of being the first female Super Hero created by a woman, June "Tarpé" Mills, herself one of the first female comics creators. Also known as Marla Drake, Miss Fury wore a skintight black catsuit and a mask. Romita shelved plans to draw a Miss Fury comic after a lukewarm editorial response to the idea, turning his attention to revamping Black Widow's costume—purposefully conceived in-story by Natasha herself.

In *Amazing Spider-Man #86*, in the first meeting of the two characters, the new-look Black Widow tries to capture Spider-Man so that she can learn more about—and possibly steal—his powers, reasoning that they were both arachnid-styled adventurers. Although at first she seems to get the better of the wall-crawler, he manages to evade her by gumming up her new wrist gauntlet

Way of the Widow
Now outside the Soviet system, Black Widow could no longer access the advanced technology of her former paymasters. This meant that all of her equipment had to be devised and built by her faithful right-hand man, Ivan Petrovitch.

weapons with his web. Black Widow decides to abandon her plan and accept that she would have to create her own identity as a hero. In her subsequent solo adventures, Natasha Romanoff would battle to earn the trust of her adopted country by helping the vulnerable, usually accompanied by her gruff partner-in-crime-fighting, Ivan Petrovitch, and later successfully teamed up with Daredevil.

Such was the impact of Romita's modish Black Widow costume that it became the classic look for the character, and would make its movie debut in the Marvel Cinematic Universe many decades later. Her 1970 relaunch ensured that Black Widow was an integral part of Marvel Comics moving into the Bronze Age and beyond, and she is now one of Marvel's most recognizable heroes. ■

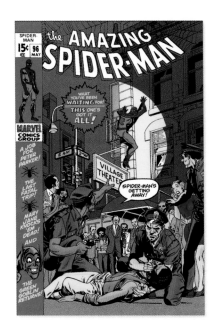

Editor in chief	Stan Lee
Cover artists	Gil Kane, John Romita Sr.
Writer	Stan Lee
Penciler	Gil Kane
Inker	John Romita Sr.
Letterer	Artie Simek
Editor	Stan Lee

On the edge
Stan Lee and Gil Kane's anti-narcotics story depicts a young man in the grip of a drug-fueled hallucination jumping off a building. Luckily for him, Spider-Man was swinging through the streets at just the right moment.

Amazing Spider-Man #96
May 1971

> ❝At a time when comics' content was suffocating under the Comics Code Authority, Stan decided to forego their approval on this stridently anti-drug story. Marvel had his back and it was the beginning of the end of the CCA's censorship authority. Good riddance.❞
>
> **Peter David**

In the early 1970s, the comic book industry increasingly began using stories to address the major social concerns of the day, including civil rights, poverty, the environment, and political corruption. However, one issue affecting young people was absent from comic books—growing drug use. This was because any mention of drugs, even if it was decrying the harm they could cause, was banned from comics produced by any publisher that had signed up to the Comics Magazine Association of America and its rigid Comics Code Authority (CCA). This had been formed in 1954 in response to a campaign by various moral arbiters that accused comics of corrupting young minds with excessive violence and horror themes.

The onus was on major publishers to sign up to the CCA, because without its approval they ran the risk of losing advertising revenue and being blacklisted by the wholesalers who put their comic books on newsstands across the US. Comics sanctioned by the CCA bore its logo on their covers so that parents could be reassured that their children's reading

material was suitably wholesome—and from the outset, every Silver Age Marvel comic had displayed the logo.

However, in 1971, Stan Lee received a letter from the US Department of Health, Education, and Welfare that would put it at odds with the CCA. Recognizing the unique reach that Marvel had when it came to young people, especially college students, the Nixon administration asked Lee to include an antidrug story in one of Marvel's titles. The obvious choice was *Amazing Spider-Man*, a book that was a major success story, reached an appropriate readership for the subject matter, and already had a history of tackling other significant social issues.

The result was the story arc "Green Goblin Returns!," running through *Amazing Spider-Man* #96–98 (May–July 1971). Gil Kane's cover art puts drug use front and center, showing the aftermath of a young man having a bad trip and thinking he can fly off a building, although readers might not have realized drugs were involved until they ventured inside the comic. In the story, Spider-Man

THEY GOTTA *SEE*-- SEE HOW I WALK ON THE *AIR*--

HAVE TO *TIME* IT JUST *RIGHT.*

THERE WON'T BE A *SECOND* CHANCE.

Saved by the web
As Spider-Man arrives on the scene, he is able to save the delusional young man from certain death. Spidey admits to himself that, although he may not understand why people take drugs, he gets his own kicks from being Spider-Man.

happens upon the unfortunate youth as he plummets from a great height to what would have been certain death if the web-slinger hadn't been on hand to catch him. The issue is peppered with antidrug messages, including Spider-Man reflecting that being addicted to drugs was far worse than fighting Super Villains. Stan Lee knew that being too preachy would turn off his readers, so he astutely integrates his gripping tale into an ongoing Green Goblin story line. The story's impact is helped in no small measure by Gil Kane and John Romita Sr.'s expressive, realistic artwork.

Another character who voices strong opposition to drugs is Randy Robertson, son of *The Daily Bugle* city editor Joe "Robbie" Robertson. Randy confronts Norman Osborn about the drugs crisis, demanding that the rich and influential should be doing more to help. He also persuasively argues that people see drugs as a problem that comes from the black community, when, in fact, it is young African Americans who are most vulnerable to the pushers.

Despite the government directing Marvel to use the story, and despite all references to drugs being wholly negative, the CCA refused approval for *Amazing Spider-Man* #96. Lee, fully supported by publisher Martin Goodman, decided that the story was too important and published without approval for the first time in Marvel's history. The comic hit the stands without the CCA logo, as did the next two issues of *Amazing Spider-Man*. Reception to the story was overwhelmingly positive and prompted the CCA to revisit its rules later that year and include a specific section about the depiction of drugs. *Amazing Spider-Man* #96 had changed the future of comic books.

As the story arc developed, readers were further shocked when the drugs problem hit Peter Parker much closer to home. His best friend Harry Osborn, feeling depressed after his girlfriend Mary Jane seems to lose interest in him, becomes addicted to pills. Peter has to deal with the fallout of this at the same time as battling his old adversary and Harry's father, the Green Goblin. ▪

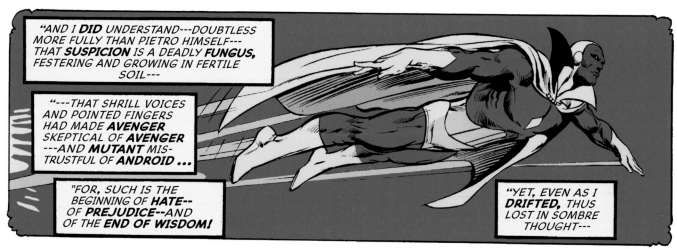

"AND I **DID** UNDERSTAND---DOUBTLESS MORE FULLY THAN **PIETRO** HIMSELF--- THAT **SUSPICION** IS A DEADLY **FUNGUS,** FESTERING AND GROWING IN FERTILE SOIL---

"---THAT SHRILL VOICES AND POINTED FINGERS HAD MADE **AVENGER** SKEPTICAL OF **AVENGER** ---AND **MUTANT** MIS- TRUSTFUL OF **ANDROID** ...

"FOR, SUCH IS THE BEGINNING OF **HATE--** OF **PREJUDICE--**AND OF THE **END OF WISDOM!**

"YET, EVEN AS I **DRIFTED,** THUS LOST IN SOMBRE THOUGHT---

"--I SUDDENLY PASSED THRU THE **GATES** OF HELL--!

AARRR

ZZZAKT!

When worlds collide
In the 1960s, Neal Adams was considered by many fans to be a comics iconoclast. His daring design sense, thrilling page composition, and realistic illustrations brought a compelling authenticity to even the most outlandish scenarios. Applied to a story that draws together several hanging plotlines and involving beloved heroes, political machinations, sly satire, warring alien empires, and even shape-shifting killer cows, the cumulative effect was utterly mind-blowing.

Avengers #93
November 1971

Editor in chief | Stan Lee
Cover artists | Neal Adams, Tom Palmer
Writer | Roy Thomas
Penciler | Neal Adams
Inker | Tom Palmer
Letterer | Sam Rosen
Editor | Stan Lee

“No one who's ever read this comic has ever forgotten it. Ant-Man's fantastic and visually stunning voyage inside the Vision was a thing of wonder. Neal Adams' body of Marvel work is small, but this is its pinnacle. ”

Mark Waid

As the 1970s began, Marvel overtook the competition to become market leader. Tastes had changed significantly since the launch of the *Fantastic Four*, and their diverse line now consisted of western, humor, supernatural mystery, fantasy, romance, and war titles. Many were reprint anthologies of classic stories, which bolstered a Super Hero division of fewer than a dozen regular titles. Then *Avengers* writer Roy Thomas conceived an epic adventure that would revolutionize mainstream comics. There had been extended story lines before, but never of the scope, sophistication, and ambition of the "Kree-Skrull War." *Avengers* #93 was the turning point in a lengthy saga that began when exiled Kree warrior Mar-Vell finally escaped the Negative Zone.

Mar-Vell originally came to Earth as a spy for the militaristic, intergalactic Kree Empire, but rebelled and became a valiant protector of humanity. After a mission to save his former homeworld, "Captain Marvel," as he was called at the time, was returning to his adopted home when he was pulled into the antimatter universe known as the Negative Zone. He found temporary release through dormant Kree Nega-Bands hidden on Earth. Atomically bonded with Rick Jones, Mar-Vell traded places with the teenager whenever danger loomed but was drawn back to the Zone after three hours. Following distressing months sharing one life, Jones and Mar-Vell finally separated, just as the Kree Empire's ruling Supreme Intelligence was overthrown by his own enforcer Ronan the Accuser.

On Earth, Ronan's actions triggered a hidden robotic Kree Sentry, which attacked Mar-Vell and the Avengers while attempting to devolve humanity to the level of cavemen. The assault was ultimately thwarted, but bystanders later revealed the panic-inducing news that extraterrestrials hid among us. Media outrage fueled public opinion, which turned against the heroes for concealing the threat of repeated alien incursions.

Incorporating a powerful allegory of the anti-Communist witch hunts of the 1950s, Thomas' script brought riots to American streets and created a political demagogue who captialized on the mayhem. Subpoenaed by the authorities, castigated by friends and the public, the current Avengers—Vision, Scarlet Witch, Quicksilver, and Goliath (aka Clint Barton, the former Hawkeye)—were helpless to prevent their mansion from being wrecked by panicked protesters. The heroes were eventually ordered to disband by founding fathers Thor, Iron Man, and Captain America. Or were they?

The crisis unfolds in this magnificent double-length tale as Neal Adams and Tom Palmer assume art duties with "This Beachhead Earth." The Vision, ambushed and reduced to a comatose state, is recovered by Thor, Iron Man, Captain America, and Hank Pym, the original Ant-Man, who plans to reboot Vision's artificial life processes via a breathtaking excursion through the synthezoid's body. The Vision is successfully revived, and he explains to his rescuers—who claim they

never benched the current team—that
his team of Avengers were checking
on Mar-Vell in a safehouse provided
by intelligence officer Carol Danvers when
they were attacked by the Fantastic Four!

Meanwhile, Mar-Vell and Danvers
awaken in shackles aboard a Skrull
starship. Scarlet Witch and Quicksilver
are also captives of the alien shape-shifters,
but Rick Jones and Goliath are still free.
As the latter are joined by the founding
Avengers, the Fantastic Four—soon
revealed as Skrulls—attack again. Inside
the ship, Mar-Vell breaks loose and sets
about constructing an Omni-Wave
Projector to contact his fellow Kree.

However, at the last minute, Mar-Vell
deduces that "Carol" is also an imposter
and destroys the device, realizing it's
a weapon that the Skrulls have coveted
for millennia. Exposed as Super-Skrull,
the powerful alien overwhelms Mar-Vell
and cuts his losses, abandoning his
own warriors and blasting into space.
Goliath comes close to stopping the
ship but loses his powers when the
Pym growth serum wears off, allowing
Super-Skrull to escape with his captives.
Defeated and despondent, the Avengers
must now deal with two hostile alien
forces infiltrating Earth when they
are at their lowest point.

This complex and audacious blend of political intrigue, cosmic conflict, and sharp characterization confirmed scripter Roy Thomas as a major creative force in comics. It also demonstrated the still-untapped potential of a largely dismissed medium. Depicting Super Heroes in such a mature manner and shading the action-packed story with literary devices showed what was possible. Each chapter references classic science fiction movies such as *This Island Earth* and *War of the Worlds*, while the political undertones of paranoia and persecution mirrored the social unrest America was experiencing at the time.

Succeeding issues would take the heroes to the hidden kingdom of Attilan, the depths of interstellar space, and the Kree and Skrull homeworlds as Thomas, Adams, and John Buscema redefined the nature of humanity in the Marvel Universe. The Kree-Skrull War even reinvigorated the faded careers of Rick Jones and Captain Marvel. At the time, this bold experiment was considered the most significant story in Marvel's history, setting the template and standard for all multipart crossovers and publishing events to come. Decades later, it remains one of the most thrilling and dazzlingly drawn sagas of its type ever conceived. ◾

Fantastic voyage
Neal Adams' revolutionary page layouts and inspired imagination ran riot as he revealed for the first time the interior landscape of the Vision, one of Marvel's most popular and enigmatic heroes. Thomas' story-within-a-story also completely reinvigorated the status and appeal of Ant-Man—one of the company's oldest characters, but one who had languished in the background for many years.

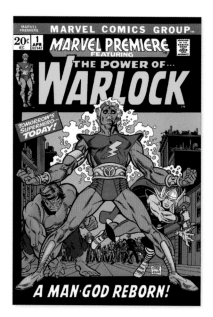

Marvel Premiere #1
April 1972

"Continuing Marvel's tradition of reimagining characters for the modern era, Thomas and Kane transform the golden humanoid Him into the messianic Adam Warlock in a revolutionary tale of truth, hate, forgiveness, sacrifice, metamorphosis, rebirth and destiny."

Bill Rosemann

Editor in chief	Stan Lee
Cover artists	Gil Kane, Dan Adkins
Writer	Roy Thomas
Penciler	Gil Kane
Inker	Dan Adkins
Letterer	Sam Rosen
Editor	Stan Lee

Unnatural selection
Obsessed geneticist Herbert Edgar Wyndham mastered the processes of evolution and created armies of ascended beings from simple animals. He only reluctantly advanced himself to virtual godhood when his mortal body was fatally wounded by his rebellious test subjects.

Super Heroes were an invention of comics' Golden Age but plummeted in popularity as the 1940s ended. They returned in force in the mid-1950s, and after Stan Lee and Jack Kirby revitalized the concept in the early 1960s, costumed characters became a mainstay of the industry. However, as the 1960s drew to a close, history seemed to repeat itself and super-powered characters went into another steep decline. Popular appetites shifted significantly, but Marvel had always offered variety and easily switched back to traditional genres such as westerns, supernatural mystery, and romance, which had worked well for the company—as Atlas Comics—in the immediate postwar era.

Employing the tactic again in the 1970s didn't signal that Marvel was abandoning Super Heroes, just that it was looking at more interesting and sophisticated ways to use them. At this time, Stan Lee was transitioning from writer-editor in chief to publisher, and Roy Thomas was being groomed to take his place overseeing the day-to-day comics publishing. With Super Heroes now a riskier proposition, they devised three new titles—*Marvel Spotlight*, *Marvel Feature*, and *Marvel Premiere*— to test new concepts and revamp old ones, with a minimum of expense and resources. These tryout titles would allow Marvel to cautiously gauge reader response before committing to full series launches.

Thanks to more thought-provoking titles like Lee and John Buscema's *Silver Surfer* and Marvel's championing of issues such as civil rights and drugs awareness, comic books had developed into a vibrant forum for debate and free expression, engaging youngsters in real-world issues relevant to them. Roy Thomas took the next logical step— and a big creative gamble—for *Marvel Premiere* #1 when he transmuted an old Fantastic Four enemy into a potent political and religious metaphor.

Debuting in *Fantastic Four #66* (September 1967), "Him" was a genetically modified, lab-grown man designed to conquer the world for his diabolical creators. He fled Earth for outer space, initiated a naive clash with Thor for possession of his girlfriend, Sif, and ultimately returned to his all-encompassing cosmic cocoon to heal and further evolve. For *Marvel Premiere* #1, Thomas, penciler Gil Kane, and inker Dan Adkins spectacularly reimagined the star-bound nomad as a fantastical interpretation of the Christ myth, placing him on a troubled world far more like that of the readers than the Earth of the Marvel Universe.

"And Men Shall Call Him... Warlock!" begins with Him's cocoon being salvaged by self-made god the High Evolutionary. While undertaking a bold new experiment, the ascended biologist interrupts his mission to investigate the strange stellar debris, allowing the creative team to retell the artificial man's origins and battles. After retrieving the cocoon, the High

Men like gods

Roy Thomas' encyclopedic knowledge of the Marvel Comics Universe allowed him to deftly mix previously unconnected characters and events into a seamless whole. And the sheer grace and force of Gil Kane's art and Dan Adkins' crisp inking imparted enormous dynamism and depth to anything the scripts required. Whether encapsulating an origin or delivering a memorable splash page, the creative team delivered maximum thrills.

Evolutionary resumes his project: constructing a duplicate Earth on the far side of the Sun. This paradisiacal planet would harbor a human race that has never experienced violence or evil. Him observes everything from within his stellar womb and sees how, at the final stage, the science-god's greatest past mistake, Man-Beast, intervenes, forcing this idealized version of mankind to repeat every mistake and atrocity of the original.

Bursting from the cocoon, the outraged Him drives off Man-Beast and his minions, and when the High Evolutionary attempts to erase his sabotaged world-building experiment, Him begs to be allowed to save humanity on this "Counter-Earth" from the wickedness in their midst and in their nature. Grudgingly, the High Evolutionary agrees and gives the would-be redeemer a gleaming stone to aid him. This Soul Gem will eventually prove the ruination of the messianic Adam Warlock, as Him would become known, and a crucial element in many future cosmic sagas.

Warlock's trials on Counter-Earth closely reflected the situations and conflicts readers were experiencing in real life, and the metaphor of super-science as modern divinity added a challenging edge of philosophical inquiry to the tale. The sombre mood and off-Earth locations make *Marvel Premiere* #1 the first truly cosmic adventure and one that set the scope and tone for all successive sagas. ∎

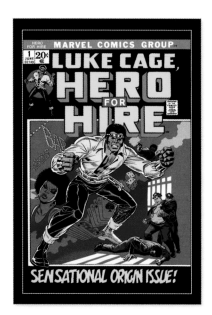

SENSATIONAL ORIGIN ISSUE!

Editor in chief	Stan Lee
Cover artist	John Romita Sr.
Writer	Archie Goodwin
Penciler	George Tuska
Inker	Billy Graham
Letterer	Skip Kohloff
Editor	Stan Lee

"SURE, WE WAS **RIVALS** OVER REVA...

... BUT STILL **FRIENDS**. AN' WHAT KINDA **MAN** WON'T LAY IT ON THE **LINE** FOR A FRIEND?

Friend in need
Luke Cage was not the kind of man to abandon a friend, and he rushed to save Willis Stryker from violent gangsters. The art by George Tuska and inks by Billy Graham capture the mean streets of Harlem and Cage's frantic, instinctive rush to fight for those to whom he is loyal.

Luke Cage, Hero for Hire #1
June 1972

> " Remember how Spider-Man learned in his first appearance that there was more to heroing than money? Luke Cage was 180° away from that. He saw it as a way to earn a living which, when you think about it, makes perfect sense. "

Peter David

In 1972, Marvel did something that no other comics publisher had done before—it gave a black Super Hero his own comic book title. *Luke Cage, Hero for Hire* #1 broke new ground, but Marvel was not just doing the right thing. The House of Ideas also considered the book a sensible business decision.

In the early 1970s, there was a new movement in cinema—the so-called "blaxploitation" genre, which in turn had been born from the previous decade's Black Power movement. On their release in 1971, movies such as *Sweet Sweetback's Baadasssss Song* and *Shaft* captured the public imagination. *Shaft*, in particular, was a breakout hit among all audiences, not just African Americans. Marvel, always quick to recognize the way the cultural winds were blowing, decided to create its own hero to tap into the same market. And, highly unusual for a Marvel Super Hero, Luke Cage actually sought payment for his good deeds.

The creators assigned to the job were writer Archie Goodwin and penciler George Tuska, with considerable input from Roy Thomas and John Romita Sr., the latter designing Luke Cage's costume: a shirt open to the waist, with various metallic accessories, including a chain around his midriff. The chain, like his new name, was intended to remind Cage of his time behind bars for a crime he didn't commit. The creative team was

further enhanced when Marvel hired African American Billy Graham to work on the title. Graham started out on inking duties, with the additional brief of adjusting Tuska's pencils where needed to accurately portray black characters. As the series continued, Graham's involvement grew, until he was contributing pencils and significant chunks of the plotting for each issue.

Luke Cage was not exactly a boy scout. Growing up on the streets of Harlem, New York City, he had survived any way he could, falling into a life of crime with his best friend Willis Stryker. While Stryker was known for his skill with knives, Carl Lucas, as Cage was then called, was unbeatable with his fists alone. Eventually, Lucas grew tired of his life, always running, always fighting, and decided to go straight. This drove a wedge between him and Stryker that was only worsened when they both fell for the same girl, Reva. At first, Reva chose Stryker, but when he was badly beaten by gangsters, she turned to Lucas for help. Stryker blamed his former friend for poisoning Reva's mind against him and set Lucas up in a drug bust. While Lucas languished in prison, Stryker wormed his way back into Reva's life, causing her death when she was caught in the crossfire of a gangland shoot-out. From his prison cell, Carl Lucas vowed revenge.

Luke Cage's origin story bears many similarities to Captain America's all those years before. Thinking it might lead to early release, Lucas volunteers to be a guinea pig for a prison experiment. He is injected with some form of virus and then shut into a chemical bath through which electricity is passed. However, as the experiment progresses, a racist guard who harbors a grudge against Lucas interferes, causing the chemical reaction to increase. Lucas bursts out of the steel container, discovering that not only does his body seem impervious to damage but that he is also super-strong. Knocking out the guard, he breaks out of jail and flees.

On the run and struggling to find work without proper ID, Cage realizes that his newly acquired strength could in fact help him become a "Hero for Hire." Adopting a new name and costume, Luke Cage even has business cards made. At the cliff-hanger conclusion of *Luke Cage, Hero for Hire* #1, his cards fall into the hands of ruthless gang boss Diamondback, who turns out to be his childhood "buddy" Stryker.

At first, *Luke Cage, Hero for Hire* performed well, but as the blaxploitation craze faded, so did sales. Sales later revived after Cage's title was united with *Iron Fist*, which had been created to capitalize on the popularity of kung fu. The partnership between the two heroes would blossom and see them feature in the Marvel Universe regularly. ▪

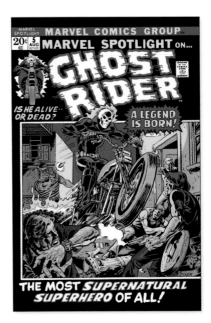

Editor in chief	Stan Lee
Cover artist	Mike Ploog
Writer	Gary Friedrich
Penciler, inker, colorist	Mike Ploog
Letterer	Jon Costa
Editor	Stan Lee

Prince of darkness
Marvel Spotlight #5 was Satan's first named appearance in the Marvel Universe. He later reveals himself as the demon lord Mephisto in one of his many hellish guises.

Marvel Spotlight #5
August 1972

❝ Ghost Rider scraped the zeitgeist of the early '70s, combining motorcycles and the occult to create a character who became more than the sum of his parts. [His] flaming skull made him one of Marvel's most recognizable icons. **❞**

Tom Brevoort

Following a 1971 revision of the Comics Code Authority (CCA) rules, comic books were allowed to include stories about classic horror characters, such as vampires, werewolves, and ghouls, although zombies were still not permitted because they were not considered part of the literary monster genre. Marvel Comics immediately began exploring the possibilities this change opened up.

At the time, Stan Lee was transitioning from writer-editor to publisher. One of the ways in which he wanted to make his mark was by starting new titles, including *Marvel Spotlight*. Lee conceived this as a place to test new characters before deciding whether they merited titles of their own. The second issue saw the debut of one of the company's new monster characters, Werewolf by Night. A few months later, *Marvel Spotlight* #5 featured the debut of a dark supernatural being, who would go on to become a major character in the Marvel Universe—Ghost Rider.

Created by writer Gary Friedrich and editor Roy Thomas, who were childhood friends, and artist Mike Ploog, Johnny Blaze was a stunt motorcycle rider who found himself on the wrong side of everyone. The character capitalized on the popularity of the real-life Evel Knievel and his daredevil motorcycle jumps, as well as the biker movies that traded on the public's fascination with rebel bikers like the Hells Angels. In fact, by the late 1960s and early 1970s, a subgenre of these films, such as *Satan's Sadists* (1969), had emerged, that mixed motorcycles with horror, satanism,

and the supernatural. Johnny Blaze would very much be tapping into the zeitgeist.

Books like *Marvel Spotlight* clearly showed Marvel starting to transition from the Silver to the Bronze Age of comics in tone and style. Ghost Rider exemplified the company's newfound confidence with horror themes, particularly satanism, which would not have been possible even 18 months previously. Satanism was beginning to carve out a presence in public awareness, both in wider society and popular culture, with the Church of Satan being founded in California in the late 1960s, not long before *Rosemary's Baby* (1968) became a critical and box-office success. And, for the moment, the heightened moral concern known as the satanic panic was still a decade away.

Marvel Spotlight #5 opens with a moody, dramatic introduction to Ghost Rider. The genius of the character is his unforgettable appearance, a cool biker with a flaming skull, which Marvel later cleverly linked to the legend of the headless horseman. The suit was inspired by the black leather outfit donned by Elvis Presley for his 1968 "Comeback Special." Artist Mike Ploog wanted to keep Ghost Rider's suit as dark as possible but included highlights so that the character's movement would still be clear. Gary Friedrich also cited Marlon Brando's iconic appearance in the biker movie *The Wild One*, as well as actor James Dean, as inspiration for Johnny Blaze when he is in human form.

After this first glimpse of the character, the issue details his backstory. After Blaze's

The Devil rides in
Mike Ploog's polished,
expressive artwork perfectly
caught the moody, supernatural
menace of the Ghost Rider.
A relative newcomer to Marvel
at the time, Ploog quickly
established a name for himself
on a number of horror titles,
including *Werewolf by Night*,
The Monster of Frankenstein,
and *Man-Thing*.

father, also a stunt rider, dies in a motorcycle
accident, young Johnny is raised by his
employers, Crash Simpson and his wife.
Growing up, Johnny falls in love with their
daredevil daughter, Roxanne. When Crash
is later found to be dying of cancer, Johnny
summons Satan, pledging his soul to save
Crash from the disease. Soon afterward,
Crash dies, not from cancer, but while
attempting a record-breaking jump, and
the devil comes to collect. Satan curses
Johnny to become his grim emissary during
the hours of darkness—the Ghost Rider.

Ghost Rider was initially considered as
a potential villain for the hero Daredevil,
but on reflection, Marvel's decision-makers
felt that the character warranted more
than just a bit part. The name had been
used for a character in western comics
back in the 1940s, and when its trademark
elapsed in 1967, Marvel picked it up for a
revival of the western hero, also created by
Friedrich and Roy Thomas. Following the
success of the motorcycle-riding Ghost
Rider, his cowboy predecessor was
renamed the Phantom Rider.

Marvel Spotlight #5, starring Johnny
Blaze as the tortured motorcyclist who had
sold his soul to the devil, was a hit with
readers, and Marvel moved swiftly to
commission a new *Ghost Rider* title, the
first issue of which was published in June
1973. While the company was still known
mainly for its straightforward Super Hero
titles, Ghost Rider showed that Marvel
could widen the scope of its offerings to
reach new readers who wanted stories
about darker protagonists. ∎

Editor in chief	Roy Thomas
Cover artist	John Romita Sr.
Writer	Gerry Conway
Penciler	Gil Kane
Inkers	John Romita Sr., Tony Mortellaro
Colorist	Dave Hunt
Letterer	Artie Simek
Editor	Roy Thomas

Tragic twist
Artist Gil Kane's shocking splash page is one of the most iconic images in comics. It is only here, on the last page, that the issue title was revealed, so that the surprise twist was not revealed too early.

Amazing Spider-Man #121
June 1973

❝[A] story that went where no previous Super Hero adventure had ever dared to go, and in the days before internet spoilers it was as shocking to the readership as anything ever done.❞

Tom Brevoort

Amazing Spider-Man #121 is one of the most famous issues in comic book history. It is so significant that many fans believe it marks the end of the Silver Age of comics and the start of the more modern, grittier Bronze Age. Titled "The Night Gwen Stacy Died," the startling plot was conceived to boost sales, which it did alongside much controversy. It also followed Stan Lee moving up to the role of publisher and handing over writing duties of the two titles closest to his heart—*Fantastic Four* and *Amazing Spider-Man*. The year was 1972, and the man who would take on the unenviable task of following both Stan Lee and Roy Thomas as Spider-Man writer was Gerry Conway, then aged just 19. His first issue would be *Amazing Spider-Man* #111 in August of that year, but Conway really made his mark the following year, when he helped devise a death that shocked readers to the core.

To reinvigorate the title, it was decided that one of the web-slinger's regular supporting characters should be killed off, and although others like Aunt May or Harry Osborn were suggested, Conway and artist John Romita Sr. felt that it should be Gwen Stacy. At the time, Gwen was less popular with fans than Mary Jane Watson, being seen as too perfect. Her dramatic departure would set up more interesting narrative possibilities as Peter Parker would suffer from guilt and loss, and a desire for revenge.

The villain who puts Gwen Stacy in harm's way is Spider-Man's old nemesis the Green Goblin (Norman Osborn), who had recently recalled Spider-Man's true identity after a bout of amnesia. He kidnaps Gwen to draw out Spider-Man, taking her to the top of a bridge (depicted as Brooklyn Bridge but described as George Washington Bridge in the text) and waits for the hero to arrive. Sure enough, Spider-Man tracks down the Goblin but cannot stop him using his glider to knock an unconscious Gwen from the bridge. Spidey shoots a web-line after her and grabs her leg, halting her fall, but the sudden stop breaks Gwen's neck and kills her.

Following Gwen Stacy's death, there was an outcry from fans. It was truly momentous for such a major character to be killed off in this manner, with the hero of the comic also failing to save her. Stan Lee, who was frequently the face of Marvel Comics at outside events, had to

Fateful decision

The controversy around Gwen Stacy's death was increased by writer Gerry Conway's decision to insert the "Snap!" sound effect next to her neck in the panel where Spider-Man's web stops her fall, leaving little doubt that it is the web that kills her. His failure to save her could be attributed to his abilities being dulled by a heavy cold, which is clearly affecting his skills earlier in the issue.

face the lion's share of criticism over the story, and so he asked the creative team to bring her back. Conway refused to simply resurrect the real Gwen in some contrived way, as he felt it would undermine the authenticity of the story, but he eventually agreed to write in a clone of Gwen. This would eventually lead to the Clone Saga story line of the mid-1990s

The issue was an instant must-read and became one of the most important parts of Spider-Man lore. The follow-up issue, *Amazing Spider-Man* #122 (July 1973), proved nearly as shocking as its predecessor. It saw the grieving hero almost beat Green Goblin to death in a vengeful rage, before the villain was accidentally impaled by his own glider as he tried to use it to kill Spider-Man. The manner of Gwen's death has been homaged many times in subsequent Spider-Man comic books and films, with other characters taking her place and Spidey, having learned from terrible experience, using multiple web strands to save them. The death is also notable for being final—although clones of Gwen Stacy have appeared since, her death as it tragically happened in *Amazing Spider-Man* #121 still stands. ∎

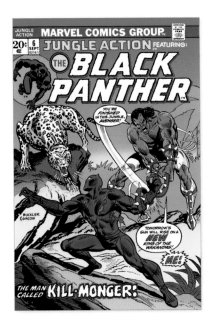

Editor in chief	Roy Thomas
Cover artists	Rich Buckler, Frank Giacoia
Writer	Don McGregor
Penciler	Rich Buckler
Inker	Klaus Janson
Colorist	Glynis Wein
Letterer	Tom Orzechowski
Editor	Roy Thomas

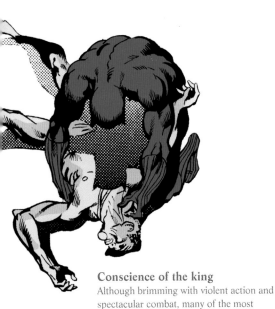

Conscience of the king

Although brimming with violent action and spectacular combat, many of the most memorable moments in *Jungle Action* #6 are fleeting, intimate scenes exploring a character's humanity. Most moving of all is T'Challa's failure to save a tortured subject: a faithful stranger he cannot name.

Jungle Action #6
September 1973

“If you enjoyed the *Black Panther* movie, this is a must-read comic: the first appearance of Killmonger that climaxes with him throwing the Panther off a waterfall. Sound familiar?”

Peter David

Seven years after debuting in *Fantastic Four* #52 (July 1966) and following sterling service as an Avenger, the Black Panther won his own solo series at a time when issues of race and equality were boiling over in America's news media and in the country's riot-riven streets. Previously, King T'Challa's appearances in the *Avengers*, *Daredevil*, and other titles had provided star writer Roy Thomas many opportunities to examine prejudice, black identity, and gang culture, but always in an American setting, with Wakanda regarded as a distant, fantasy paradise.

For *Jungle Action* #6, writer Don McGregor and penciler Rich Buckler took their cues from international events, concentrating on everyday life in that scientifically advanced African country. They portray the isolated, secretive kingdom of Wakanda as an emergent nation and part of a continent in transition. Their radical vision establishes the Black Panther as more than a Super Hero. He is also a leader with the burdens and obligations that entails, guiding millions of people. Set in a land that has never known white men, this also affords the creators' opportunity to work with a cast of almost exclusively non-white characters—a first in modern comics.

Since coming to America, T'Challa had been torn between his duties as an Avenger and his regal responsibilities. That all changes when a charismatic demagogue named Erik Killmonger foments rebellion in Wakanda, making the Black Panther's decision far clearer,

and he returns to his beleaguered homeland. A shrewd and ruthless foe, Killmonger possesses superior technology and employs well-armed, and even super-powered, minions. He also trades on and stokes growing anxieties among Wakandans that the world is changing too quickly and that T'Challa, their secular and spiritual leader, has abandoned them.

The opening chapter "Panther's Rage" sees T'Challa stumble upon Killmonger's soldiers torturing an elderly villager. Despite his best efforts to stop them, he is too late. The devout, devoted subject dies in his arms, swearing he never lost faith in his chieftain. In the palace, the king is plagued by guilt and harangued by his own inner circle. They may have helped him modernize Wakanda, but all still cling to tribal ways and traditions. Ideological wrangling and criticism of his actions is further exacerbated by T'Challa's choice of companion. American singer and social activist Monica Lynne might be the king's chosen consort, but as an outsider, she is resented by many in his inner circle.

However, there's no time for strained feelings as Killmonger's forces strike again, destroying a village sympathetic to the ruling Panther Cult. When word arrives that his wily, elusive enemy waits at the sacred Warrior Falls, T'Challa rushes into battle but is shockingly and swiftly defeated, hurled over the precipice to his doom by his hulking, ferocious foe and his attack-leopard Preyy.

One of Marvel's earliest multipart epics, "Panther's Rage" also remains one of the most powerful. Spectacular battles

McGregor and Buckler worked closely on "Panther's Rage," discussing scenes long into the night as McGregor posed for many of the cast. Both fervent anti-racists, they were greatly concerned about utilizing a savage villain who seemed to confirm many unwelcome racial stereotypes. The iconic result was a complex enemy who epitomized everything the rationalistic, spiritual T'Challa opposed.

are deftly counterbalanced by intimate insights into family life, destabilizing culture shocks, and a desperate search for identity in an all-too-rapidly changing world. Crucially, all these themes are introduced in this opening installment and carefully built upon over the next two years by McGregor and Buckler, and the latter's artistic successors Gil Kane and Billy Graham. The fierce war of wills for Wakanda's body and soul concludes where it started, at Warrior Falls, in *Jungle Action* #17 (September 1975), with a chilling and moving epilogue detailing the price of defeat and the cost of victory in the subsequent issue.

Killmonger is a terrifying villain with lucid, credible motives underpinning his remorseless, Machiavellian actions. His subordinates are complex, capable individuals and a match for Wakanda's king and his equally well-characterized loyalists. The protagonists and antagonists' internal conflicts are also maturely handled with McGregor's introspective approach allowing readers access to the private thoughts of all involved.

"Panther's Rage"—the comic story and the novel it became—offered sophistication seldom seen before in comics. Here were engaging characters defined by more than a change of color palette: heroes with flaws, villains with redeeming qualities, and friends and lovers acting like real people in times of extreme crisis. All this is depicted in a comic story that maintains the demands of Super Hero storytelling by being hugely exciting and unforgettably exceptional. ■

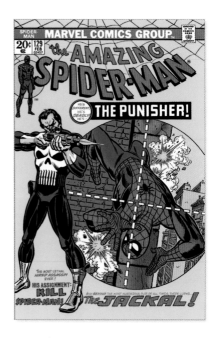

Amazing Spider-Man #129
February 1974

"This issue introduces the Punisher—one of Marvel's most recognizable characters—and the Jackal—a villain who'd haunt Spidey for decades. But it also looks at how tragedy, grief, and rage can affect even our greatest heroes."

Ryan Penagos

Editor in chief	Len Wein
Writer	Gerry Conway
Penciler	Ross Andru
Inkers	Frank Giacoia, Dave Hunt
Colorist	Dave Hunt
Letterer	John Costanza
Editor	Roy Thomas

After Stan Lee gave up his regular scripting assignments to become Marvel's publisher in 1972, and following a short stint on *Amazing Spider-Man* #101–104 (October 1971–January 1972) by writer Roy Thomas, teenaged science-fiction novelist and relatively untried comics scripter Gerry Conway took over helming two of Marvel's biggest draws: Thor and Spider-Man. Conway's tenure on the latter resulted in some of the most significant story lines in the hero's long and storied history. One issue in particular stands out as a watershed moment.

Amazing Spider-Man #129—illustrated by Ross Andru, Frank Giacoia, and Dave Hunt—sees the web-slinger in a downward spiral as Peter Parker mourns the loss of his murdered girlfriend, Gwen Stacy. He is also being harassed by his boss, J. Jonah Jameson, who is behind a media campaign to paint Parker's wall-crawling alter ego as Norman Osborn's killer. Peter thinks he is the only one who knows the truth: Osborn, as the Green Goblin, died due to his own murderous actions. Spider-Man doesn't know that his best friend Harry Osborn witnessed the final fight and is slowly descending into a madness as deep, deadly, and goblin-tainted as his father's.

In this charged atmosphere, "The Punisher Strikes Twice!" abruptly debuted two new characters—both motivated by hatred and revenge—who would make the wall-crawler's life a living hell and reshape the Marvel Universe itself. Both would also remain enigmas for months to come. In this fast-paced tale, the Punisher is a mysterious justice-obsessed judge and executioner in a pact with costumed mastermind the Jackal. Their mission is to kill Spider-Man—ostensibly for murdering Norman Osborn.

After an inconclusive clash between Spidey and the Punisher—who, in this first foray, uses fancy gadgets rather than simply bullets—Jackal murders the gunman's private armorer and frames the web-slinger for the deed, in the hope of motivating his conflicted accomplice. Following another brutal battle, Spidey shows the Punisher that the Jackal had set them both up and they call an uneasy truce. Spider-Man returns to his troubled life, pitying the unstable vigilante, who stoically returns to the shadows, adding Jackal to his list of prospective kills.

Later issues would reveal the Jackal as Parker's mentor and college tutor Professor Miles Warren. He had developed a fixation with Gwen and, blaming Spider-Man for her death, set upon a path of bloody retribution. Warren also discovered the hero's identity after classroom genetics experiments, and cloned both Gwen Stacy and Peter Parker, precipitating decades of confusion by creating a horde of killer clones, including aberrant arachnid heroes Ben Reilly and Kaine Parker.

The Punisher made even greater waves. Conceived by Conway and first realized by Marvel art director John Romita Sr. and

Ambush predator
As befits his cunning nature, the Jackal's fist meeting with Spider-Man is a punishing and near-fatal sneak attack. In fact, the embattled wall-crawler never once lays eyes on the manic mastermind in the entire issue!

artist Ross Andru, he was originally dubbed "The Assassin," a comic book response to a popular trend in action novels in the early 1970s. These all featured returning Vietnam veterans using their training to battle crime as urban vigilantes. After more than a decade as an increasingly popular guest star in many Super Hero titles, in 1986, The Punisher won his own comic, and changed the definition of what a hero meant in the Marvel Universe. The soul-searching, self-critical, driven, former marine had no backstory as yet, and when it arrived later in the decade, horrific family tragedy was once

more used to show how a good man can turn bad. In years to come, the Punisher's relentless, ruthless spirit would see him take on and best most of the Marvel Universe.

Later Spider-Man stories revealed that Norman Osborn had not died, and he soon returned as the Green Goblin to once again plague Spider-Man. Similarly, Miles Warren would also rise from the grave several times in his ever-escalating war against Peter Parker and his loved ones, employing a hidden empire of clones, monsters, and even multiple copies of Gwen Stacy. ■

Acts of vengeance
"The Punisher Strikes Twice!" is a study in pain, with the leads consumed by retaliation and retribution. At this stage, readers are unaware why the Punisher and Jackal are so obsessed with vengeance, but its grip on them has made them fanatics. In contrast, although Spider-Man has exacted revenge for Gwen's death, it has brought him no peace, only anguish and emptiness.

Captain Marvel #33
July 1974

"In just 18 mind-bending pages, Starlin and Englehart [assembled] all these classic characters... for a cosmic trip of desperate heroes and mad gods that still inspires storytellers today."

Bill Rosemann

Editor in chief	Len Wein
Cover artist	Jim Starlin
Writers	Jim Starlin, Steve Englehart
Penciler, colorist	Jim Starlin
Inker	Klaus Janson
Letterer	Tom Orzechowski
Editor	Roy Thomas

Captain Marvel is a name that carries comic book prestige but was one that Marvel did not utilize until its 1968 expansion. Since applying for the trademark in October 1967, the House of Ideas has always had a character attached to the name—ranging from alien warriors to earthborn Super Heroes.

In an era of growing social unrest and anti-war sentiment, Stan Lee, Roy Thomas, and artist Gene Colan created a dutiful but disaffected alien soldier named Mar-Vell. Sent by the intergalactic Kree Empire to spy on Earth, he gradually rebelled against his militaristic training to become a life-affirming Super Hero. For much of his time on Earth, Mar-Vell was physically and psychically bonded to teenager Rick Jones while his body languished helpless in the Negative Zone. He could only escape for brief periods thanks to the atom-switching properties of ancient Kree Nega-Bands. Although the series was fresh and engaging, it never really caught on with fans, and was canceled and relaunched several times, establishing some permanence only when writer-illustrator Jim Starlin took over. He fashioned a cosmic saga of conquest, death, obsession, and love that introduced one of comics' most enduring, complex villains: Thanos of Titan.

Starlin's epic affected every corner of the Marvel Universe, spanning *Captain Marvel* #25–33 (March 1973–July 1974) and included key episodes involving Iron Man, the Thing, Daredevil, and the Avengers. The saga also introduced new characters Drax the Destroyer, Eros (aka Starfox) and Mentor of Titan, and reshaped former villain Madame MacEvil as heroic demi-goddess

Moondragon. Ultimately, reality's fate hung on an uneven final battle between Mar-Vell and Thanos. As the "Thanos War" progressed, Mar-Vell was transformed from a warrior hero into a cosmically aware, divinely appointed Protector of the Universe, destined to be a champion of life in its darkest hour. The Mad Titan was a fanatical lover of Mistress Death and hungered to give her Earth as a betrothal gift. Using a reality-warping Cosmic Cube, he turns himself into a supreme being controlling all reality and removing all opposition to his reign. However, Thanos' gloating overconfidence allows the cosmically enhanced Mar-Vell to outmaneuver and eventually defeat his near-omnipotent foe.

As well as a master class in plotting and nonstop action, *Captain Marvel* #33, the saga's concluding chapter, sharply expressed Starlin's philosophical and spiritual beliefs, which struck a chord with young readers at a time when they were increasingly questioning the status quo. Starlin's run on the title also proved to be a creative peak for the character. Although a string of subsequent creators dispatched the hero across the universe with varying success, the cosmic spark was never fully rekindled. Eventually, editorial decisions led to the creation of a new Captain Marvel and the demise of Mar-Vell. Starlin was asked if he would do the honors: the result was *The Death of Captain Marvel* (April 1982), the first Marvel Graphic Novel. Its publication would further signify the transition of comics from cheap disposable entertainment to a valid literary medium with a mature readership. ■

Cosmic combat
Although mind-blowing concepts and bizarre situations bombard readers at every turn in the epic finale, Starlin adheres to the prime directive of Super Hero storytelling. A big finish demands dramatic and dynamic illustration.

Love and Death

Although comics are a marriage of image and text, often the most effective moments come when dialogue is absent. Here, in a multi-panel cinematic sequence zooming out and back in to an extreme close-up, Starlin sums up Thanos' warped obsession as forever doomed and ultimately pointless. Mistress Death, the personification of eternal rest, always has the last laugh.

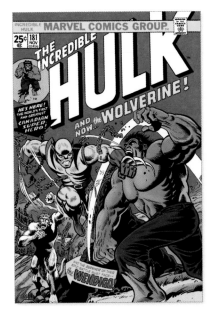

Incredible Hulk #181
November 1974

"No one knew at the time that we were seeing the introduction of one of Marvel's most popular characters... Wolverine became the most renowned X-Man in the Marvel stable."

Peter David

Editor in chief	Roy Thomas
Cover artists	Herb Trimpe, John Romita Sr.
Writer	Len Wein
Penciler	Herb Trimpe
Inker	Jack Abel
Colorist	Glynis Wein
Letterer	Artie Simek
Editor	Roy Thomas

Incredible Hulk #181 is now one of the most valuable comic books in existence. It attained this status for one important reason—it is the first full appearance of the character Wolverine. The creators did not know it at the time, but the Canadian mutant would go on to become one of Marvel's most popular characters ever. Wolverine was created by writer Len Wein and Marvel art director John Romita Sr., while the art duties on this issue fell to regular Hulk penciler Herb Trimpe. At the time *Incredible Hulk* #181 was published, mutants had fallen from favor in Marvel's books, with the *X-Men* title printing only reprints of older stories. But Hulk writer Len Wein decided to take a chance on introducing a new mutant character— an uncannily astute call as it turned out.

Editor Roy Thomas asked Wein to create a new character, named Wolverine, who would be short of stature and temper, like the Canadian animal from which he took his name. John Romita Sr. designed Wolverine's costume, giving him a black nose and whiskers on the mask, to resemble the markings of a real wolverine, as well as his trademark Adamantium claws. While his claws were fully extended throughout this issue, Romita later confirmed that he intended them to be retractable, worrying about how Wolverine would perform simple tasks without injuring himself.

Wolverine's first appearance was in the last panel of the previous issue, but it was not until *Incredible Hulk* #181 that fans really got to see what he could do. Despite his size, Wolverine unhesitatingly attacks either the monstrous, almost invulnerable

Wendigo or the mighty Hulk, who has traveled to Canada. Hulk is puzzled by the "little man" but decides that if he is attacking the Wendigo, then they can be friends. So he is all the angrier when Wolverine turns on him after the Wendigo's defeat. Hulk eventually gets the better of Wolverine on this occasion.

The creators were not sure at the time of publication whether Wolverine would go on to have a life of his own in comic books, or whether he was doomed to be a minor character in the Hulk's adventures. But just in case, they included an important part of his backstory in this first appearance. The main narrative cuts away to a Canadian military installation to reveal that Wolverine is also known as "Weapon X" and has been honed, on government orders, into a formidable fighter. The people who sent Wolverine after the Hulk reveal that they are still worried about his mental state, hinting not only at the character's unpredictability but also the suffering he may have experienced in life.

Wein felt that volatility was at the heart of Wolverine's nature. He later said that Wolverine always professed not to care about anything, but his actions made it clear that he cared deeply for those around him. Wein had suffered from poor health from the time he was a young child and first fell in love with comic books when reading them while he was in hospital. Wolverine's popularity with fans was cemented when Wein used him as part of the hugely successful X-Men reboot in 1975. Since then, the character's position among Marvel's greats has been undisputed. ▪

Face off
An intense close-up enables Herb Trimpe to capture the anger on Hulk's face before zooming out to take in the fight between the two formidable but short-tempered antiheroes.

Tag team
Hulk and Wolverine impressed each other on their first meeting with their mutual strength against the formidable Wendigo. These panels, drawn by Herb Trimpe, almost shake with the effects of the titanic battle, while Len Wein's captions reveal that Adamantium was part of Wolverine's story from the very start.

Mutants united

Past and present unite to make the X-Men bigger and better than ever, thrillingly depicted in this splash panel by Dave Cockrum, with inks from Cockrum and Peter Iro, and colors from Glynis Wein. The fight against the mutant island Krakoa is the first time the all-new, all-different X-Men have came together in battle, and, having freed the original X-Men, all the mutant heroes put their differences aside to defeat the living island.

Giant-Size X-Men #1
May 1975

> **"** The first appearance of the modern-day X-Men. Storm, Nightcrawler, Colossus... never have so many popular heroes been introduced in one issue. It led to the relaunch of the monthly comic and there was no stopping the mutants from that point on. **"**

Peter David

Editor in chief	Marv Wolfman
Cover artists	Gil Kane, Dave Cockrum
Writer	Len Wein
Penciler, inker	Dave Cockrum
Colorist	Glynis Wein
Letterer	John Costanza
Editor	Len Wein

There are few comic books more pivotal to the history of Marvel than *Giant-Size X-Men* #1. In 1975, the X-Men were in the doldrums, their title having been used only for reprints for five years. But the team's status as one of the less popular Marvel properties was about to change in a major way.

Marvel president Al Landau was at the time maximizing the company's potential in international markets, and he believed that there would be money to be made with new characters hailing from some of the countries where Marvel comics were sold. He met with editor in chief Roy Thomas, who suggested the X-Men as the perfect vehicle for such a diverse group of new heroes. Writer Len Wein, who had already created the Canadian mutant Wolverine for just such an occasion, was brought on board to come up with more global mutants, as was in-demand young artist Dave Cockrum.

Wein and Cockrum devised four entirely new characters for the X-Men: the Russian Colossus, the German Nightcrawler, the Kenyan Storm, and the Native American Thunderbird. They also brought in three characters who had already been created for use in other titles—Banshee, an Irish mutant; the Japanese Sunfire; and, of course, Wolverine. The new team was dubbed "All New, All Different," a phrase that became an integral part of the Marvel lexicon.

The new team debuted in *Giant-Size X-Men* #1, which, as the name suggests, was larger than standard comics and contained 68 pages, some of which carried reprints. The opening story introduces readers to the new lineup, as Professor X travels around the world making contact with some extraordinary mutants and recruiting them to the team. The second chapter sees the new X-Men back at Professor X's Westchester mansion, meeting Cyclops, the only member of the original team still there. The absence of the others is used as a plot device to bring the new characters into the fray, as Professor X and Cyclops need them to help rescue the other original X-Men from the island of Krakoa.

At the mansion, the team is outfitted in new costumes, the creation of which was one of artist Dave Cockrum's special skills. Cockrum would come up with multiple different options for each new outfit, tweaking small details over and over until he got it just right. However, one aspect of the heroes' attire that was not Cockrum's idea was the elongated points on Wolverine's new cowl. This was a mistake by Gil Kane, the artist who drew part of the cover for the issue, but Cockrum liked the effect so much that he reworked all the panels he'd drawn for the inside pages, altering Wolverine to match Kane's "error." On the cover, Cockrum drew the old X-Men almost in shadow, while their new counterparts, drawn by Kane, appeared to burst through the page. It is a classic cover composition that has been much homaged in later X-Men books.

The early interactions of this exciting new team were characterized mainly by bickering, as the individual members quickly got to know each other and found out who they hit it off with and who rubbed them the wrong way. Writer Len Wein included an early hint of the tension that would always exist between Wolverine and Scott Summers— even before Jean Grey is on the scene. Grey and the other original X-Men are trapped inside the island, which the others soon realize is a mutant itself. Krakoa is feeding off their energy and deliberately let Cyclops escape so that he would bring more mutants for it to feed on. The two teams join forces to defeat Krakoa before returning to Westchester, their destinies now forever linked as teammates and X-Men.

Wein's original intention was to continue the adventures of these new X-Men in the quarterly, giant-size format. However, *Giant-Size X-Men* #1 was such a massive hit that plans were quickly changed, and Marvel brought the *X-Men* title back as a bimonthly standard comic. Writing *Incredible Hulk* and performing his editing duties left Len Wein little time to be writing another new title, however, and he passed the X-Men on to writer Chris Claremont. The latter had contributed to the editing of *Giant-Size X-Men* #1, and so was more than ready to step in and take the team forward. Claremont would remain with the title, taking it to even greater heights, for an extraordinary 16 years.

The impact of *Giant-Size X-Men* #1 was such that it caused a wave of mutant mania among comic book fans. Indeed, some commentators see the release of this issue as the true start of the Bronze Age of comics—an era-defining moment. It built the foundations that would catapult the X-Men to the top rank of Marvel heroes, ensuring the misunderstood mutants a bright future for decades to come on both page and screen. ∎

Offer of a lifetime
Artist Dave Cockrum's simple, bold panels capture a historic mutant moment, when Wolverine meets Charles Xavier for the first time. Although Wolverine does not exactly welcome Professor X's approach with open arms, he is eager to escape the clutches of the Canadian military.

Editor in chief	Marv Wolfman
Cover artists	Gil Kane, Frank Giacoia
Writer	Gerry Conway
Penciler	Ross Andru
Inker	Mike Esposito
Colorist	Janice Cohen
Letterer	Annette Kawecki
Editor	Marv Wolfman

Separate paths
Gwen Stacy's clone realizes that she is not the true Gwen Stacy, and so neither she nor Peter Parker are the two young people who had been in love years before. Artist Ross Andru captures the poignancy as Peter bids "Gwen" goodbye for a second time, as she leaves to make a fresh start.

Amazing Spider-Man #149
October 1975

" Amazing Spider-Man #149 concludes what is sometimes known as "The Original Clone Saga." Gerry Conway [tied] up his story arc with a strong finish. His introduction of the Spider-Man clone, and the backstory of the Gwen Stacy clone, would have long-lasting effects on Spider-Man's future. "

Melanie Scott

Writer Gerry Conway had already made an indelible mark on Spider-Man history after scripting the death of Gwen Stacy in *Amazing Spider-Man* #121 (June 1973). By summer 1975, Conway was coming to the end of a long stint on Spider-Man, and *Amazing Spider-Man* #149 would be his last issue before he moved on to other titles. It turned out to be another hugely significant part of the wall-crawler's mythos.

Reaction to the death of Gwen Stacy had been mixed. While it was a milestone moment in comic book history, with far-reaching ramifications, many readers had been disappointed to see the demise of Gwen. One of those "readers" was Marvel publisher Stan Lee. He urged Conway to bring Gwen back somehow, but the writer was loath to simply resurrect the character exactly as she had been. He felt that it would weaken the original story and that fans might also feel cheated by an easy "do-over," and editor in chief Roy Thomas and *Amazing Spider-Man* #121 artist John Romita Sr. agreed.

Conway's ingenious solution was to create a clone of Gwen Stacy, identical in nearly every respect to the original. The clone was introduced in *Amazing Spider-Man* #144 (May 1975), although Spider-Man himself didn't learn that she was a clone until three issues later.

The villain in *Amazing Spider-Man* #149 was the Jackal, another Conway creation. Although he had first appeared a year earlier, his secret identity was not revealed until the end of *Amazing Spider-Man* #148 (September 1975). Miles Warren was Peter Parker and Gwen Stacy's brilliant college biology professor, who had debuted in *Amazing Spider-Man* back in 1965. After his unmasking as the Jackal in the previous issue, Warren explained to Spider-Man how he had secretly always loved Gwen Stacy and, grief-stricken by her shocking death, set about creating her clone. His plan was to assume his Jackal identity and defeat Spider-Man to punish the hero for causing the real Gwen's death—while the "new" Gwen watched.

However, *Amazing Spider-Man #149* was most significant for revealing that Gwen Stacy was not the only person whom the unstable Miles Warren cloned. After Spider-Man was drugged by the Jackal, he woke to find himself looking at... himself. This was the first appearance of the Spider-Man clone who, although not named in this issue, would go on to reappear decades later as the Scarlet Spider (Ben Reilly). Although both the clone and the Jackal seemingly died at the end of the issue, Warren's elaborate machinations behind the scenes ensured that they would both feature again in Spider-Man's adventures.

Amazing Spider-Man #149 concludes what is sometimes known as "The Original Clone Saga." Gerry Conway wanted to tie up his story arc—and his run on the title—with a strong finish. His introduction of the Spider-Man clone, and the backstory of the Gwen Stacy clone, would have long-lasting effects on Spider-Man's future. But the very end of the issue belongs to another important thread of Peter Parker's story—his relationship with Mary Jane Watson. Still in its infancy at the time the Gwen Stacy clone reappeared, the couple's future togther seemed to have been placed in serious jeopardy. The last panels see Peter return to his life with MJ after bidding farewell to "Gwen" and putting his love for her into the past.

Yet one crucial thread left unresolved was the true fate of Spider-Man's clone. As Spider-Man and the clone faced off at Shea Stadium, the Jackal caused an explosion in which he and one of the Spider-Men were apparently killed. It was assumed that it was the clone who had died and the original Peter Parker who had lived. However, when Gwen Stacy's clone asked the survivor how he could be so sure that he was the true Spider-Man and not the clone, he couldn't answer. After all, they had both believed themselves to be Spider-Man. This ambiguity created a loophole that would be famously exploited in Clone Saga of the 1990s. ▪

Double take
Miles Warren's transformation into the insane Jackal happens at the same time as he is using his biological genius to create clones of Gwen Stacy and Peter Parker. The ensuing Spidey encounter with himself is one of the most important in the history of Spider-Man comics.

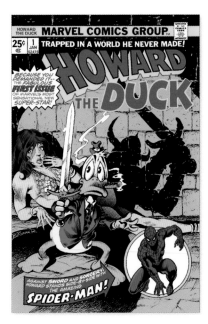

Howard the Duck #1
January 1976

66 A wildly subversive book tapping into the underground comics ethos of the time, Howard brought satire to the Marvel Universe through the eyes of its most grounded character... who just, you know, happened to be a duck. 99

Chip Zdarsky

Editor in chief	Gerry Conway
Cover artists	Frank Brunner, Glynis Wein
Writer	Steve Gerber
Penciler, colorist	Frank Brunner
Inker	Steve Leialoha
Letterer	John Costanza
Editor	Marv Wolfman

Where credit's due
Steve Gerber took satirical pot shots at consumer excess and even his Marvel bosses as Howard discovers the tower is built on credit card debt.

Howard the Duck is perhaps the most notable example of how Marvel Comics in the 1970s vastly expanded its remit to encompass the most weird and wonderful characters. Howard was a very bad-tempered alien from a planet called Duckworld, populated by talking ducklike beings with arms instead of wings. He first appeared in *Adventure into Fear* #19 (December 1973), alongside the Man-Thing, and intended to be just a joke about absurdity. But the character struck an immediate chord with readers and was used again in both *Man-Thing* and *Giant-Size Man-Thing*. Howard's apparent death prompted outrage among fans and so he was brought back for his very own title in January 1976.

Writer Steve Gerber, who created Howard with artist Val Mayerik, was one of the comic book world's wild cards. His work was a mixture of tragicomedy, social and political satire, and absurdity. Howard the Duck proved to be an ideal conduit for Gerber's vision, an outsider who could look at Earth and its inhabitants with a mix of detached cynicism and incredulity. Howard's predicament was summed up by the tagline most frequently used on the covers of his adventures: "Trapped in a world he never made."

Howard was a revolutionary character in the Marvel Universe. Although he was extra-ordinary by virtue of being from another planet, he had no super-powers

at all, and was not exceptionally brave, intelligent, or heroic. So whenever he confronted and even defeated a villain, it was usually by accident or luck. He also didn't live in New York City like most other Marvel heroes but was stranded in Cleveland, Ohio, from where he subverted comic book traditions and tropes.

The story in his debut issue was a smart spoof of another, highly successful, Marvel character at the time—Conan the Barbarian. Based on a character created by pulp writer Robert E. Howard in the 1930s, Conan was a consistently top-selling title produced by some of Marvel's elite talents. In *Howard the Duck* #1, the cantankerous mallard is swept up in a sword-and-sorcery adventure with a difference. He dons armor and a horned helmet to take on the evil wizard Pro-Rata, who is trying to become the most powerful accountant in the universe.

The cover for the issue was drawn by Frank Brunner with colors from Glynis Wein and depicts the main female character, Beverly Switzler, in an outfit closely resembling that of iconic Conan character Red Sonja. Joining Beverly and Howard on the cover is Spider-Man, woven into the story to encourage a wider reading audience for this new title. Fan favorite artist Brunner and inker Steve Leialoha adopt a lushly rendered cartoon-like style for the interior pages, the subject matter of which is clearly aimed at an adult audience. The opening

scenes show Howard driven to such despair
that he plans to kill himself by jumping
from a tall tower. When he begins climbing
the tower (unlike Earth ducks, Howard
cannot fly), he discovers that it is actually
made from thousands of credit cards—
a monument to capitalism and debt.

Clambering through a window,
Howard discovers a young woman being
held prisoner by a madman. The woman
is Beverly Switzler, who, as the series
progresses, becomes Howard's companion
and possible love interest. The two are
sent by Pro-Rata to another dimension
to retrieve a key for the financial wizard's
cosmic calculator. They obtain the key,
and Pro-Rata brings them back but also
lets in a monstrous Bahndbird by mistake.
As Pro-Rata and Howard argue over the
key, Spider-Man stumbles upon the scene.
It turns out that his alter ego Peter Parker
has been sent to Cleveland by *The Daily
Bugle* to photograph a rumored talking
mutant duck. Howard rescues Spider-
Man from Pro-Rata's magic and is
about to sacrifice himself to kill the
wizard when Spidey returns the favor
and saves the duck's life.

The genuinely trailblazing *Howard the
Duck* #1 was an instant hit, notching up
exceptional sales figures. Howard now
occupied a beloved niche in the Marvel
pantheon, becoming a cult classic who
has even made cameo appearances in
the Marvel Cinematic Universe. ∎

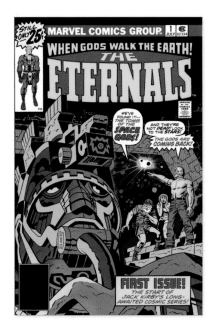

The Eternals #1
July 1976

"Kirby unleashed! This premiere issue marked the return of "The King" to Marvel, and he blew fans' minds with over-the-top art and colossal concepts as he introduced us to the world of the immortal Eternals."

C. B. Cebulski

Editor in chief	Marv Wolfman
Writer, penciler	Jack Kirby
Inker	John Verpoorten
Colorist	Glynis Wein
Letterer	Gaspar Saladino
Editor	Marv Wolfman

Evolutionary leaps
The forced elevation of primordial apes to a higher biological status is a potent, recurring theme in Marvel comics. Variations of this process created The Inhumans, transformed Greer Nelson into Tigra, and underpinned the experiments of the High Evolutionary.

In 1968, the publication of Erich Von Däniken's bestselling book *Chariots of the Gods* sparked a wave of global interest in the hypothesis that humanity had been visited in ancient times by extraterrestrials, who bestowed their advanced technology on the civilizations of the time. A few months later, Stanley Kubrick explored similar concepts in his seminal science fiction film *2001: A Space Odyssey*. The idea was eagerly leapt upon by contemporary psuedoscience and made global headlines in populist media.

Marvel was unusually late to jump on the trend with their take on the subject in "Man Gods from Beyond the Stars" in their first mature-reader *Marvel Preview* magazine in July 1975. But the following year, Jack Kirby, Marvel's foremost artist and conceptualist ran with the idea. He wrote and drew not only a treasury-sized adaptation of Kubrick's cinematic classic and a new series extending the movie's story but also his own mythic saga *The Eternals*. Melding current theories about early alien visitations with his own ideas about the origins of life and heroic legends, Kirby crafted a dramatic First-Contact adventure that pulsed with a sense of wonder and rewrote the history of the Marvel Universe.

When Kirby returned to Marvel at the end of 1975, he was granted editorial free rein on his projects. These included the aforementioned licensed adaptations, new runs on established characters he had co-created—Captain America and Black Panther—reuniting with Stan Lee for an out-of-continuity reimagining of the Silver Surfer, and devising three new series: *Devil Dinosaur*, *Machine Man*, and *The Eternals*.

The Eternals #1, "The Day of the Gods," finds aging anthropologist Daniel Damian and his daughter, Margo, exploring a lost city in the Peruvian Andes. Here, they make a remarkable discovery, thanks to their enigmatic guide, Ike Harris, who walks them through vast chambers filled with derelict statues, time-worn friezes, and immense machinery, all confirming Damian's theories that aliens visited Earth in ages past. Harris' knowledge of the find is explained as he relates how extraterrestrial visitors known as Celestials evolved proto-hominids into three distinct species: human beings; monstrous, inventive Deviants; and godlike super-beings, the Eternals. The guide's real name is Ikaris, and he is an Eternal. He joined the researchers to activate an ancient beacon and confirm that Celestials are returning imminently to check up on their experiments.

Throughout prehistory, Eternals faced opposition from Deviants. These genetically unstable, infinitely variable horrors ruled the planet in the antediluvian past, their dire actions and appearance imprinting

themselves upon humans as the basis of monsters and devils. After several millennia in the shadows, the Deviants, too, are active once more, tracing Ikaris' location in a desperate attempt to prevent the Celestials' return. They are too late.

In many ways, *The Eternals* #1 is reminiscent of the first issue of *Fantastic Four*. The heroes wear no costumes, the story simply introduces the players and sets the stage, leaving readers in huge anticipation of the returning Space Gods, who begin their landing approach only on the final page. Moreover, the diabolical, monstrous Deviants completely steal the show. Kirby saw his tale as occurring outside Marvel continuity, and only sparingly incorporated familiar elements such as S.H.I.E.L.D. and a robot replica

of the Hulk in later issues. However, successive creators incorporated Celestials, Deviants, and Eternals into the fabric and structure of their own stories, which would ultimately come to underpin the entire cosmology of the Marvel Universe.

The Eternals perfectly encapsulated and examined Jack Kirby's manifold fascinations—deities, the cosmos, the origins of myth, and the forces of Supernature—all viewed through the lens of flawed, deeply human observers. The breathtaking scope of Kirby's storytelling, refined by his successors, have been rewarded with popular acclaim in recent years. In 2020, *The Eternals* will become the 25th Marvel Cinematic Universe release, bringing Kirby's expansive vision to a wider audience. ▪

Eye of the beholder

Jack Kirby's *Eternals* succeeds through a thrilling combination of scope and scale, both in concept and imagery. The sheer power of the uncovered artifacts and the potential for disaster as the Space Gods arrive are visually majestic. The shock and awe only increase in later issues when the Celestials are revealed to be more than 2,000 feet tall!

Editor in chief	Archie Goodwin
Cover artists	Gil Kane, Joe Sinnott
Writer	Jim Shooter
Penciler	Gil Kane
Inker	Klaus Janson
Colorist	George Roussos
Letterer	Denise Wohl
Editors	Archie Goodwin

Death of a hero
After overcharging his armor to battle Hulk and the Sub-Mariner, Tony Stark sacrifices his last ergs of energy to reenergize and save dying comrade Giant-Man. The crucial power transfer fatally drains his own life-sustaining chest plate and Iron Man perishes.

What If? #3
June 1977

> **"**One of the best-written, best-looking Marvel comics of the decade. Jim Shooter's raw-edged story gave the early Avengers a new depth of character, and the art of Gil Kane and Klaus Janson was electrifying.**"**
>
> **Mark Waid**

From its earliest days, Marvel Comics embraced many fascinating and fanciful science-fiction concepts that have since gained scientific credence and popular acceptance. The most story-rich has always been the idea of alternate worlds and parallel dimensions. In comic book terms, the notion of various versions of favorite Super Heroes clashing with "themselves," or the most memorable villains acting as noble champions is irresistible. After years of stories about convergent planes and divergent futures with alternate Ben Grimms, Squadron Supremes, or Doctor Dooms, the concept was formalized by editor in chief Archie Goodwin at the end of 1976. The result was a series of extra-long (usually) stand-alone stories under the umbrella title *What If?*

Written by future Marvel editor in chief Jim Shooter and illustrated by Gil Kane and Klaus Janson, *What If? #3* remains one of the most moving and memorable of the series. "What If the Avengers Had Never Been?" returns to the pivotal moment the Hulk petulantly quits the team during its second adventure. The divergence manifests when, instead of hunting for him as they did in *Avengers #3*, Thor, Iron Man, Giant-Man, and Wasp argue about what to do next. When Hulk teams up with Namor the Sub-Mariner to smash his former allies, the Thunder God is absent. A last-minute reconciliation between the human heroes and the addition of Rick

Jones cannot balance the enormous power disparity. Even augmented with Stark technology, the makeshift squad are unable to control their armored suits and again decide to go their separate ways.

With no other choice, Iron Man rashly overcharges his own armor and tackles the outlaws alone. Despite the last-minute arrival of his former comrades wearing the armor he made for them, and the unstable Hulk turning on Namor, the outcome is death for Tony Stark and the escape of both savage foes. In their wake, they leave behind heartbroken allies who will carry on in Iron Man's name but never be the founders of Earth's Mightiest Heroes. Packed with blistering action, powerfully told, and vividly illustrated, "What If the Avengers Had Never Been?" is a resonant, thought-provoking drama perfectly recapturing the fractious temperament and unpredictably abrasive natures of the characters at the time.

What If? was hosted by cosmic chronicler Uatu the Watcher, representative of an immortal race of godlike beings who began recording all universal events soon after the birth of creation. The Watchers debuted in *Fantastic Four #13* (April 1963) as the first of many hyper-advanced extraterrestrials in the Marvel Universe. With his observatory located on Earth's moon, Uatu, like the rest of his race, adopts a strict code of non-interference—though he invariably breaks that oath as often as not to protect the humans he has been assigned to observe.

Marvel masterwork
Gil Kane was a master of dynamic anatomy, peerless in depicting the sheer power embodied in Super Heroes. Refined and augmented by Klaus Janson's dramatic inking, the fleeting moment of triumph when Tony Stark's technology and courage beat the unstoppable Hulk has huge visual impact.

Uatu's brief also included watching all of Earth's adjacent dimensions and possible futures. This allowed readers to witness key moments in Marvel history that diverged from recorded continuity. The concept is potent and evergreen. Many one-off *What If?* stories have been retrofitted into the greater whole, such as Jane Foster becoming the female Thunder God Thordis, the Avengers beginning in the 1950s, or the ongoing career of second-generation Spider-Girl Mayday Parker. All of these were eventually spun off into their own mainstream series. With the huge success of the Marvel Cinematic Universe, *What If?* has also been co-opted for the small screen, with major movie moments being revisited and taken in strikingly different directions.

The ever-extendable concept has also allowed occasional moments of brilliantly surreal absurdity in stories such as Jack Kirby's "What If the Fantastic Four were the Original Marvel Bullpen?," Frank Miller's "What If Daredevil was Deaf instead of Blind?," and cartoonist Fred Hembeck's grab bag of spoof yarns in *What If?* #34 (August 1982), which included "What If Black Bolt got the Hiccups?"and "What If the Watchers in all the Realities got Together and Watched Watchers Watching Watchers...?" Since its debut in February 1977, the multitude of characters created over 13 volumes of *What If?* have been designated as inhabitants of alternate Earths in an infinite Marvel Multiverse, one in which Earth-616 is where mainstream Marvel continuity takes place. ▪

"HOPELESSLY **GROUNDED** IN THE STAGNANT, BRINE-FILLED POOL, THE HULK WRITHED IN **UTTER** AGONY AS IRON MAN SENT A HIGH-VOLTAGE **ELECTRIC CHARGE** CRACKLING FROM HIS TRANSISTORIZED GAUNTLETS!"

Avengers Annual #7
August 1977

Marvel Two-in-One
Annual #2
December 1977

> ❝These annuals represent the climax to the first and best series of story lines featuring Thanos. The Mad Titan was killed here with finality, and would stay dead for ten years, until his creator Jim Starlin was convinced to bring him back for another go-round.❞
>
> **Tom Brevoort**

Editor in chief	Archie Goodwin
Cover artist	Jim Starlin
Writer, penciler	Jim Starlin
Inker	Josef Rubinstein
Colorist	Petra Goldberg
Letterers	Tom Orzechowski (*Avengers Annual*), Annette Kawecki (*Marvel Two-in-One*)
Editor	Archie Goodwin

For most of its existence, the comic book industry has operated on the principle of never-ending story lines. In an ideal world, the absorbing dramas and spectacular battles would run forever from issue to issue. However, that seldom happens as reading tastes or other economic factors usually afford most creations a fixed longevity and shelf life. When Marvel began, the traditional game plan for comics publishers was to develop the best characters and craft interesting adventures around them for as long as possible. However, as an interlinked continuity grew, a new idea formed: heroes with a finite life span and whose demise would be a crucial aspect of their appeal.

Although never declared as such, the hyper-evolved artificial human Adam Warlock was always shrouded in the brooding solemnity of a tragic hero. When Jim Starlin assumed creative control of his tangled life story, the saga of the troubled interstellar nomad attained mythic proportions as it was steered toward a darkly nihilistic and definite ending.

In an issue of his own series, Warlock had even participated in the moment of his future self's death, and although his title was canceled soon after, readers wouldn't have to wait long to experience that prediction coming to pass in a grand crossover crisis. Marvel had long-ago pioneered guest shots where established stars met to collaborate or clash, and this had quickly led to story lines that began in one title and carried over into another. Ultimately, these far-reaching, sales-boosting crossovers, which also reinforced the impression of a shared universe, would evolve into epic events such as "The Infinity Crusade" and "The War of the Realms." These events would impact on and unfold in nearly every Marvel title simultaneously.

The Warlock crossover by Starlin and inker Joe Rubinstein began in *Avengers Annual #7* with "The Final Threat." The story saw Kree Protector of the Universe, Captain Marvel, and psychic goddess of Titan, Moondragon, drawn back to Earth with a vague presentiment

When heroes rise
Although Jim Starlin's most popular works address issues of death and other metaphysical quandaries, he never neglects to deliver pulse-pounding Super Hero action. However, even though the greatest heroes of Earth and their allies can take down space thugs, they are helpless against an all-powerful Thanos. Stopping the Mad Titan will need the intervention of a champion from beyond death.

THE EXPLOSIVE FLASH BLINDS EVERYONE MOMENTARILY, BUT EVEN WHEN THEIR VISION CLEARS, NONE ARE QUITE SURE THEY SHOULD BELIEVE WHAT THEIR EYES SEE.

of impending cosmic catastrophe. Meeting at the Avengers Mansion, their ominous premonitions are confirmed when Adam Warlock arrives bearing news that death-obsessed Thanos has amassed an alien armada from the criminal dregs of many worlds and built a Soul Gem powered weapon to snuff out the stars. Tracking down the invasion fleet and boarding Thanos' ship, the united heroes battle mightily to thwart the plan and prevent the Mad Titan from destroying Earth's Sun—but they win only at the cost of Warlock's life. As he had foreseen, the final moment was a welcome ending and allowed the weary warrior to find his deserved rest beside all his dead friends within his own predatory Soul Gem.

It appeared the threat was over, but *Marvel Two-in-One Annual #2* proved otherwise as "Death Watch!" finds Peter Parker bedeviled by prophetic nightmares. These reveal how Thanos has snatched victory from defeat and now holds the Avengers captive while again preparing to extinguish Sol as an offering to his beloved Mistress Death. Anguished, disbelieving Spider-Man borrows a spacecraft from the Fantastic Four and heads into space, accompanied by the Thing who also has a history with Thanos. Although completely outmatched, the duo upset Thanos' plans

long enough to free the Avengers, which allows the Great Powers of Creation time to resurrect Warlock. Destined to become the Universe's Champion of Life, he seemingly ends the Titan's threat forever before returning to the peace of the grave.

At the time, this powerful story appeared to complete a mythic cycle of heroism, and even deliver a just end for one of Marvel's most experimental and long-suffering characters. Warlock was a tormented hero who battled corruption, intolerance, universal evil, and even his own dark nature. Under Jim Starlin's guidance, he had grown into a truly intriguing, soulful character for whom fans came to care deeply. His fittingly dramatic and poetic death was carefully orchestrated and beautifully rendered by Starlin and inker Josef Rubenstein. Editor in chief Archie Goodwin ensured its revered status by allowing the extended, stand-alone story to span two annuals.

Warlock's welcome embrace of death presaged Starlin handling of Mar-Vell's passing years later. Yet, ultimately, sales dictate whether even the most fallen heroes are recalled to life if a fresh approach can be found and readers demand it. Both Warlock and Thanos were resurrected—more than once—with Starlin returning to the cosmic fold to spin their epic tales. ■

BEFORE THEM HAD STOOD *THANOS*, PROUD, POWERFUL, RUTHLESS, AND MERE HEART-BEATS FROM *VICTORY*. NOW IN THAT EXACT SPOT, MOMENTS LATER, STANDS THE MASSIVE TITAN TRANSFORMED INTO SOLID *GRANITE*.

Fitting finale
Filled with portents of foreboding and the threat of galactic Armageddon, the story of Adam Warlock's second death culminates with his ascension into a fiery avatar of life and Thanos' transformation into cold unfeeling stone.

Iron Man #128
November 1979

66 This is the issue that first [saw] Tony hitting the bottle a bit too heavily, which would later be greatly expanded on. His armor could protect him from everything... but himself. **99**

Peter David

Editor in chief	Jim Shooter
Cover artist	Bob Layton
Writers	David Michelinie, Bob Layton
Penciler	John Romita Jr.
Inker	Bob Layton
Colorist	Bob Sharen
Letterer	John Costanza
Editor	Roger Stern

Iron Man #128, aka "Demon in a Bottle," is quite simply one of the most famous comic book story lines of all time. It had such a major impact on the portrayal of Tony Stark that it is impossible to imagine him now, in comics or on screen, without this being part of his past, his psychological makeup. In the late 1970s, writer-artist Bob Layton and his good friend, writer David Michelinie, were relative newcomers at Marvel, but they were nonetheless given free rein on *Iron Man*. Layton later said that they made a great creative team on Iron Man as he was a longtime fan of the character while Michelinie was not, so they combined in-depth knowledge with a fresh perspective. And they decided that they wanted to examine the man inside the armor a little more closely.

Tony Stark was a man who seemed to have everything, so what happens when things go wrong? *Iron Man* #128 was the culmination of a nine-issue story arc that had seen all aspects of Stark's life spiral into crisis. His company was facing a hostile takeover, his Iron Man armor kept malfunctioning, and he was personally under threat of assassination. Layton and Michelinie had noted that Stark was well known for his billionaire playboy lifestyle and the social drinking that might entail, so they felt alcohol would be an obvious way for him to try to relieve his stress. As Tony drank more, it began to have serious ramifications, including firing his loyal and long-serving butler, Jarvis, at the end of *Iron Man* #127 (October 1979). Alcoholism, not some exotic Super Villain, was his worst enemy, and it was one that his genius could not easily conquer.

Iron Man #128 sees Stark reach a new low when he dons his armor while drunk and attempts to help the police with a derailed train carrying dangerous chemicals. Iron Man fails to properly judge the weight of the tanker he's lifting, and it crashes to the ground, leaking poisonous gas. The Avenger flees the scene in disgrace. At home, drowning his sorrows in a bottle again, Stark is confronted by his bodyguard Bethany Cabe, angrily telling him to let his friends help before he kills himself. Although his instinct is to push her away, Tony breaks down, begging her for help. She stays with him while he goes cold turkey and finally gets a handle on his alcoholism. Later, he apologizes to and reinstates Jarvis, and resolves to deal with his problems without the "courage" he derives from hard liquor.

The issue was unprecedented in its depiction of how far its titular hero had fallen. Although addiction had been dealt with a few times in comic books in the 1970s, it had never been the main character who was the addict. Bob Layton's striking cover for *Iron Man* #128 was truly shocking, showing Tony Stark, partially clad in his Iron Man armor, staring in horror at his own disheveled reflection, an open bottle beside him. When Layton and Michelinie had gone to Marvel editor in chief Jim Shooter to run their controversial story line past him, he had given them the green light, albeit with one condition—do it well. The critical reaction to "Demon in a Bottle," which included an Eagle Award for Favorite Single Comic Book Story, and its important legacy for not only *Iron Man* but for comic book history as a whole confirms that they did indeed do it well. ∎

X-Men #137
September 1980

Editor in chief	Jim Shooter
Cover artists	John Byrne, Terry Austin
Writers	Chris Claremont, John Byrne
Penciler	John Byrne
Inker	Terry Austin
Colorist	Glynis Wein
Letterer	Tom Orzechowski
Editors	Jim Salicrup, Louise Jones

> **What** *Amazing Spider-Man* #121 had been to a prior generation, *X-Men* #137 was to the successive one, as the long-running saga of the Dark Phoenix culminates in the self-sacrifice of Jean Grey... an unforgettable classic. **"**

Tom Brevoort

Fitting death
Jim Shooter's 11th-hour request to suitably punish Dark Phoenix's heinous actions pushed Chris Claremont and John Byrne to excel themselves, resulting in an issue packed with emotional strength and narrative purity.

"Once upon a time, there was a woman named Jean Grey, a man named Scott Summers. They were young. They were in love. They were heroes." *X-Men* #137 is arguably writer Chris Claremont's finest work on the title he spent more than 16 years on, and the tragic culmination of the Dark Phoenix Saga that had begun in *X-Men* #129 (January 1980).

The story line commences with Jean Grey, one of the original X-Men, being possessed by the incredible cosmic power known as the Phoenix. However, the Phoenix proves too much for any human to contain, and Jean is overwhelmed and transformed into the Dark Phoenix. Ranging through the universe, the Dark Phoenix consumes a star to satisfy its hunger, destroys an inhabited planet in the process, and then, shortly afterward, a Shi'ar warship. Returning to Earth, Professor X manages to use his psionic powers to subdue the Phoenix and allow Jean Grey to reassert control.

However, the terrible crimes she has committed need to be answered for. In the opening scene of *X-Men* #137, all the X-Men are forcibly brought aboard the warship of the Shi'ar empress Lilandra so that Jean Grey, the vessel of the Dark Phoenix, can face justice. Professor X requests a duel of honor— a fight between the X-Men and the Shi'ar Imperial Guard—to decide the issue. Empress Lilandra agrees, and the X-Men spend the night agonizing over whether fighting for someone who has killed billions is acceptable, even if she is their teammate. Eventually, they all decide to stand beside her, seeing the Jean Grey they know and love as separate from the Phoenix force and therefore not guilty of crimes committed while under its control.

On the following day, the two sets of combatants face each other in the Blue Area of the Moon. The Shi'ar Imperial Guard are formidable fighters, and eventually only Jean Grey and Cyclops

are left standing for the X-Men. When Cyclops is hit, Jean's fear and anger cause the Phoenix to rise again, and Professor X realizes that he has to command any X-Men who is able to attack their teammate.

What happened next was the result of much discussion in the Marvel bullpen. Editor in chief Jim Shooter had agreed to the story line of the Dark Phoenix saga in principle, as he had been interested in exploring the idea of a hero going bad, rather than a villain turning good as had already happened in other Marvel comics. However, when he saw the issue proofs for *X-Men* #135 (July 1980), which showed Dark Phoenix destroying a planet, he told Chris Claremont that she had to be appropriately punished—she could not just go back to "normal." Although imprisonment was suggested, Claremont believed that the X-Men would just keep trying to rescue her, and the problem would be prolonged. The writer then suggested killing Jean Grey, an extremely

daring move for a major character, and Shooter surprisingly agreed. Although it was too late to change *X-Men* #135, *X-Men* #137 was still in production, and so the creative team was able to rework the final few pages, changing the draft that had originally shown Jean returning to the X-Men.

As the published issue played out, Jean Grey chose to end her own life rather than risk Dark Phoenix claiming any more innocent lives. Claremont and artist John Byrne created a truly heartbreaking but morally understandable conclusion to the dilemma that faced Jean and the rest of the X-Men. *X-Men* #137 was a double-sized issue, a clear sign that Marvel felt it would be a milestone. Indeed, the story was a hit, an instant classic that is still numbered among the greatest comic books of all time. It is even sometimes credited for being the catalyst that revitalized the comic book industry at a time when it was in decline. ∎

Close encounter
John Byrne's arresting double-page spread, enhanced by Terry Austin's intricate inks and vivid colors from Glynis Wein, starts *X-Men* #137 as it means to go on, with feelings running high and the stakes set at life or death for Jean Grey.

Daredevil #168

January 1981

> "It's hard to overstate just how seismic Frank Miller's run on Daredevil was."
>
> **Wil Moss**

Editor in chief	Jim Shooter
Cover artists	Frank Miller, Klaus Janson
Writer, penciler	Frank Miller
Inker	Klaus Janson
Colorist	D. R. Martin
Letterer	Sam Rosen
Editors	Denny O'Neil, Mark Gruenwald

A finite romance
Matt's carefree college days end forever after romancing intriguing Greek émigré Elektra. Still concealing his abilities from friends like Foggy Nelson, Matt has no desire to become an action hero—until death and criminality blight Elektra's life.

Since his debut in 1964, Daredevil has operated on the fringes of the Super Hero world, confronting crime and protecting his neighborhood of Hell's Kitchen, New York City. Raised by his father, aging boxer and reluctant gangland enforcer "Battlin' Jack" Murdock, Matt Murdock was a natural athlete with an inclination for fighting. Bullied by other kids, who dubbed him "Daredevil" for his scholarly pursuits, Matt secretly honed his body and skills. These abilities helped him save an old man from a runaway truck, but at the cost of his sight after the vehicle's contents—radioactive waste—hit him in the face. The contamination hyper-amplified his other senses and created a "radar" pulse that could map his surroundings. Matt's intellect took him to Columbia University to study law, but he never escaped the crime-ridden streets. After Battlin' Jack was murdered, Matt created a costumed identity to punish the killers who thought themselves beyond the reach of justice.

Largely operating outside Marvel's mainstream continuity over the years, *Daredevil* was a steady, if not exceptional, seller, whose sales began growing after writers Jim Shooter and Roger McKenzie began introducing darker, grittier stories. In 1979, when a young Frank Miller came aboard as artist on *Daredevil* #158, those sales spiked and climbed steadily, his moody artwork intensifying the foreboding tone of the title's edgier story lines. With *Daredevil* #168, Miller also took over scripting the title, his "Elektra" story arc tweaking the hero's origin and changing his character forever.

As Daredevil hunts a criminal fugitive fleeing a mysterious bounty hunter, a vicious clash reveals his opponent to be someone he knows intimately. While being knocked unconscious, the hero recognizes a voice and recalls the girl he loved and lost years ago. Back at Columbia University, he fell for a beguiling ambassador's daughter, Elektra Natchios, and the two became inseparable for a year. Matt even shared with her the secret of his hyper-senses, but everything fell apart when she and her father were kidnapped by terrorists. Desperate to help, Matt donned a mask for the first time and attacked, but the situation soon escalated out of control, and Demetrios Natchios was killed by a panicked police SWAT team. In the aftermath, Elektra vanished, but now here she was, a hired assassin, embodying everything Matt despises. Despite the shame he feels over his tragic failure and her loss, Daredevil swears to bring Elektra to justice at all cost.

This radical overhaul of Daredevil's motivations—with a masked Murdock's unique, super-sensory gifts reinforced by martial arts skills while he was still a student—becomes more believable when we learn he was already taking the law into his own hands years ago. Creating a guilty secret and a lover with a troubled past added emotional depth to a hero, who, until then, was generally considered somewhat dull. Miller's thoroughgoing conversion of Daredevil to a crime-noir tinged, flawed hero made the Man Without Fear far more credible. Future innovations would dial back Super Villains in favor of organized crime, ninja mysticism, and a blind sensei shaping Daredevil's development. ■

HE REELS, DIMLY AWARE OF A WOMAN'S FORM--

--A MOMENT BEFORE SHE STRIKES HIM A BLOW THAT ROCKS HIS BRAIN AND STRETCHES THE CORDS IN HIS NECK.

HE FALLS. HE STRUGGLES TO REMAIN CONSCIOUS, SOME-HOW, HE HEARS FLEEING FOOTSTEPS...

...HEARS HIS ATTACKER WHIRL, AND THROW HER WEAPON...

...HEARS THE WEAPON STRIKE A WALL...

...HEARS THE SPLINTERING OF BONE AS IT SMASHES AN UNPROTECTED JAW.

THEN, HE HEARS HER SPEAK...

THERE IS A BOUNTY OUT IN EUROPE FOR ALARICH WALLENQUIST, BILGE--

--A BOUNTY I INTEND TO COLLECT.

YOU ARE GOING TO HELP ME CAPTURE HIM, OR I AM GOING TO KILL YOU.

IT IS AS SIMPLE AS THAT.

THAT VOICE--

ELEKTRA?!

Love hurts

Seeking to clear a framed man, Daredevil hunts a witness and becomes embroiled in an assassination plot involving a European bounty hunter and his old foe Eric Slaughter. Daredevil's resolve is shaken to the core upon realizing his first love, Elektra, is back and that his precipitous actions during their college days have caused her to become a killer for hire.

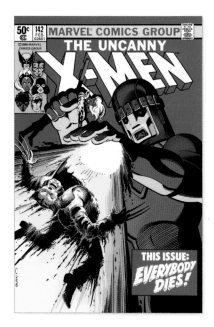

Uncanny X-Men #142
February 1981

" Hot on the heels of the unforgettable Death of Phoenix story line, Claremont and Byrne took matters to an almost absurd level, in which the X-Men of the future were wiped out by the Sentinels... and only the time-displaced mind of Kate Pryde could save the day. **"**

Tom Brevoort

Editor in chief	Jim Shooter
Cover artists	Terry Austin, Danny Crespi
Writers	Chris Claremont, John Byrne
Penciler	John Byrne
Inker	Terry Austin
Colorist	Glynis Wein
Letterer	Tom Orzechowski
Editors	Louise Jones

By the early 1980s, the X-Men were hot property at Marvel, having fully hit their stride after a mid-1970s reboot. The creative team of writer Chris Claremont and writer-artist John Byrne were delivering story lines that would become all-time classics, and one of the very best of these was "Days of Future Past." This game-changing tale played out over just two issues, with *Uncanny X-Men* #142 providing the conclusion. Incredibly, it came just a few issues after another celebrated arc, the "Dark Phoenix Saga." Marvel Comics at that time, led by editor in chief Jim Shooter, preferred to keep its story lines relatively short to make an impact in one or two issues and leave the readers wanting more.

The future of the X-Men was apparently bleak, as revealed to readers in *Uncanny X-Men* #141 (January 1981). In the year 2013, mutants have been ostracized from society and are in constant peril of being killed by the giant, mutant-hunting robot Sentinels that patrol North America. The mutants' powers have been neutralized by inhibitor collars, rendering them unable to fight back against their oppressors. Worse still, the Sentinels are about to trigger a global nuclear war. The surviving X-Men hatch a plan to send Kate Pryde's consciousness back in time to inhabit her younger self, Kitty, to try to change history so that their terrible future would never come to pass. They identify the assassination of Senator Robert Kelly in 1980 as the key moment when anti-

mutant legislation and the creation of the Sentinels becomes inevitable.

In *Uncanny X-Men* #142, the X-Men have rushed to Washington, DC, to prevent the senator's murder. The issue opens with them confronting the Brotherhood of Evil Mutants, in this iteration led by the shape-shifting Mystique. Even the future Kitty Pryde does not know who will be responsible for the killing, only that it is said to have been a mutant. As the opposing sides brutally clash, the onlooking military seem unconcerned about whether the mutants they are trying to take down are on their side or not. It is a hint of the anti-mutant sentiment that already exists and would morph into something even more terrible over the ensuing decades.

While the present-day battle scenes were thrillingly drawn and told by artist John Byrne, it is the evocative glimpses of the future that really make this issue stand out. It is a true dystopia, populated by misery and with virtually no hope of anything better. The previous issue had emphatically underlined what had been lost when Kate Pryde returned to her internment camp and walked through a graveyard containing headstones for almost all the heroes of the Marvel Universe. The cover of *Uncanny X-Men* #142 made no secret of the fact that things were very bleak, proclaiming "This Issue: Everybody Dies!" The dramatic image accompanying this grim promise was, for many X-Men fans, the

book's most shocking moment—when a Sentinel succeeds in killing Wolverine, beyond any hope of his incredible healing powers bringing him back to life.

Wolverine's death is not the only important X-Men moment in this story. *Uncanny X-Men* #141 had seen the debut of Rachel Summers, a Claremont and Byrne creation who is the daughter of Scott Summers and Jean Grey in that terrible alternate future. Eventually, Rachel Summers would return to the past to become a popular character in the main X-Men team. Another significant character beat, although not revealed in detail in *Uncanny X-Men* #142, is the revelation that the mutant Nightcrawler is related to Mystique. Claremont was always careful to place as much emphasis on the relationships between characters as he did to the big set-piece battle scenes.

Claremont had spent time working on a kibbutz in Israel, where he met many survivors of the Holocaust. He has

mentioned that the experience of being around people who had lived through the most extreme prejudice and oppression stayed with him, and informed some of the thrust and details in "Days of Future Past." The story was also partly inspired by an episode of the classic British science fiction TV series *Doctor Who*, and he chose the name as a play on the Moody Blues album *Days of Future Passed*.

"Days of Future Past" was the first time-travel story in the X-Men's world. Its success paved the way for several other major story arcs of this type and new characters spinning out of them such as Cable, Bishop, and Stryfe. The dystopian future it portrayed was intended by the creators to show what was at stake for mutants, both to readers and the X-Men in story. It played into the essence of the X-Men: "Feared and hated by the world they are sworn to protect," and still ranks as one of the greatest X-Men stories ever told. ▪

Fight for the future
Kitty Pryde plays a key role as she tries to avert a tragic event that will cause a horrific future, in this all-time classic X-Men story by legendary creators Chris Claremont and John Byrne. The searing saga would also inspire a hit X-Men movie of the same name.

Avengers Annual #10
October 1981

> "...this landmark issue shows the beginning of Carol Danvers' lifelong friendship with Spider-Woman and the debut of Rogue, who all but wipes the floor with the Avengers... [signaling] how important she would become one day."

Kelly Thompson

Editor in chief	Jim Shooter
Cover artists	Al Milgrom, Irv Watanabe
Writer	Chris Claremont
Penciler	Michael Golden
Inker	Armando Gil
Letterer	Joe Rosen
Editors	Chris Claremont, David Kraft

Saving Ms. Marvel
Avengers Annual #10 reintroduced Carol Danvers to the Marvel Universe in shocking fashion, with Spider-Woman saving her life as she falls from the Golden Gate Bridge. Writer Chris Claremont used the book to confront a traumatic episode from Ms. Marvel's past and pivot her character toward a resolutely independent and self-reliant future.

Writer Chris Claremont was best known for his long stint on *The X-Men*, but in the late 1970s, he also wrote *Ms. Marvel* and *Spider-Woman*. *Ms. Marvel* was canceled just before Claremont planned to introduce a new character—Rogue—and have her use her mutant ability to steal Ms. Marvel's powers. So when he was slated to write *Avengers Annual* #10, he seized the chance to revive this defunct story line.

Avengers Annual #10 also became a very public rejection of the events of an earlier comic, *Avengers* #200 (October 1980), the last issue in which Ms. Marvel had appeared. Claremont had a reputation for creating strong female characters such as Rogue and Mystique, which also extended to writing stories for existing characters like Spider-Woman (Jessica Drew) and Ms. Marvel (Carol Danvers). The way Ms. Marvel, a character he was especially attached to, had been let down by her teammates in *Avengers* #200 had not sat well with Claremont. The issue had also been criticized by some readers for a story line in which Ms. Marvel became pregnant by a mysterious being, Marcus, who admitted using mind-control devices on her. When Marcus took Ms. Marvel with him at the end of the issue, the Avengers did not think to question whether or not she was going of her own free will.

Claremont ended *Avengers Annual* #10 with Carol Danvers confronting her former teammates and calling them out on their behavior toward her. They are shocked at first, but after listening to what she had to say, they realize that they had been blind to the trauma she had suffered. Danvers would remain with the X-Men—and therefore continue to be written by Claremont—while she tried to regain her powers and find a new place in the world. After a long and difficult road, she would eventually become Captain Marvel, one of the Marvel Universe's main heroes and the first female Marvel hero to star in her own movie.

Another character from *Avengers Annual* #10 who would go on to great things was Rogue. Created by Claremont and artist Michael Golden, Rogue started out as a villain and protégée of Mystique in the Brotherhood of Evil Mutants. Rogue had permanently taken Ms. Marvel's powers, "off-panel," just before the story started in *Avengers Annual* #10, and would go on to steal Captain America and Thor's powers too. It made her the most powerful character in the story until Iron Man managed to take her down. Later, joining the X-Men, Rogue would become one of the team's most popular members among readers.

Avengers Annual #10's classic status was cemented by gorgeous art from the great Michael Golden, whose detailed pencils and luminous colors were enhanced by Armando Gil's bold inking. Later, writer Brian Michael Bendis cited this comic book as one he treasured and its smart portrayal of Spider-Woman as key to making Jessica Drew one of his favorite characters. ∎

Hex power
This full-page splash was one of the key action sequences in *Avengers Annual* #10. Artist Michael Golden uses perspective to emphasize the task facing Scarlet Witch as she takes on the villain Pyro's giant fire beast. But despite her diminutive size, the Scarlet Witch's hexes prove too much for the monster.

AS THE MAIN EXPLODED, PYRO SEIZED CONTROL OF THE BURNING GAS, MOLDING THE FLAMES INTO A **GIANT CREATURE** OF LIVING FIRE. HIS INTENTIONS WERE BRUTALLY SIMPLE: TO TURN HIS MONSTER LOOSE AGAINST THE AVENGERS AND INCINERATE THEM.

SEEING THE DANGER, THE SCARLET WITCH CAST A SECOND HEX, AND A THIRD, AND A FOURTH--POURING HER HEART AND SOUL INTO EACH ONE WITHOUT BEING COMPLETELY CERTAIN OF WHAT WILL HAPPEN AS A RESULT.

UNDER HER DESPERATE ON-SLAUGHT, REALITY TWISTED, SHATTERED, REFORMED. BEFORE PYRO'S DISBELIEVING EYES, THE VERY SUBSTANCE OF HIS CONSTRUCT CHANGED FROM LIVING FLAME TO UNLIVING STONE.

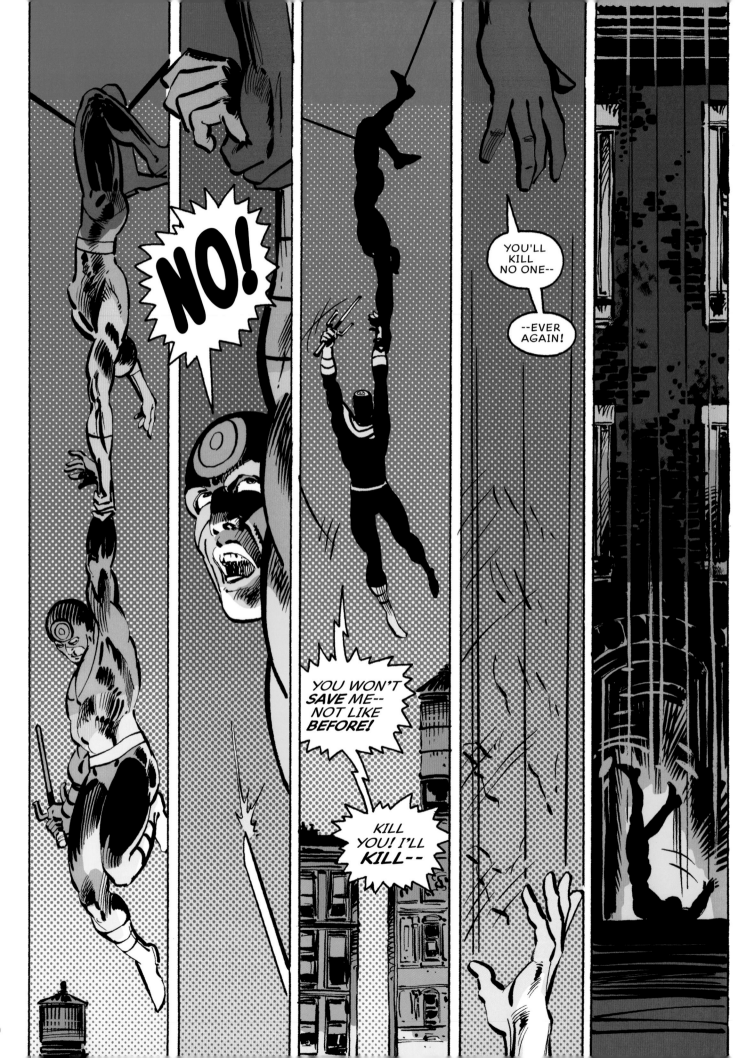

Daredevil #181
April 1982

"One wins. One dies." was not hyperbole. A shocking story where Frank Miller brought so many of his grim, gritty plotlines to a head [changing] these characters' lives forever.**"**

C. B. Cebulski

Editor in chief	Jim Shooter
Cover artist	Frank Miller
Writer, penciler	Frank Miller
Inker	Klaus Janson
Letterer	Joe Rosen
Editor	Denny O'Neil

◀ **Equal and opposite**
Frank Miller spent a lot of time and effort building Bullseye into Daredevil's moral antithesis and stressing the sheer overwhelming threat he posed. A hero is defined by his enemies, so when Daredevil ultimately defeats the most dangerous man alive, we see the bereaved, enraged hero at his deadliest.

Daredevil #181 is one of the most shocking comics books of the 1980s—and, indeed, Marvel history. In "Last Hand," Frank Miller's revelatory reinvention and redefinition of sightless Super Hero Daredevil pivots on the moment that the increasingly hard-pressed, distressed, and demoralized vigilante faces an ethical meltdown. The dramatic outcome changed the man behind the mask forever and reshaped how Super Hero comic stories would be viewed from that point forward.

Daredevil's transformative crisis of conscience follows months of increasingly uncompromising encounters, with the hero confronting hard-hitting social issues—suicide, child criminals, the blurry fault lines between justice and vengeance—as well as dealing with the shock return of his tempestuous first love, Elektra Natchios. Such relentless physical and emotional provocation pushes the hero to the limits of endurance. So when Elektra unexpectedly arrives in New York, Matt Murdock's world is turned upside down. Shaped by years of heartbreak and the murder of her father—a tragedy in which young Murdock was cruelly involved—Elektra reenters Daredevil's life as a ruthless hired killer with unclear connections to a mystic ninja cult called The Hand.

Frank Miller's most formative creative influences were manga (Japanese comics) and American crime fiction, with his art style initially borrowing from former Daredevil illustrators Gene Colan and Gil Kane—particularly the latter's expressive, balletic poses and dynamic figure work.

After drawing scripts by Roger McKenzie, Miller took over writing and illustrating duties on the series with *Daredevil* #168 (January 1981). Blending a darker, film noir sensibility with more mature themes and characterizations of Marvel heroes and villains proved an immediate hit. In an echo of Raymond Chandler's famous line, Miller sent his hero down Manhattan's mean streets, "(as) a man who is not himself mean... tarnished or afraid," plunging him into territory familiar to fans of director Martin Scorsese's own *Mean Streets* (1973). Set against a vibrant yet chilling backdrop of dark alleys and gleaming towers, the Man without Fear's life became ever more grim and tormented as he took on the worst of humanity: drug dealers, petty thugs, vigilante killers, assassin cults, and his bête noire, the lord of organized crime, Wilson Fisk, aka the Kingpin.

Daredevil #181 sees Elektra, now employed by Fisk, ordered to kill Murdock's best friend Foggy Nelson. At the same time, Kingpin's former assassin Bullseye breaks out of prison while recovering from brain surgery. Determined to take revenge on Daredevil and kill Elektra, the woman who usurped his rightful position, he viciously adds to his sky-high body count to prove his intentions. As he studies his prospective targets, the maniacal Bullseye realizes that Matt Murdock is Daredevil, but is unable to convince anyone of his conclusions. Stalking Elektra, he observes the moment she redeems herself by allowing Murdock's law partner Foggy Nelson to live, before engaging her in a furious dance of death that leaves her bleeding out and painfully crawling back to her former lover to die in his arms. In the aftermath, a gloating Bullseye falls for a simple trap set by Murdock, leading to a staggering, silent battle across the city that ends with Daredevil forced to decide whether the villain lives or dies. And then the hero does what no comics reader ever expected a Marvel Super Hero to do... he lets the raving Bullseye fall to his apparent death.

As he both wrote and drew the saga, Miller became more of a director and stage designer, employing sharp filmic cuts, abrupt location changes, and unconventional "camera angles" to accentuate action and pace, tone, and mood. Panels became page-wide or deep like manga, which, combined with terse dialogue, sped up the rate at which the stories were read. Miller also experimented with layout to enhance emotional impact. The final three pages of "Last Hand" are compositionally identical, giving readers intimate and foreboding insight into the individual reactions of the story's three survivors: Fisk, Murdock, and the crippled, unrepentant Bullseye.

Groundbreaking, utterly compelling, and simply unforgettable, this unflinching character study of the impulses that drive heroes and villains showed them at their very best and worst—and underscored the thin line that often separates them. The introduction of Elektra and her tragic demise shifted Daredevil from costumed crime-busting and science-fiction adventures to a world of organized crime, dark magic, and religious symbolism. Characterized by a savagely intense, if stylized, depiction of violence, "Last Hand" heralded a new, adult-oriented sensibility that soon provoked controversy in some quarters. However, what commentators and readers could agree on was that American comics weren't just for kids anymore.

As the series progressed, Miller began concentrating more on scripting and scene setting, providing fewer and less detailed pencils as inker Klaus Janson stepped up to contribute an even faster-paced, looser energy to the stories. Frank Miller's last contribution to his first run was *Daredevil* #191 (February 1983). He would return in *Daredevil* #219 (June 1985), to commence another celebrated, game-changing sequence of stories. ■

Brutal ballet
As a writer, Miller wanted pictures to tell the stories. He minimized characters' dialogue to brief outbursts, banished authorial captions, and dropped thought balloons in favor of internal monologues. The battle sequences are particularly innovative: brutal, graceful, largely devoid of banter, and deadly serious.

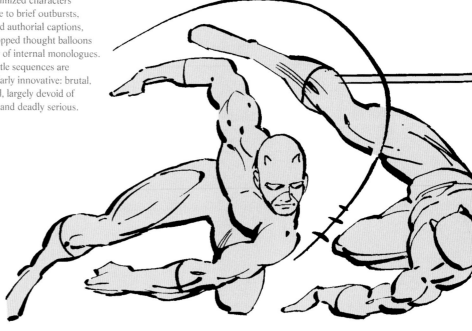

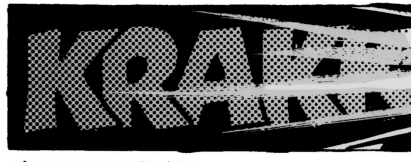

Marvel Graphic Novel #1
April 1982

Editor in chief	Jim Shooter
Cover artist	Jim Starlin
Writer, penciler, inker	Jim Starlin
Colorist	Steve Oliff
Letterer	James Novak
Editor	Al Milgrom

In the early 1980s, the comics industry battled adverse economic conditions and a persistent perception that comics had little artistic merit and were of fleeting value. Industry creatives and professionals had struggled for years to foster the attitudes of Europe and Japan, where sequential narrative was accepted as a valid art form, but despite some early independent graphic novels, progress was very slow. That attitude began to shift after Jim Starlin returned to Marvel to craft an enduring, classic conclusion to the story and life of a character with whom he was inextricably associated.

Jim Shooter had become Marvel's editor in chief in 1978 and, as well as expanding its output and pushing the company toward more licensed titles, he wanted to reproduce the style and success of French comics with a line of prestige albums offering more mature fare to readers. Much emulated by many competitors since its inception, the game-changing Marvel Graphic Novel line began in 1982 and ran until 1993. It published European album-format, stand-alone trade paperbacks that featured both licensed and creator-owned properties as well as debuting new Marvel Universe characters who would then continue in their own monthly titles. The first book, however, dealt with the last adventure of a beloved fan favorite, starkly entitled "The Death of Captain Marvel."

From 1973 to 1974, writer-artist Jim Starlin revitalized the character during a two-year tenure that spanned *Captain Marvel* #25 to #34. On Starlin's watch, the Kree spy-turned-hero, Mar-Vell, underwent cosmic metamorphosis, became Protector of the Universe, and defeated the Mad Titan Thanos in a battle preordained since life began. When Starlin moved on, despite the efforts of many creators, Mar-Vell again slipped from favor and a decision was made to grant the name to another hero, Monica Rambeau. In time, Rambeau graduated from Captain Marvel to Photon and then Pulsar, before becoming Spectrum.

In 1982, Starlin reentered the scene. The creator had long explored themes of death and metaphysics in his work, and he was invited to kill off Mar-Vell, with Marvel agreeing that the hero would not be resurrected. As Starlin worked on the book, however, real-world tragedy intruded—his own father died of a lingering terminal illness. The author's reactions shaded his creativity, even as it gave him an avenue for dealing with his own feelings. The result is an eloquent and profoundly moving recapitulation of Mar-Vell's eventful life, leading to his untimely death.

In the last issue of his earlier run on *Captain Marvel*, Starlin introduced the Super Villain Nitro. The villain was defeated, but Mar-Vell was exposed to the experimental nerve gas Compound 13.

Last rites
Despite the greatest efforts of the wisest minds, even the mightiest of heroes must perish in the end. Although Mar-Vell always thought he would die alone in one last battle, his truth is more glorious: he is loved and admired, and his passing is mourned by the most powerful champions in the universe.

Years later, in *Marvel Graphic Novel* #1, just as he finds love and contentment, the Kree discovers that the contamination has caused cancer, which has metastasized and mutated into something completely incurable. Experiencing the Kree version of the Kubler-Ross Cycle—grief, denial, anger, bargaining, depression, and acceptance—Mar-Vell can only watch as all his many friends and comrades try desperately to find a cure before death comes for him. Yet even they are finally forced to accept the grim reality of Mar-Vell's condition—and, indeed, their own mortality. As he hovers on the edge of death, sworn foes like the Skrull pay their respects, and he is even visited by his greatest enemy, Thanos, who accompanies him to... "the beginning."

Starlin's story is a clear-eyed, heartfelt examination of the process of dying as experienced by a born warrior, who never thought he would die in bed. It argues forcefully that even in a universe where miracles are commonplace, sometimes death may be welcome.

Although told within the framework of traditional Super Hero comics, in a genre built upon dramatic action and often bombastic storytelling, this is a quiet, intimate, and introspective tale—and all the more powerful for that. "The Death of Captain Marvel" demonstrated how Super Hero fare could achieve the same quality and maturity as the finest European comics and has been rightly hailed as one of the best Marvel stories of all time. ■

Warrior spirit
In his last moments, delirium grips Mar-Vell as he rages against the dying of the light and makes one last stand against Thanos, his most relentless enemy and lover of the one person he has to face with resolute acceptance—Death. As the Mad Titan taunts him during pitch battle: "Death should never be easy. It must be earned." Mar-Vell's final metaphysical fight scene is lucidly illustrated and superbly choreographed, and ends on an uplifting grace note.

Editor in chief	Jim Shooter
Cover artist	Michael Golden
Writer	Roger Stern
Penciler	Michael Golden
Inker	Terry Austin
Colorist	Glynis Wein
Letterer	Jim Novak
Editor	Allen Milgrom

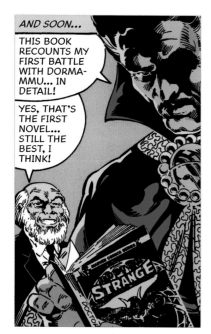

Identity crisis
Already in mental anguish, Stephen Strange is pushed to the brink when a disguised demon tells him that "Doctor Strange" is a fictional character and his whole reality is just a delusion.

Doctor Strange #55
October 1982

❝Quite possibly one of the trippiest issues ever, it starts out as a riff on *It's a Wonderful Life* but then tips over into a twisted, demented, "Wait, what?" story line that keeps you guessing about what's really happening until the very end.❞

Peter David

Writer Roger Stern had a hard act to follow when he took over *Doctor Strange* in the late 1970s. His esteemed predecessor, Steve Englehart, enjoyed a legendary run with the character, working with great artists closely associated with the character such as Steve Ditko and Gene Colan. Stern himself was originally slated to start *Doctor Strange* with Frank Miller on art duties, but this potentially epic pairing sadly never happened. Nonetheless, Stern's own lengthy run on the title saw some of the most acclaimed Doctor Strange stories of all time and showcased the work of some of the finest comic book artists of the era.

Doctor Strange #55 was a stellar example of both storytelling and art, with the renowned artist Michael Golden signing on for penciling duties on the one-off comic. Stern saw the issue as an appropriate epilogue of a story arc that ended the involvement of the character Clea in Doctor Strange's world. Clea was both a lover and pupil of Strange, a long-term, uneven liaison Stern wanted to shake up. Having decided to write out Clea—a controversial move among some readers—Stern introduced a new character, Morgana Blessing, as a more equal romantic interest for Strange.

This examination of Doctor Strange's relationships was classic Stern. As a writer,

he was interested in Stephen Strange as a person as much as he was in the Sorcerer Supreme's mystical prowess. He felt it was important to bring to the forefront those elements of Strange's life that occurred when he was among ordinary humans, as well as his otherdimensional battles with demons and spirits.

In *Doctor Strange #55*, readers see the Sorcerer Supreme at his lowest ebb following the departure of his beloved Clea, who had voluntarily left him after Morgana had entered his life. Refusing to see anyone, Strange is visited by a spirit, who shows him what his world might have been like if he had never chosen to study magic. What follows is both a homage to classics like *A Christmas Carol* or *It's a Wonderful Life* and a remorseless dismantling of everything Doctor Strange has ever believed in—his entire reality.

Pushed to the brink of madness by the visions the spirit shares with him, Doctor Strange is at rock bottom and almost ready to give in when he discovers that he wants to live and rejects everything the spirit has shown him. He strikes back with a powerful spell and finds that he had been tricked—the spirit is in fact the demon D'Spayre, who has seized on his vulnerable state to try and destroy him. A high-stakes magical battle ensues, in which Strange manages to triumph

Demonic struggle

Michael Golden's lavish pencils and cinematic storytelling, intricately delineated by illustrious inker Terry Austin, contribute heavily to *Doctor Strange* #55's classic status. This dramatically realised triptych of panels emphasises Strange's extreme disorientation as he battles the demon D'Spayre for his very sanity.

by using one of his oldest weapons, the Crimson Bands of Cyttorak, to trap the demon. By the issue's end, Strange is at peace with himself. Having been on an emotional journey that had also led him into great danger, he found the mental strength he needed to resume his wondrous ordinary life.

Roger Stern was forging his own path with Stephen Strange, but he and Michael Golden included an affectionate hat tip to his creators in *Doctor Strange* #55. While D'Spayre is trying to convince him that his reality is false and he is, in reality, just a fictional comic book character, Strange is introduced to the writer and illustrator who allegedly created him—"Les Tane" and "Ted Tevoski"—aka Stan Lee and Steve Ditko.

Doctor Strange #55 is still regarded as a true classic, in large part thanks to Michael Golden and inker Terry Austin's breathtakingly beautiful art. Despite never working on a regular Super Hero title, Golden is considered by many to be one of the greats of the comic book medium. He was only ever a guest penciler on *Doctor Strange*, but the art he produced for the title was of a quality that stands up to scrutiny beside the likes of Ditko and Colan. That *Doctor Strange* #55 is one of only two issues of the title drawn by Golden makes it all the more special. ▪

Thor #337
November 1983

> **"**...the idea of anyone else wielding Thor's hammer Mjölnir was unthinkable. And yet Walt Simonson thought of it—[shattering] Thor's familiar world, opening it to new and bizarre friends, enemies, perils, and drama.**"**
>
> **Mark Waid**

Editor in chief	Jim Shooter
Writer, penciler	Walter Simonson
Inker	Tom Palmer
Colorist	George Roussos
Letterer	John Workman Jr
Editor	Jim Shooter

POWER ENOUGH TO SHAKE THIS PLANET TO ITS FOUNDATIONS!

Breaking the boundaries
Beta Ray Bill's introduction is a brilliant piece of lateral thinking, acknowledging that other heroes can be as worthy as Thor. The notion eventually culminates in Captain America wielding the power in Secret Empire and Jane Foster becoming Mighty Thor.

Since his 1962 debut, Mighty Thor has been one of Marvel's bestselling stars, blending riveting Earth-based Super Hero action with mystical fantasy. However, any long-lived series can experience occasional doldrums, which generally end when a new creator arrives with a fresh vision and a hunger to shake things up. That has never been better demonstrated than when Walter Simonson took control of the Thunder God in *Thor* #337.

Simonson had briefly illustrated *Thor*, written by Len Wein, in the late 1970s, but he was now scripting as well. And his aim was to rekindle Jack Kirby's compelling, majestic synthesis of mythology, science fiction, and humanist philosophy. Sharing Kirby's love of legends and high fantasy, Simonson, brought his own unique style and sensibility to the series, resulting in a groundbreaking body of work (*Thor* #337–382; November 1983–August 1987), which redefined the canon and inspired the 21st-century film franchise. Simonson envisaged a major story arc and extinction-level threat culminating in *Thor* #350 (December 1984), with a radical change to all Nine Realms. The sweeping epic began with a shattering shake-up of the status quo.

"Doom!" starts with a shadowy cosmic demon forging a universe-rending sword. Meanwhile, in Chicago, complacent Doctor Donald Blake is approached by S.H.I.E.L.D. Director Nick Fury to investigate an Earth-bound starship that refuels by absorbing suns! Ignoring the disturbing fact that the super-spy knows his secret identity, Thor intercepts the warship, only to be defeated in combat by its occupant: a bionically augmented warrior named Beta Ray Bill. As they fight, Thor drops his hammer and, losing contact with it for more than a minute, reverts to his human form. As the ship crashes to Earth, the alien co-opts Mjölnir's magic and is transformed into a bizarre duplicate of Thor. While S.H.I.E.L.D. attacks the downed vessel, All-Father Odin, mistaking Beta Ray Bill for his actual son, summons the new hammer-wielder to Asgard to defend the Realm Eternal. Trapped on Earth as powerless Don Blake, the true Thor can only scream his frustrations to the heavens.

This story revolves around a rereading of the spell inscribed on Thor's magic hammer: "Whosoever holds this hammer, if he be worthy, shall possess the power of Thor." Introducing a very different champion with equal right to the power was merely the start. Ultimately, Thor would regain his divine birthright and unite with Bill—who was built to protect the survivors of his Korbinite race from a demonic horde—to save Earth from the monsters. Along the way, Thor would update that transformation spell, retire his Donald Blake persona, and even modify his Shakespearian speech patterns.

Simonson's complex tale involving the fire demon Surtur triggering Ragnarok and the Asgardian sacrifices needed to save Earth was only the start of a campaign to make Thor relevant and fun again. And he achieves this while also fully integrating the character and his mystical realms into a greater, more unified Marvel Universe. ∎

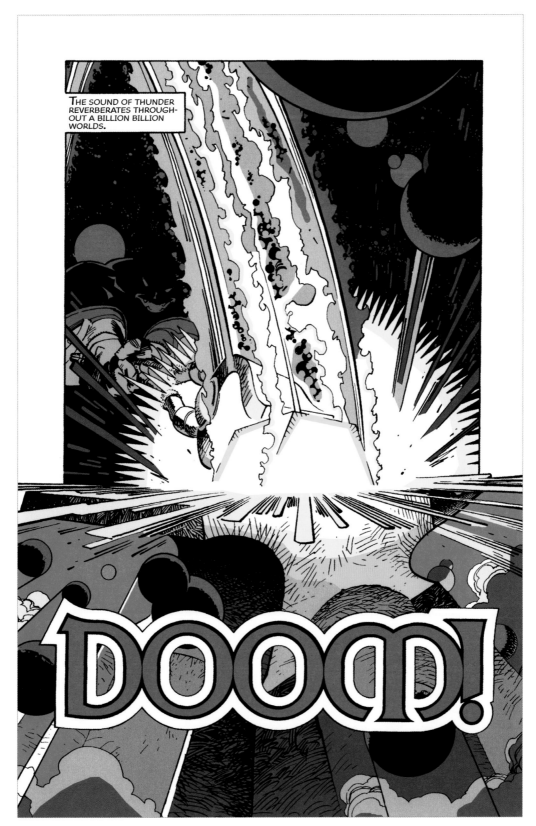

Grand design

Simonson's bold storytelling and illustrative style are epic in scope, but arguably his strongest asset is incorporating calligraphy and lettering into his page designs. The variety of letterforms and sound effects by John Workman Jr. greatly enhances the mood and drama of the mystical proceedings.

ORORO...

...IT'S FORGE.

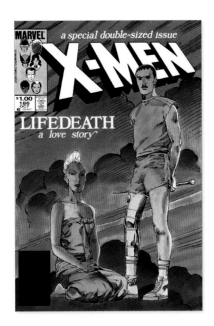

Uncanny X-Men #186
October 1984

" Barry Windsor-Smith's Incredible artwork combines with Chris Claremont's rich character-work to produce one of the most remembered issues of the writer's run. "

Jordan D. White

Editor in chief	Jim Shooter
Cover artist	Barry Windsor-Smith
Writers	Chris Claremont, Barry Windsor-Smith
Penciler	Barry Windsor-Smith
Inker	Terry Austin
Colorists	Glynis Wein, Christie Scheele
Letterer	Tom Orzechowski
Editors	Ann Nocenti, Peter Sanderson

◄ **Storm passed**
Barry Windsor-Smith's art sensitively conveys the delicate emotional state of the once-mighty Storm. Shorn of her powers, she cannot even summon the energy to get out of bed as she wonders who she is if she is no longer a Super Hero.

Uncanny X-Men #186, subtitled "Lifedeath," was a standout issue of writer Chris Claremont's run even during a period that also included the "Dark Phoenix Saga" and "Days of Future Past." It was a very different kind of comic book, one that examined themes of loss and identity, and mixed sublime visuals with quiet introspection. Those dazzling visuals came from the pencil of acclaimed artist Barry Windsor-Smith, lending the issue an almost painted look that set it apart from other Super Hero comics of its time. Claremont stated that he had always wanted to work with Windsor-Smith and praised his notes during the creative process, which described characterization and relationships in detail. Although Windsor-Smith often did his own inking, those duties in *Uncanny X-Men* #186 were performed by the estimable Terry Austin.

Although the story falls within regular X-Men continuity, the double-sized issue feels like a pause button has been pressed. Storm, one of Claremont's key characters throughout his long run on the title, had lost her powers in the previous issue. *Uncanny X-Men* #186 shows her trying to come to terms with this loss with the help of mutant genius Forge. The two become closer as the tale progresses—in fact, its cover billed it as a "love story"—but at the end, Storm is horrified to discover that the weapon that had robbed her of her powers had been designed by Forge.

The issue opens with Windsor-Smith sensitively depicting the devastating effect Storm's depowering had on the hero. She is shown lying listlessly in bed, as Forge, feeling terrible guilt, tries to care for her and encourage her to have hope. Having lived with her powers for so long, they were bound up with Storm's sense of herself. Forge reveals to her, and readers, that he, too, knows what it was like to lose something of yourself. He had been badly wounded in Vietnam and had put his inventive genius to good use building a prosthetic leg and hand for himself.

His talents are also evident in the design and functionality of his high-tech penthouse suite, which uses holograms to "remove" the floors and walls, creating a dizzying sense of space. These effects enabled Windsor-Smith to add dramatic elements to the sequences of Storm and Forge talking, which were otherwise very understated, with facial expressions and body language conveying the intimacy and depth of the story.

Forge was a new character, having been introduced by Claremont and artist John Romita Jr. in *Uncanny X-Men* #184 (August 1984), so this issue was used to reveal elements of his backstory, like his Native American heritage. Although Forge would later become a valued member of the team, *Uncanny X-Men* #186 does not paint him in a wholly positive light, with his deception of Storm and his apparent willingness to sell out mutantkind by making weapons for those who hunt them.

"Lifedeath" would have a sequel in *Uncanny X-Men* #198 (October 1985). Also by Claremont and Windsor-Smith, it finds a still powerless Storm return to Africa, where she rediscovers her heroic instincts and will to live. ■

Punisher #1
January 1986

> **❝** *Punisher* #1 changed Marvel forever, splintering the Marvel Universe into a world of bright Super Hero adventure that also has a dark underside: hard, single-minded, and deadly. **❞**

Win Wiacek

Editor in chief	Jim Shooter
Writer	Steven Grant
Penciler	Mike Zeck
Inker	John Beatty
Colorist	Mike Zeck
Letterer	Ken Bruzenak
Editor	Carl Potts

An early movie headliner and one of Marvel Comics' biggest stars from the late 1980s onward, the Punisher was an unlikely and uncomfortable hero for comic books. A compulsively vengeful antihero, the Punisher's methods were uncompromising, and his excessively violent solutions were usually permanent. Unlike most heroes debuting as villains or antagonists, such as Black Widow or Wolverine, the Punisher became more immoral, antisocial, and murderous, not less. And he seemed to always be in tune with his fiercely loyal readership. The hard-hitting Punisher never toned down or cleaned up his act.

Originally dubbed "The Assassin," the Punisher was created in 1974 by writer Gerry Conway, and artists John Romita Sr. and Ross Andru as a Spider-Man antagonist. His first outing was a muted, Comics Code compliant response to the then popular, taking-the-law-into-their-own-hands school of antiheroes such as Don Pendleton's Mack Bolan: The Executioner, Clint Eastwood's Dirty Harry, and Charles Bronson's avenging vigilante in the *Death Wish* franchise. The Executioner, in particular, was part of a rising fictional wave of returning Vietnam vets turning their training and talents to cleaning up the streets and wiping out organized crime in 1970s America. Publisher Stan Lee came up with the designation "Punisher" (recycled from a robot used by Galactus), and another complicated, complex character was born.

Later revealed as former Marine Frank Castle—who lost his entire family to mob violence—his brutal, self-righteous mission to eradicate criminals repeatedly brought him into conflict with everyone's favorite neighborhood web-slinger following his debut. However, Marvel was, at the time, reluctant to spin him off into his own series in its comic book line. Despite his tragic motivations, the Punisher's ruthless actions made him a villain, not a hero. Other than two solo stories in Marvel's black-and-white, mature reader magazine line, Castle was never intended for stardom. However, his many fans loved him and he worked as a sharp counterpoint to Super Heroes such as Captain America, Daredevil, and Spider-Man, in whose titles he guest starred.

As tastes shifted and older readers grew in numbers, editor in chief Jim Shooter relented to countless requests, commissioning a Punisher miniseries. However, writer Steven Grant and penciler Mike Zeck had an uphill struggle convincing editors to let them portray the psychologically disturbed vigilante in all his unrestrained glory. and series editor Carl Potts was even informed that he would bear full responsibility for any negative repercussions.

The initial miniseries ran from January to May 1986 and turned the industry on its head. There was plenty of controversy, especially as the tale featured a protagonist who was sexually promiscuous and executed his enemies in cold blood. Another big headache for the censorious

Switch hit
Unfolding like a crime movie, "Circle of Blood" brilliantly switches between hard-hitting action and conspiracy thriller mode. Mike Zeck's slick, smart storytelling seamlessly adapts to the shifting game play: brutal violence one minute, moody intrigue the next.

Kiss kiss, bang bang

Crucial to the Punisher's success was the art of Mike Zeck, a newly acclaimed superstar after his stint illustrating all-ages mega hit *Marvel Super Hero Secret Wars*. As the Punisher switched between the gritty world of crime thrillers and costumed capers, Zeck and inker John Beatty's clean, sleek, semi-cartoonish portrayal sustained a connection to Marvel's Super Hero house style.

was the suicide of a major character and the murder of innocent children. Marvel mitigated potential fallout with a fairly low-key promotional campaign, but that didn't stop the Punisher series from becoming a barnstorming success.

With a subplot revealing that many of his previous appalling actions were caused by him being poisoned by psychotropic drugs, "Circle of Blood" sees a now clean and clear-headed Frank Castle locked in Ryker's Island prison with every inmate out to kill him. Before long, he has turned the tables, terrifying his fellow inmates and challenging the status of old foe Jigsaw, who had drugged him. Vengeance is deferred, though, as mob godfather Don Cervello has special plans for Castle, and the Punisher needs to be free to continue his war on crime.

When a mass jailbreak frees all convicts, Castle seizes his moment, foiling the escape, and dealing with Jigsaw and the Don. Expecting to be recaptured, he is instead allowed to escape by the Warden, who offers him membership in an organization of right-minded, law-abiding citizens who approve of his actions and want to back his crusade against crime. Castle accepts but knows "The Trust" cannot be trusted.

Punisher #1 changed Marvel forever, splintering the Marvel Universe into a world of bright Super Hero adventure that also has a dark underside: hard, single-minded, and deadly. In time, Frank Castle would show just how dangerous he was by taking on and eliminating every Super Hero and Super Villain in the Marvel Universe, including himself. ∎

Daredevil #231
June 1986

Editor in chief | Jim Shooter

Cover artist | David Mazzucchelli

Writer | Frank Miller

Penciler, inker | David Mazzucchelli

Colorist | Max Scheele

Letterer | Joe Rosen

Editor | Ralph Macchio

> "Never before had a hero's life been so thoroughly torn apart by an enemy, and never before had a hero's return from the brink been so exhilarating... every note is pitch-perfect."
>
> **Tom Brevoort**

Reunion and redemption
In "Born Again," Miller and Mazzucchelli underscore the religious allegory of Matt Murdock's fall and rebirth by incorporating Christian imagery into the art. After Karen Page risks her life to warn the man she betrayed, she is embraced by Murdock with love and forgiveness for her sins.

Frank Miller's first tenure on *Daredevil*, from 1979 to 1983, was undoubtedly transformative for the writer-artist and the character. Commercially successful and critically acclaimed, Miller moved on to other projects, his work on the title applauded for the many relationships he had rewoven and revitalized for the sightless swashbuckler. Resurrected first love Elektra, arch nemesis and intellectual equal Wilson Fisk, and evil mirror-image Bullseye all became more intricate and even sympathetic characters, as did supporting cast members Foggy Nelson, Karen Page, Melvin (the Gladiator) Potter, and *The Daily Bugle* reporter Ben Urich.

Three years after leaving the title, Miller returned for another momentous, self-contained story arc, which graced the pages of *Daredevil* #226–233 (January–August 1986). Working closely with celebrated artist David Mazzucchelli, Miller crafted what is considered by many to be the definitive Daredevil tale. "Born Again" redefined the parameters of heroism. Implacable, seemingly invincible villainy was confronted and defeated, but the depths plumbed by embattled protagonist, Matt Murdock, as he fought his way back from dark despair and madness, changed how Super Hero comics were perceived.

Matt Murdock's ultimate crisis begins after his true love, Karen Page, resurfaces as a fading adult film star and junkie in Mexico, selling Daredevil's secret identity for one more fix. The revelation makes its way to Fisk, and he plans epic vengeance. Murdock suffers a string of bad luck: an IRS audit, missed mortgage payments,

accusations of bribing witnesses, and committing perjury. His friends are attacked and his legal career wrecked. Daredevil goes on a rampage, beating underworld small-timers in search of the mastermind behind Murdock's woes. It falls into place when his house is blown up—at last the besieged lawyer knows who is behind his impossible ill fortune.

In the heart of a bitter New York winter, Murdock vanishes. Penniless, homeless, and pushed beyond rational limits, his mind shuts down. On the edge of a nervous breakdown, Murdock confronts Kingpin in his palatial penthouse apartment and is almost beaten to death. However, no corpse is found and Fisk begins to worry. Broken and beyond hope, Murdock roams back alleys, unaware that Ben Urich has been quietly digging away to find the truth. Lost on the streets as Christmas arrives, Murdock endures another brutal beating from petty thugs and crawls off to die. In a church hospital ward, he emerges from near death, tended by a nun who might be his long-missing mother.

Elsewhere, although Kingpin's constant machinations keep Urich silent and Matt Murdock's friends occupied, the big man is not content. His victory is incomplete, but hopefully his vanquished foe will return. Fisk then makes an ill-judged decision and starts calling in carefully hoarded favours from the city's high and mighty establishment who he believes he owns. Recuperating in the church, Matt has no idea Karen is about to reenter his life, nor that Urich, fed up with being

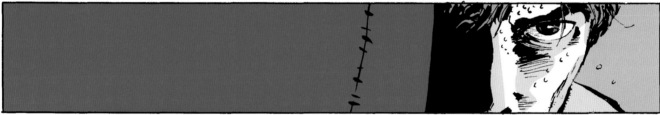

terrorized, is speaking both to the police and on record in *The Daily Bugle*.

"Saved," the final chapter of "Born Again," begins with a clear-headed Murdock battling back to fighting fitness in time to save Urich from an assassin. He reaches out to costumer Melvin Potter, and a resurrected Man Without Fear makes his first move against Fisk, foiling a plot to blacken Daredevil's reputation through the use of a violently insane imposter in a Daredevil suit. It's the beginning of the end for Fisk who will burn all his bridges with the government and bring war to the streets of Hell's Kitchen in his obsessive attempts

to systematically destroy Murdock's life. The result is chaos and a clash with not just a reborn Daredevil but also Captain America and the Avengers. From that point on, Kingpin's fate is sealed.

Gritty, realistic, and packing a potent emotional punch, David Mazzucchelli's evocative artwork and storytelling matches Miller's hard-boiled prose beat for beat. Chilling, intricate, and deeply satisfying, this tale of defeat, despair, and redemption proved comics could be as smart, sophisticated, and resonant as any novel or movie, and set a more mature tone for Daredevil—and Super Heroes in general—for years to come. ◼

Dark reflections
"Born Again" is a personal turf war between Matt Murdock and Wilson Fisk, not Daredevil against the Kingpin. Miller and Mazzucchelli portrayed the struggle by mirroring the simultaneous activities of each protagonist as they maneuvered toward their final showdown.

The 'Nam #1
December 1986

Editor in chief	Jim Shooter
Cover artist	Michael Golden
Writer	Doug Murray
Penciler, colorist	Michael Golden
Inker	Armando Gil
Letterer	Phil Felix
Editors	Larry Hama, Pat Redding

Hero in spite of himself
PFC Marks' journey from timid newcomer to combat veteran is a classic transformation parable. The bemused everyman perfectly embodies the hero-in-waiting: honest, likable, willing, and capable of great deeds, despite his own lack of belief in himself.

Revered today for its revolutionary reinvention of Super Heroes in the 1960s, Marvel, in its first incarnation as Timely Comics, was a comics powerhouse from the 1940s onward. During World War II, Timely pitted its heroes—masked mystery men and adventurers like Headline Hunter or G-Man Don Gorman—against Axis agents and armies, but by the end of the decade had dialed back Super Heroes and switched to a broader canvas. In the 1950s, the company, now reconstituted as Atlas Comics, focused on human heroes and anthologized stories in genres such as horror, humor, western, and war stories.

When the Korean War started in June 1950, publisher Martin Goodman rushed into production comics dealing with the conflict. The result was *War Comics* #1 (December 1950), the vanguard of several similar titles. Between mid-1952 and mid-1953, Atlas released 153 war comics over 19 titles with names like *Battle Action* and *Men in Action*. When Atlas finally became Marvel Comics in 1961, public tastes had re-embraced Super Heroes. Some of these heroes interacted with the ongoing Vietnam war, with the only war titles—*Sgt. Fury and His Howling Commandos* and *Captain Savage and His Leatherneck/Battlefield Raiders*—still fighting in the historically distant WWII.

In practical terms, the Vietnam conflict lasted for almost two decades, from November 1, 1955, to April 30, 1975,

when the conflict was brought to a dramatic end with the fall of Saigon and the withdrawal of US forces from the country. In 1986, Marvel editor Larry Hama—who, like many other Marvel staff and freelancers, had fought in Vietnam—was tapped by editor in chief Jim Shooter to create a comic series about the war. He wanted to publish a title that honored those who had served: an honest portrayal of the war—as much as possible under restrictions imposed by the Comics Code—and a prestigious project not dictated by economics or buying trends.

Marvel expected controversy but was unprepared for extraordinary popular acclaim. Told in real time but removed by 20 years, *The 'Nam* shared the perspective of a succession of soldiers, each serving out their tours of duty. Stories paralleled analogous events of the war on a month-by-month basis. From December 1986 to September 1993, 84 issues covered 1966 to 1973, the years of America's largest involvement and greatest losses, as witnessed by "grunts" and "boots on the ground." The title also didn't shy away from the treatment of returning soldiers. Later issues even incorporated elements of the Marvel Universe as Marine Frank Castle's pre-Punisher experiences were detailed.

The 'Nam drew in readers who never read comics and was welcomed by many veterans who used it to show their

families what they could never share about the war or how the conflict shaped their generation. Hama had overseen similar material in Marvel's mature-reader magazine *Savage Tales*, where writer Doug Murray and artist Michael Golden created "The 5th of the 1st," which inspired the color series, jokingly dubbed the world's longest miniseries.

Transferred to the mainstream, Murray and Golden introduce readers to naïve Private First Class Ed Marks in *The 'Nam* #1. "'Nam: First Patrol" follows Marks through his basic training and an eventful flight to Saigon, where he is stationed with the 23rd Mechanized Infantry. Marks, based on Murray's own first days "in-country," fails to realize when he's being asked for a bribe in return for a soft assignment and is sent to a frontline unit. Adopted by veteran Mike Albergo, Marks is soon trudging

through paddy fields and survives his first firefight with the loss of his dignity but thankfully nothing else. During his trial by combat, he is somehow transformed: no longer a gullible innocent but a jaded, fully adapted survivor, even able to watch a movie while being relentlessly shelled by the ever-present enemy.

The series also owed its much praised status, in no small part, to Michael Golden and Armando Gil's cartoonish, semi-realistic artwork. The exaggerated body language of the participants undercuts the gritty seriousness of the subject matter, softening the impact of war for younger readers, while allowing for exacting precision in depicting the machinery, material, and locations. Its success spawned a black-and-white sister title *The 'Nam Magazine*, which from 1988 to 1989 reprinted the first 20 issues of Murray and Golden's exemplary run. ▪

Shock and awe
Channeling imagery from iconic war movies, such as *The Deer Hunter*, *Apocalypse Now*, and *Platoon*, and a generation of television news documentaries, Michael Golden and Armando Gil's stylized illustration simplified the complexities of life during wartime. This was especially true when depicting the staggering capabilities of the American military and the chaotic urgency of missions in the service of rescuing its own troops.

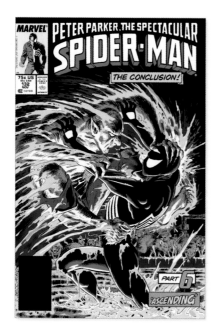

Peter Parker, the Spectacular Spider-Man #132
November 1987

> **"** The gripping, frantic, distraught, bloody, and ultimately somber finale to "Kraven's Last Hunt," one of the most revered Spider-Man stories of all time. And yeah, it lives up to the hype. **"**

Ryan Penagos

Editor in chief	Tom DeFalco
Cover artists	Mike Zeck, Bob McLeod
Writer	J. M. DeMatteis
Penciler	Mike Zeck
Inker	Bob McLeod
Colorist	Janet Jackson
Letterer	Rick Parker
Editor	Jim Salicrup

Brave heart
Peter Parker, the Spectacular Spider-Man #132 ends on a happy note as an exhausted Spider-Man is finally able to do what he has been longing for throughout the intense story arc—reunite with his new wife, Mary Jane. Her relief at having him home safe illustrates the difficulties of being the spouse of a Super Hero who has to put his life on the line every day.

By the mid-1980s, Spider-Man's huge popularity had led to three separate titles: *Amazing Spider-Man, Web of Spider-Man,* and *Peter Parker, the Spectacular Spider-Man.* Usually each title's stories would be unrelated, but in 1987 one arc was deemed so important that it would cross over between all three Spidey books. This was "Kraven's Last Hunt."

Conceived by writer J. M. DeMatteis, "Kraven's Last Hunt" would use the title villain to explore how others perceived Spider-Man. Kraven saw his failure to defeat Spidey in their previous encounters as the defining moment in his quest to be the world's greatest hunter. He would rectify this by only not hunting and killing the web-slinger but also by becoming Spider-Man himself. Having apparently achieved this in *Amazing Spider-Man #294* (November 1987), Kraven took his own life as there was nothing more he could attain. Earlier issues of the saga featured Spidey's seeming death, burial, and subsequent clawing his way out of his own grave. Artist Mike Zeck used this striking image for the cover of *Amazing Spider-Man #294* first, then drew the other covers for the six-part story line before working on any interiors.

Peter Parker, the Spectacular Spider-Man #132 concluded "Kraven's Last Hunt." Subtitled "Ascending," Spider-Man had escaped his "grave" to confront Kraven, but he had not witnessed the hunter's suicide since he was busy chasing down Vermin. His ratlike quarry had been released by Kraven to go on a murderous rampage and lure Spidey away. The issue opens with Spider-Man pursuing Vermin through New York City's sewer system. There is no light to brighten the subterranean gloom, no color even from the web-slinger's black suit, which replaced his traditional costume when the latter was destroyed. After being buried alive, Spidey has to battle his own fear in the tunnels' confined space while also fighting Vermin—before eventually fleeing the sewers. As Vermin follows him into the bright, bustling city streets above, the crepuscular villain becomes so disoriented that Spidey is finally able to capture him and turn him over to the authorities.

By using Kraven as a substitute Spider-Man—one far more violent than the original—DeMatteis highlighted the unique, inimitable qualities that made Peter Parker a hero. Although he was super-strong and unfailingly courageous, it was Peter's humanity and innate kindness that made him a hero and struck a chord with his legions of fans since his 1960s debut. As *Peter Parker, the Spectacular Spider-Man #132* draws to a close, with Kraven being buried on his family estate, DeMatteis pointedly paraphrases William Blake: "Spyder, Spyder, burning bright, in the forests of the night... What immortal hand or eye could frame thy fearful symmetry?" ∎

Buried alive

The opening six pages of *Peter Parker, the Spectacular Spider-Man* #132 solely focus on a lone Spider-Man, struggling to overcome his fear as he searches the claustrophobic sewers for the murderous Vermin. Artist Mike Zeck's measured storytelling underscores the wall-crawler's panic and mental confusion as his mind flits between his present predicament and his earlier traumatic battle to escape the grave—intercut with unsettling panels of a gravedigger in action.

Silver Surfer #1
December 1988

" Worlds collided as Stan Lee teamed up with European legend Moebius to create this beautifully illustrated tale of two titans—the Silver Surfer and Galactus—but takes time to reflect on what it means to be human. **"**

C. B. Cebulski

Editor in chief	Tom DeFalco
Cover artist	Moebius
Writer	Stan Lee
Penciler, inker, colorist, letterer	Moebius
Colorist	John Wellington
Editors	Archie Goodwin, Margaret Clark, Tom DeFalco, Jean-Marc Lofficier

In 1966, Jack Kirby created the Silver Surfer for a story line about a voracious planet-devouring space god in *Fantastic Four* #48 (March 1966). The alien sky-rider's naïveté and strident virtue made him the perfect commentator on humanity, especially during the socially turbulent 1960s, and a potent symbol of the peaceful ideals and fellow-feeling to which humankind might aspire—the better angel of our nature. Used sparingly, and primarily scripted by Stan Lee, the Surfer retained an aura of quality and exclusivity for decades thereafter.

The early comics industry survived on high sales and low costs. Thanks to rapid response to market trends and constant experimentation, in 1972, Marvel became the leading comic book publisher in America. By the 1980s, its position was unassailable. A downturn in newsstand sales at the time was countered by the rise of specialty comic shops and distributors: a direct market for serious fans and collectors. Marvel quickly embraced the new marketplace, devising prestigious series and formats, launching its Original Graphic Novel line, and making some titles "direct sales only." In 1982, editor in chief Jim Shooter founded the Epic Comics imprint specifically for the Direct Sales sector. Overseen by veteran writer-editor Archie Goodwin and prolific artist-writer-editor Al Milgrom, Epic generated more adult-oriented material—much of it creator-owned—and became a byword for innovation and excellence.

In 1982, a one-shot Silver Surfer comic by Stan Lee, John Byrne, and Tom Palmer was an early hit for the Direct Sales market, proving the character still had many fans, and it led to a new mainstream series in 1987. By now, Marvel was a truly international presence, employing a global workforce, with many stories crafted explicitly for overseas readerships in Britain, Europe, and Japan. When publisher Lee met legendary French comics auteur Jean "Moebius" Giraud that year, they agreed to work together on a prestige project. The result was a remarkable two-issue Epic limited series starring the Silver Surfer.

This was not new territory. The Surfer was already an outreach character, star of an all-new saga by Lee and Kirby in 1978. The Marvel Fireside Books edition—rereleased as *The Silver Surfer: The Ultimate Cosmic Experience*—was one of the earliest graphic novels. Sidestepping Marvel continuity, the one-off book allowed the creators to focus on his uniquely philosophical nature and his ravenous master, Galactus, without the distraction of Super Heroes to dilute its message. These qualities intrigued Moebius, a deeply spiritual man and a paragon of European comics, whose visionary science fiction/fantasy comics leaned toward the mysterious and the metaphysical. When the two-issue, Silver Surfer tale was released in December 1988 and January 1989, it was like no Surfer story any American reader had ever seen.

The coming of Galactus
Wreathed in primal storm fury and uncanny technology, the towering alien introduces himself to humanity. Most readers anticipated that the space god would try to consume Earth, but here the abiding threat is to free will and self-determination.

Loving the alien

Although set in the future, "Parable" explores how contemporary humanity responds to contact with alien forces. Whether Galactus is god or devil, humankind will react ignobly and selfishly, praying for a savior to fight its battles only to turn on the redeemer in the end.

Set in the near future on an Earth with no Super Heroes in sight, the first issue reveals how astronomers detect a massive space ship approaching. Panic ensues with terrified humankind descending into riot and mayhem. Residing unnoticed in the grimy streets, a shabby derelict recalls a lost love on a distant world. As cops target the vagrant, the starship arrives and colossal Galactus addresses the planet. The alien has come to save the world from terror, poverty, conscience, and free will. Religions spring up worshipping him, and an ambitious televangelist declares himself prophet and voice of Earth's newest god. As civilization crumbles, the derelict is revealed as the Silver Surfer, who valiantly defies his creator, Galactus, on behalf of a species that has become too cowardly to fight and too venal and lazy to think for itself.

Moebius' beliefs resonated with the messianic purity of the gleaming fallen angel, resulting in a unique story dynamic balancing theocratic debate with shattering action. The concluding chapter sees Galactus rampage through cities like a B-movie monster, demanding his former herald's return to servitude. Tragically, the turning point comes after the pointless death of a true innocent: a woman who begs the Surfer to intercede on behalf of humankind. The series was repackaged as "Parable," a stunning 80-page hardcover volume, with creators' notes and added extras. The compliment of bonus features is now standard in graphic novel collections, and this pioneering collaboration stands as a triumph in the evolution of comics. ■

Incredible Hulk #377

January 1991

" David and Keown complete a character evolution that, unlike many in Super Hero comics, won't be reversed—bringing the dichotomy of Banner and the Hulk to a logical (and psychological) conclusion. **"**

Al Ewing

Editor in chief	Tom DeFalco
Cover artists	Dale Keown, Bob McLeod
Writer	Peter David
Penciler	Dale Keown
Inker	Bob McLeod
Colorist	Glynis Oliver
Letterer	Joe Rosen
Editor	Bobbie Chase

By the early 1990s, a few years into a run that would last more than a decade, Peter David had already ensured his reputation as one of the Hulk's definitive writers. *Incredible Hulk #377* was one of the very best issues of his long stint on the title, an exploration of Bruce Banner's psyche that got right to the heart of the character. The comic's classic status was helped in no small measure by its superstar artist, Dale Keown, who enjoyed a critically lauded creative partnership with David on *Incredible Hulk* that lasted for 27 issues.

Peter David's take on the Hulk was notable for its focus on Bruce Banner the man and how his transformation into the Hulk was both a cause and effect of his psychological and emotional issues. The writer went beyond "the angrier I get, the stronger I get" scenarios to delve deeper into Banner's relationships, going right back to his childhood.

Earlier in his run, David had introduced the gray Hulk, who took the nickname Joe Fixit. This version of the Hulk was smarter than the green iteration, more cunning, but also not as strong. He was outgoing, funny, and always in pursuit of pleasure, unlike the quiet and studious Banner. The choice of skin color harked back to the character's debut in 1962, in which he had gray skin before printing problems forced the change to

green in later issues. Another aspect of Joe Fixit that was inherited from the very first incarnation of the Hulk was that his transformation happened only at night.

So Bruce Banner's psyche was now getting quite crowded. As well as Banner, the reserved, introspective, "puny" genius, there was Hulk, the giant, green smashing machine, and Fixit, the gray party animal. *Incredible Hulk #377* separates these three personas, making them confront each other in Banner's mindscape, the result of a hypnotism session by the reforming villain Ringmaster. The session is organized by longtime Hulk and fellow gamma-ray-mutated character, Doc Samson, in an attempt to "cure" Banner.

Inside his psyche, Banner and the two Hulks witness harrowing scenes from the scientist's childhood, where he is menaced by a terrifying monster. Both the Hulks fear it, yet they try to attack it and are both destroyed. As his mother tries to leave the house with Bruce to save him from the creature, it kills her. The monster is Bruce's father, and its horrifying appearance is a manifestation of the effect he has on his young son. It is in this tormented atmosphere that Bruce learns to bottle up his emotions, pushing his rage and terror deep within himself.

As the hypnotic dream continues, it becomes clear that only Banner himself can face this dreaded avatar of an abusive

Betty Ross—and the Hulk's
legions of fans—got a first
look at the new "merged
Hulk." This was writer Peter
David's way of addressing
the increasingly crowded and
fragmented nature of Bruce
Banner's traumatized psyche.
Artist Dale Keown expressively
and masterfully combined
the best attributes of all
the Hulks into one.

childhood, as even the super-strong
Hulks are no match for it. At his mother's
graveside, Bruce admits that his lack
of emotion was part of a desire not to
turn out like his brutal, insane father.
The monster shrinks to appear just like
an ordinary man and is then replaced by
a vision of Bruce's mother, who urges all
her "sons"—Banner, Hulk, and Fixit—
to come together for their mutual benefit.
As Bruce wakes from his hypnotic state
in the real world, he emerges as a new
kind of Hulk, the so-called "merged
Hulk," within which all his personalities
and attributes are combined.

Artist Dale Keown rose brilliantly to the
challenge of bringing real emotions to not
one but two Hulks, as the green and gray
iterations experienced the horror of their
monstrous father and their sorrow and
guilt at losing their mother. His panels
depicting the psychic monster unsettlingly
illustrates how childhood traumas can
loom over a person throughout their life.

The cover of *Incredible Hulk #377*
featured a special fluorescent green ink
that cleverly resonated with the bright
acidic colors that featured prominently
on the clothes and accessories of the
time. Later print runs would feature two
alternative covers with different but still
eye-catching color treatments—another
reason why this issue was one of the most
collectible of all Hulk comics. ■

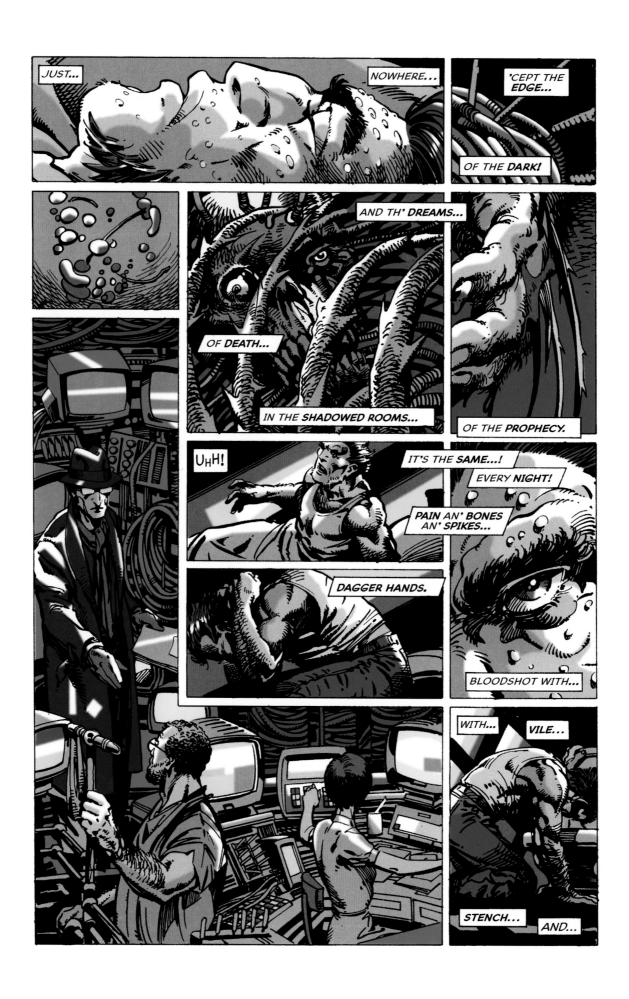

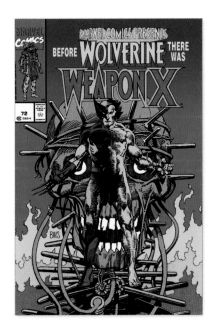

Marvel Comics Presents #72
March 1991

66 Although Wolverine's true intended origin is disputed, this issue launched the now accepted revelation that Logan was originally Weapon X, part of a Canadian program to create living weapons out of helpless subjects. 99

Peter David

Editor in chief	Tom DeFalco
Cover artist	Barry Windsor-Smith
Writer, penciler, inker, colorist, letterer	Barry Windsor-Smith
Editors	Terry Kavanagh, Kelly Corvese

◄ **Psycho drama**
Logan's biologically generated claws are a recurring visual motif throughout Barry Windsor-Smith's meticulously crafted tale. They indicate mood and reading direction, become prison bars reinforcing Logan's captivity and helplessness, and are a terrifying reminder of his feral power when unleashed. The claustrophobic jigsaw design of the page acutely reflects Logan's fractured frame of mind.

Joining the new X-Men in 1975, the taciturn mutant berserker Wolverine's popularity grew steadily as reading tastes turned darker and edgier throughout the 1980s. Much of his appeal came from an aura of mystery, when surprising details of his past suddenly emerged, such as his unexplained knowledge of Japanese culture. For three decades, his origins remained undisclosed, with readers gleaning only hints and even contradictory insights, because Logan's history was obscured even from himself. Sporting fearsome claws and a killer attitude, he rode, and helped, the meteoric rise of the outcast X-Men before gaining his own series. Starting with the first issue, he assumed lead position in the fortnightly anthology *Marvel Comics Presents*. Soon after, a solo monthly title confirmed his independent status and set him on a path to comics and cinematic stardom.

In 1991, superstar creator Barry Windsor-Smith began filling in some of the missing pieces. Already affiliated with the *X-Men* for illustrating feted stories such as the Chris Claremont scripted "Lifedeath" in *X-Men* #186 (October 1984), Windsor-Smith's serialized part-work "Weapon X" at last disclosed how the bestial mutant gained his Adamantium-laced skeleton and claws. Writing, drawing, inking, coloring, and in places even lettering the 13 eight-page chapters, which appeared in *Marvel*

Comics Presents #72–84 (March–July 1991), Windsor-Smith brought a fine-art sensibility combined with a thriller director's discipline to the tale. The story delved deeply into Wolverine's hitherto unexplored genesis and motivations but shrewdly left readers guessing at the full truth and even hungrier for further revelations.

At 120 pages, the story should be read in one sitting (collected in *Wolverine: Weapon X*, March 2009). It details how a burned-out secret agent is abducted by ruthless scientists working for an undisclosed backer. Their intent is to build perfect Super-Soldier assassins, but previous attempts have met with agonizing failure. Their project takes an unexpected turn when their latest unwilling acquisition is found to be superhuman: a mutant with enhanced senses. However, what really interests the scientists is Logan's rapid-healing powers and the shocking fact that—unknown even to himself—he can extend razor-sharp bone claws from his knuckles. Both abilities suggest that his body should be able to tolerate infusions of unyielding super-metal Adamantium. And if the excruciating process destroys his mind, that just assists their eventual aim of brainwashing him into a compliant slave. Of course, with a spirit as fierce and unbreakable as Logan's, things do not go according to plan.

During the procedure, Logan is reduced to snarling bestiality and let loose on a variety of animal test subjects. Yet some deeply buried vestige of the man within struggles to emerge. Ultimately, however, it's not his humanity that saves Logan, but his savagery, which overcomes all attempts at programming. He eventually frees himself to exact vengeance and claw his way to freedom and self-awareness. Sadly, his triumph is short-lived, and by the time he carves his way through an army of soldiers, his memories are drastically damaged.

The Weapon X saga's prologue in *Marvel Comics Presents* #72 sets the pervasive tone of bleak anxiety. Flashbacks to Logan's capture and flash-forwards to his technologically maltreated, forcibly augmented body floating in liquids are unsettlingly juxtaposed. Images of a troubled, weary operative, quitting his dirty job and dreaming of a clean, simple life in the Yukon are intercut with Logan's present torment. As he fights and drinks and dreams, shadowy men with an appalling agenda close in on him and change his life forever.

With complete control of his page, Windsor-Smith uses every opportunity to create tension and drama in this masterpiece of terror. Small, interconnected panels relay detailed yet elliptical information. Captions deliver ambient dialogue, not authorial comment, and sound effects are tightly tied to words and actions, leading the reader to the next moment—even against the traditional flow of comics narratives. The overall effect is one of disorientation and dread. This is no ordinary Super Hero story. In fact, there are no costumed characters in sight. This is an espionage/horror story unfolding in relentless installments as one of the most indomitable heroes in Marvel history endures and eventually overcomes his lowest ebb.

Key aspects of Windsor-Smith's saga were transplanted to the big screen in *X-Men Origins: Wolverine* (2009), in which Logan's nemesis, the mad scientist Abraham Cornelius, appears as a main player in his transformation. In 2014, Cornelius reprises his role in the comic book miniseries *The Death of Wolverine*, as he attempts to revive the process for making Adamantium-enhanced killer cyborgs. The villain suffers a just end, but his malicious actions remove Logan from the Marvel Universe for years. ■

KNEES GIVIN IN--

DON'T GIVE UP!

The horror within
Initially perceived as a creature of savage excess and high-tech augmentation, Logan is broken down and rebuilt as a man who overcomes the horror of his own mutation and the merciless exploitation of true monsters. Tragically, his formidable resolve is constantly undercut by his revulsion for the claws lurking within his body.

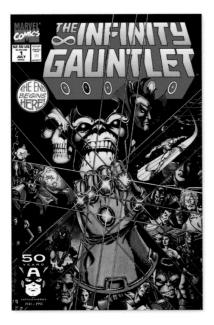

Infinity Gauntlet #1
July 1991

“Most people today recall this story for the snap of fingers with which Thanos extinguishes half the living beings in the universe. But for readers at the time, the most exciting thing about *Infinity Gauntlet* #1 was the return of artist George Perez to Marvel after a decade away.”

Tom Brevoort

Editor in chief	Tom DeFalco
Cover artist	George Pérez
Writer	Jim Starlin
Penciler	George Pérez
Inkers	Josef Rubinstein, Tom Christopher
Colorists	Max Scheele, Ian Laughlin
Letterer	Jack Morelli
Editor	Craig Anderson

Since his debut in *Iron Man* #55 (February 1973), Jim Starlin's fearsome cosmic villain Thanos had grown immensely in popularity and reputation. A breakthrough character creation and critical success after his universe-shaking battles with Captain Marvel, the Avengers, the Thing, and Spider-Man, his deserved destruction at the hands of sometime ally and long-term pawn Adam Warlock was a thrilling peak in Super Hero storytelling. With such great triumph comes great pressure from fans, and even creators, for more. And so Thanos' inevitable resurrection came in February 1990, in *Silver Surfer* #34, as Mistress Death—perceiving a universal imbalance in the current number of living beings compared to all those who have ever died—returns the Mad Titan to life to balance the books for her.

Thanos' attempts to satisfy her demands brings the villain into conflict not only with the Surfer but also most of the heroes in the Marvel Universe. The extended story line ran until *Silver Surfer* #59 (November 1991), encompassing intertwined crossover events, such as Infinity Gauntlet, Infinity War, and Infinity Crusade, a spin-off *Warlock and the Infinity Watch,* and the crucial prequel miniseries *Thanos Quest*. Here, the driven death-worshipper was diverted from his purpose while acquiring the six rare Infinity Stones that underpinned the totality of creation and—when used in conjunction—granted control of every aspect of existence to the being who held them. With all life endangered, the higher powers of reality began marshaling their forces to counter Thanos and Death.

The Infinity Gauntlet was a six-issue miniseries drawing together all those disparate story strands, while putting in place credible heroic opposition to Death's plans. As the saga opens in *The Infinity Gauntlet* #1, an omnipotent Thanos has made himself the supreme being—in his terms, "God"—but is uncharacteristically uncertain how to proceed now that nothing is beyond his power and awareness. His ruminations manifest as idle acts of spectacular creation and destruction, peppered by ingratiating suggestions by infernal tempter Mephisto, who has attached himself like a parasite to the almighty one.

Meanwhile on Earth, a traumatized Silver Surfer crashes into Doctor Strange's Greenwich Village Sanctum Sanctorum to warn Earth's heroes of imminent disaster. At the same time, in upstate New York, three criminals perish. Their lives are over, but reality needs their bodies as vessels for agents—to be released from a sanctuary within an infinity stone—chosen to battle Thanos.

Despite wielding ultimate power, Thanos learns even God can't find contentment or satisfaction. Mistress Death continues to spurn his affections, and nothing he offers or manifests can

Call to arms
Hidden forces subtly work against Thanos throughout the story. As the resurrected Titan dons the Infinity Gauntlet, Life's Champion Adam Warlock and his greatest allies are ejected from Paradise within the Soul Gem to thwart his terrible plans.

Fist of God

Although action-packed, *The Infinity Gauntlet* is also a romantic tragedy about hubris. Following years of struggle, Thanos finally wins the power to do whatever he wishes, but he still cannot win the favor of his one true love, Death. His ascension to "godhood" is witnessed by the Silver Surfer who warns Doctor Strange of the Mad Titan's nihilistic designs.

sway her. With Mephisto still seductively whispering in his ear, Thanos resolves to finally fulfill the mission she gave him, and with a snap of his fingers, half of all life in the universe vanishes.

As friends and foes dematerialize, Earth's remaining heroes realize some terrible cosmic crisis has occurred. Simultaneously, Pip the Troll and Gamora, the deadliest woman in the galaxy, have fully resurrected in the bodies of three recently deceased criminals. Suddenly, Gamora vanishes, and as Pip checks on a reborn Adam Warlock, he realizes with horror that the one being destined to stop Thanos has inexplicably retreated into a cocoon to further transform.

Portrayed as a modern iteration of Macbeth, Starlin's Mad Titan is one of the few instances in comics of a villain succeeding as a protagonist. Only Doctor Doom and Magneto have the gravitas and emotional complexity to carry a readership with them without actually reforming their characters. Meticulously rendered by superstar illustrator George Pérez and sympathetically burnished by inkers Josef Rubinstein and Tom Christopher, *Infinity Gauntlet*'s trenchant examination of greed, need, and obsession forever escalated the stakes and scale of Super Hero epics. The saga's key moments were thrillingly adapted in the critically acclaimed and box-office shattering Avengers movies *Infinity War* and *Endgame*. ▪

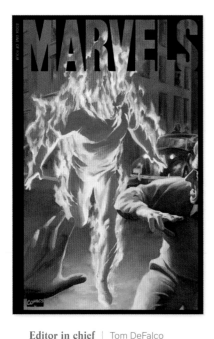

Marvels #1
January 1994

Editor in chief	Tom DeFalco
Cover artist	Alex Ross
Writer	Kurt Busiek
Art	Alex Ross
Letterers	Richard Starkings, John Gaushell
Editors	Marcus McLaurin, Spencer Lamm

A new normal
Marvels showed the dawn of the age of Super Heroes from the perspective of ordinary people, such as photojournalist Phil Sheldon, who had to come to terms with a new reality in which they were vulnerable to the actions of far mightier beings.

The four-issue miniseries *Marvels* was a radical departure for Marvel that triggered a wave of nostalgia for heroes of the past. Older readers were entranced to see beloved characters brought back to stunning life by Alex Ross. The artist was only just starting out in comics at the time and was trying to kick-start a project that would enable him to draw classic Marvel characters such as the android Human Torch, Namor the Sub-Mariner, and Captain America, as well as later legends of the Silver Age. Working with writer Kurt Busiek, they came up with the idea of presenting the stories of early Marvel heroes through the eyes of an "everyman."

Taking this idea to Marvel's then editor in chief, Tom DeFalco, resulted in the creation of photojournalist Phil Sheldon, who would observe critical events that were part of Marvel lore. In *Marvels* #1, this meant the "birth" of the Human Torch, the emergence of Namor into public consciousness, and the coming of Captain America, as World War II gripped the US. *Marvels* #1 conveyed the natural reaction from ordinary people when confronted with the reality of super-powered beings— nicknamed "Marvels"—suddenly appearing in their lives. At first, they were disbelieving, and then fearful. They thought they were the pinnacle of creation but now realized that they were almost helpless compared to these Marvels. They were forced to reassess their place in the world. Down at street level, the carnage caused by the clashes between the Human Torch and Namor caused terrible injuries and damage.

Unlike regular comics, the fights were often hidden behind buildings as onlookers strained to get a glimpse of the mighty beings. Longtime Marvel readers would already have been familiar with the events being depicted, but *Marvels* gave them a fresh perspective, putting them in the position of a regular person on a New York sidewalk. While the lead, Phil Sheldon, was newly created, some familiar characters made up the supporting cast, such as young reporter J. Jonah Jameson; Betty Dean, a recurring character from the Sub-Mariner's 1940s adventures; and even a young, wide-eyed Nick Fury eager to get involved in the impending war.

Ross's fully painted artwork set a new benchmark for depicting Super Heroes and the world in which they existed. The Golden Age of comics and the lost world of prewar New York City is brought back to glorious life with near-photorealistic flair. Ross was influenced not only by legendary comic book artist George Pérez but also by the famous painter-illustrator Norman Rockwell, whose snapshots of ordinary life seemed to recreate the essence of 20th-century America.

Marvels was marked for classic status from the start, being published in a prestige format, with high-quality paper interiors and acetate covers. It was a hit with readers as well as critics, being nominated for five Eisner Awards in 1994 and winning three: Best Finite Series, Best Painter (for Ross), and Best Publication Design (for Comicraft, the lettering services provider). The series firmly established the industry reputations of both Ross and Busiek. ■

Golden heroes

The closing image of *Marvels* #1 gave artist
Alex Ross the chance to assemble an array of
Golden Age heroes. The lineup brings to mind the
World War II team, the Invaders, created at the
end of the 1960s by Roy Thomas and Sal Buscema.
With the outbreak of World War II, Super Heroes
had rallied to the cause of the Allies, making them
far more welcome among ordinary citizens.

Editor in chief	Bob Harras
Cover artist	P. Craig Russell
Writer	Marc Andreyko
Penciler, inker	P. Craig Russell
Colorist	Lovern Kindzierski
Letterer	Galen Showman
Editor	Bob Harras

Dr. Strange: What Is It That Disturbs You, Stephen?
October 1997

> 66 Gorgeously rendered and breathlessly paced, this is a twisting, sprawling, genre and panel-bending love-letter to the weird and wonderful corners of the Marvel Universe that Strange floats, stumbles, and casts his way through. 99

Ryan Penagos

Doctor Stephen Strange is rare among Marvel Super Heroes. He may be the Sorcerer Supreme, but he is also human and afflicted with all the foibles of a mere mortal. A self-made man who destroyed his life through hubris and excess, and rebuilt it through humility and hard work, he stands as humanity's watchman against all manner of otherworldly malfeasance. As such, Strange is constantly on guard against threats to others but suffers from a kind of myopia when the target of mystical mischief is himself.

Such was the case in the twice-told tale "What Is It That Disturbs You, Stephen?" a beguiling collaboration between up-and-coming artist P. Craig Russell and writer-editor Marv Wolfman, initially published in *Dr. Strange Annual* #1 (December 1976). In "… And There Will Be Worlds Anew!," Strange is lured to the mystical dimension of Phaseworld and into a three-way battle between evil queen Lectra, her sister, Phaydra, and the angel Tempus. The tale of love, abduction, and obsession was based on and an early example of Russell's abiding fascination with translating classical fantasy opera themes into comics form. Although the story became a cult favorite, the creators were unhappy with the final result, and the characters involved were never used again.

Fast forward 20 years, Russell—now a celebrated comics creator—was invited to return to the story. He decisively fulfilled the brief, and then some. Russell expanded, redrew, and, working with scripter Marc Andreyko, even rewrote sections of the Dr. Strange annual. Vibrant new colors by Lovern Kindzierski and fresh calligraphic effects and lettering from Galen Showman added subtle emotional shading that helped transform the original tale into a foreboding yet beautiful fable, perfectly in tune with Russell's operatic sensibilities. The result was an artistic high watermark of the maturing comics artform, released as a one-shot prestige format graphic novel.

The story—winner of a prestigious Eisner Award—was also a fitting tribute to the work and influence of Dr. Strange and Spider-Man cocreator Steve Ditko. Alternatively entitled "Mourning Becomes Electra," the story reveals how a profusion of coincidences contrive to repeatedly ask Strange a baffling question: "What Is It That Disturbs You, Stephen?"

As Sorcerer Supreme of Earth, duty and responsibility to others are his enduring burdens, with personal concerns duly disregarded. Despite a warning from his mentor the Ancient One, Strange starts searching for his devoted associate Wong, who has mysteriously vanished from the

Mystical misdirection
Doctor Strange's constant exposure to uncanny coincidences and arcane signals betray him as Electra lures him to her world with a whispered question. Galen Showman's ornate, ethereal lettering enhances the mystic master's disorientation.

Sanctum Sanctorum. The trail leads to
a band of slaughtered monks, a demonic
ambush that is easily dealt with, and,
ultimately, to an unknown, but perilously
unstable and endangered magical dimension.

On arrival in this realm, Strange battles
the powerful sorceress Electra. His equal
in magic, this ruler of a doomed city holds
Wong hostage, and demands Strange's
surrender. Electra wants his power and
ultimately his love as her consort, all to save
her city. However, Strange suspects she is
misleading him. Compliant while gathering
information, the mystic master learns that
Electra originally coruled this realm with
her sister, Celeste. When angelic magician
Galtus chose Celeste over her, Electra
ensorcelled them both and seized control.
Now, through subterfuge and treachery,
she plans to consolidate her own power by
stealing that of the Sorcerer Supreme, but
she is brought low when Strange succeeds
in freeing the bewitched lovers. Confronted
with her past sins, Electra goes mad and
brings about the suicidal destruction of
everything she professed to love.

Originally drawn in a consciously art
nouveau-style, the revised story's simplified
line work, evocative use of flat colors,
and dramatic storytelling demonstrates
Russell's greater confidence in orchestrating
all facets of the medium. He conjures a tale
of deceit and passion imbued with all the
baroque force of a magical opera, while
also displaying the breadth, scope, and
maturity to which Super Hero comics
can aspire—and achieve. ∎

Daredevil #1
November 1998

66 [Building on] themes of sin, salvation, repentance, and confession, Smith and Quesada... offered one of the most penetrating glimpses of the man behind the mask. 99

Win Wiacek

Editor in chief	Bob Harras
Cover artist	Joe Quesada
Writer	Kevin Smith
Penciler	Joe Quesada
Inker	Jimmy Palmiotti
Colorist	Dan Kemp
Letterer	Liz Agraphiotis
Editor	Nanci Dakesian

For most of his comic book career, sightless swashbuckler Daredevil has remained on the fringes of the Marvel Universe. An innate loner due to the nature of his unique powers and super-senses, he was not the kind of costumed champion to regularly work in teams, except in special circumstances or the most critical of crises.

In the late 1990s, during a period of economic turbulence in the comics industry, Marvel moved Daredevil as well as a number of other outlier heroes, such as Black Panther, the Punisher, and the Inhumans, into a separate imprint that worked adjacent to but slightly removed from the regular shared continuity. Aimed at older readers, the Marvel Knights line would feature experimental stories and mature themes, many by creators not usually associated with Marvel. The line would by overseen by Jimmy Palmiotti and future Marvel editor in chief and chief creative officer Joe Quesada. Marvel Knights not only revitalized *Daredevil* and other "outsider" heroes, it also restored Marvel's financial fortunes, repositioning the company for a 21st-century readership and ultimately paving the way for the Marvel Cinematic Universe.

Daredevil's first series was canceled with *Daredevil* #380 (October 1988), and the new Marvel Knights reboot launched a month later, illustrated by Quesada and Palmiotti, and scripted by fan-favorite screenwriter, director, and comics aficionado Kevin Smith. The initial eight-part story arc "Guardian Devil" explores the finely balanced relationship between driven legal crusader Matt Murdock and his vigilante alter ego, and how both are informed by the character's Roman Catholic faith. This incisive and consequential insight into The Man without Fear's often conflicted frame of mind would be expanded on in subsequent stories by creators David Mack and Brian Michael Bendis.

Unlike Frank Miller's legendary, mold-breaking tenures, Kevin Smith wasn't concerned with tearing down and rebuilding the hero. Instead, he focused on shining a contemporary light into neglected corners of Daredevil's past, reminding jaded fans why the character had lasted so long, while also presenting him afresh to new readers.

The opening story arc "And a Child Shall Lead Them All" begins as Murdock reels from the news that longtime lover Karen Page has left him for a broadcasting job on the West Coast. Six months later, he is still coming to terms with being abandoned, and even a confession to his priest offers no solace. The first inklings of something strange afoot occur after Daredevil saves a teen with a baby from thugs who have already ceremonially murdered her parents. As he dispatches them, the girl disappears, only to appear in Murdock's office later. Her name is Gwyneth, and she claims her child is the result of immaculate conception. She has sought Murdock out to protect the baby until the time comes for her to begin her work redeeming the world.

Murdock's heightened senses make him a human lie detector, so he knows

"...IS A LEAP OF **FAITH**."

Stan Lee presents DAREDEVIL in

GUARDIAN DEVIL

PART ONE:

"...AND A CHILD SHALL LEAD THEM ALL."

KEVIN "You asked for him, you got him" SMITH WRITER

JOE "Smoovie Q" QUESADA PENCILER

JIMMY "Who's your daddy?!" PALMIOTTI INKER

BRIAN HABERLIN STUDIOS
DAN "The Baron" KEMP
COLORS

RS & COMICRAFT'S
LIZ "Dagon's only middle name" AGRAPHIOTIS
LETTERING

NANCI "Married to sorority" DAKESIAN
EDITOR

BOB "You couldn't pay us enough to do his job" HARRAS
EDITOR IN CHIEF

Gwyneth thinks she's telling the truth. The fact that she's being relentlessly pursued by fanatics also makes her credible. What's harder to accept is that she says she knows he is Daredevil because an angel told her so. Later issues reveal how a religious zealot believes the child is not the Messiah but the Antichrist, and if Daredevil doesn't kill her, the world is doomed. Passing weeks drag the tortured hero through much emotional turmoil and test his faith as he strives to do the right thing. His personal life and that of his friends become living hells, and even old enemies resurface.

Ultimately, Murdock tragically loses his one true love, but eventually his rationalistic mind finally realizes he has fallen prey to a vicious scam by a long forgotten foe, a scam to which he is particularly susceptible because of his strong religious convictions.

Powerfully building on Miller's use of resonant Roman Catholic themes of sin, salvation, repentance, and confession, Smith and Quesada's affecting tale offered one of the most penetrating glimpses of the man behind the mask. It also enhanced Daredevil's outsider status, effectively proving why he will always be the ultimate lone avenger. ■

Signs of faith
Religious metaphors in Kevin Smith's script are carefully augmented by Quesada and Palmiotti's complex page designs. The artists use found Christian iconography, reference illuminated manuscripts, and overlap small panels to resemble stained glass windows to great effect.

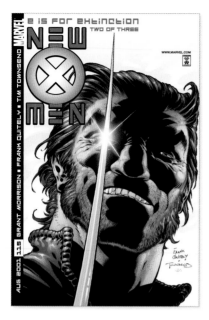

Editor in chief	Joe Quesada
Cover artists	Frank Quitely, Tim Townsend
Writer	Grant Morrison
Penciler	Frank Quitely
Inkers	Tim Townsend, Mark Morales
Colorists	Brian Haberlin, Hi-Fi Design
Letterers	Richard Starkings, Saida Temofonte
Editors	Pete Franco, Mark Powers

Beyond evil
Created by Grant Morrison and Frank Quitely, the remorseless Cassandra Nova is determined to wreak destruction on all mutants. She is a "mummudrai," a parasitic life form from the astral plane, who becomes telepathically entangled with the future Charles Xavier, granting her psionic powers.

New X-Men #115
August 2001

> **"** One issue after Morrison and Quitely made mutants cool again, they bring their world crumbling down with an act of horrific genocide, setting the stage for the title straight through to the present day. **"**

Chip Zdarsky

New X-Men #115 was the second in the "E for Extinction" story arc, and also the second issue of Grant Morrison's radical shake-up of the X-Men. The multiple titles featuring the mutant characters were crowding the market by the turn of the millennium—diluting their impact. However, with fan interest in the X-Men riding high after the blockbuster *X-Men* movie had hit cinemas in 2000, Marvel decided that a revamp was needed to capture the mutant cool seen on the big screen. So editor in chief Joe Quesada persuaded acclaimed writer Grant Morrison—a creator well known for his bold, idiosyncratic approach to classic comic book characters—that he was the right person for the job.

Morrison accepted and became the definitive "man with a plan." He wrote a manifesto outlining his views on the X-Men comics and what should be done to reinvigorate them. Key to his masterplan was the idea that the characters needed to keep changing in order to stay relevant. He suggested retitling the flagship comic from *X-Men* to *New X-Men* so that readers were left in no doubt that a fresh era was dawning. To lead the X-Men into this brave new era, Morrison chose a core group of X-Men for his team: Professor X, Beast, Cyclops, Jean Grey, Wolverine, and, most surprisingly, the reformed psychic villain Emma Frost.

The most obvious change was evident on the cover of Morrison's first issue, *New X-Men* #114 (July 2001): the team had been given updated uniforms. Gone was

the traditional spandex, to be replaced by modern leather-like outfits that had much in common with the appearance of the team in the *X-Men* movie. Another visual change was the mutation of Beast (Hank McCoy), whom Morrison and artist Frank Quitely reimagined as being more lion like than simian. This was explained in the story as "secondary mutations," which allowed established characters to develop new powers. In *New X-Men* #116 (September 2001), it was revealed that Emma Frost had gained the ability to turn her skin diamond-hard, a power that was almost a direct replacement for Colossus, who was deceased in the current continuity.

New X-Men would feature familiar aspects of the X-Men's world, like the Sentinels, Shi'ar, and Magneto, but Morrison would place an emphasis on creativity above continuity, searching for new angles on venerable concepts. This was evident in "E for Extinction," when readers were introduced to the concept of the wild Sentinels—a spin on the mutant-hunting robots—which assembled themselves out of whatever technology and parts were available. This opened up far more possibilities for the appearance and capabilities of Sentinels, and more storytelling potential.

These wild Sentinels were used to devastating effect in *New X-Men* #115 by a new Morrison-created character, Cassandra Nova. The parasitic "twin" of Charles Xavier, Cassandra wants nothing less than to eradicate mutants to prevent them from rendering *Homo*

sapiens extinct. She uses Sentinels activated unwittingly by a distant relative of Bolivar Trask, the robots' original creator, to launch a devastating attack on the mutant-inhabited island of Genosha. Sixteen million mutants were killed in what amounted to an act of genocide.

The shocking events of *New X-Men* #115 exemplified and kick-started Morrison and Quitely's now-iconic run on the title. The old order was swept away, and the X-Men were forced to confront (and adapt) to a new reality. Quitely, a frequent collaborator of Morrison's and arguably the artist whose style and vision best matches the writer's ambitious storytelling, brought a clean, modern aesthetic to the mutants' world. His stylized, unconventional pencils captured a new way of looking at the X-Men, in which they were part of a cool, contemporary counterculture. ◼

Extermination event

The destruction of Genosha is captured in a powerful full-page splash with pencils by Frank Quitely and inks by Tim Townsend and Mark Morales. This event becomes a seminal moment in the comic book history of the X-Men, relaunching the team for the new millennium and making *New X-Men* #115 a certifiably modern classic.

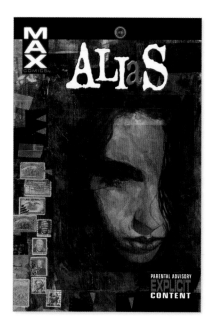

Alias #1
November 2001

Editor in chief | Joe Quesada
Cover artist | David Mack
Writer | Brian Michael Bendis
Penciler, inker | Michael Gaydos
Colorist | Matt Hollingsworth
Letterer | Richard Starkings
Editors | Stuart Moore, Kelly Lamy, Nanci Quesada

> **"** *Alias #1* was a smart but much darker look at the underbelly of Super Heroes. Jessica Jones' detective noir mixed with capes changed everything. And the way I thought about Super Hero comics after that was never the same—in the best of ways. **"**
>
> **Kelly Thompson**

In 2001, Marvel Comics stopped submitting its titles to the Comics Code Authority, instead implementing its own ratings system so that readers could make their own decisions about the content they wanted to buy and read. At the same time, Marvel debuted the new MAX comic book imprint for mature readers, which featured uncensored cursing, nudity, sexual content, drug use, gritty violence—and pretty much anything else.

Alias was the first title to be launched under the MAX imprint. It was a slightly risky choice, since its lead character was one new to the Marvel Universe, not an established name like Nick Fury or War Machine, who would gain their own MAX titles soon afterward. *Alias #1* introduced readers to Jessica Jones, and although her backstory would be revealed only gradually, the debut issue left readers in no doubt that Jessica was a character unlike any other in the Marvel Universe.

Created by Brian Michael Bendis and Michael Gaydos, Jessica was a former Super Hero turned private eye. She had been in the Avengers, although was no longer with the team for reasons that were not divulged in this first issue. Bendis astutely told Jessica's story in a way that made it seem as though she had always been in the Marvel Universe, maybe just out of shot, not quite visible in previous comics. He would later refer to her as "Queen of the Marvel 'B' characters."

Bendis was a rising star at Marvel after his successes with the Ultimate line of comics, which provided creators with more freedom on non-continuity stories. He also had considerable experience writing crime titles, which gave him a solid grounding for creating the milieu for Jessica Jones' new career as a sleuth-for-hire. For *Alias*, the writer wanted to examine what would happen if someone just wasn't very good at being an Avenger. What would happen next? In Jessica Jones' case, it was to use her powers in a less ostentatious way, investigating minor mysteries at the fringes of the Super Hero world.

The other major theme of *Alias* was Jessica's very obvious struggle with her own personal issues and her difficult progress toward some sort of recovery. *Alias #1* showed her in a bad place, dealing with lowlifes and drinking heavily to try to blot out some as yet unnamed trauma. As the series progressed, each of Jessica's cases would lead both she and

Marvel noir
Artist Michael Gaydos clearly
signaled that *Alias* operated
at a different level to many of
Marvel's other Super Hero titles.
Narrow panels focused on the
ordinary streets in which Jessica
Jones worked, evoking a
noir sensibility that befits her
status as a private detective.

the reader to learn a little more about her past life and the root of her turmoil.

What made Jessica such a hit with readers was her convincing "realness"— she was a rounded and flawed character. Just as in her short-lived Super Hero career as Jewel, so too in her private and professional life, she did not always make the right calls. Artist Michael Gaydos, who had been at college with Bendis, captured a modern noir sensibility, while also having the feel of an independent comic rather than a title published by one of the comic industry's big hitters.

Alias became one of the most critically acclaimed comic books of the early 21st century, picking up multiple industry awards. Jessica Jones has become an established Marvel character, crossing over into mainstream Marvel titles, and has also starred in her own TV series. The way her character, and that of her partner Luke Cage, is portrayed still owes much to *Alias*. The title was revolutionary in making its lead a troubled woman who wore regular clothes, not a skimpy costume, and was in reality a bit of a mess in all aspects of her life. *Alias* was a world away from the normal Super Hero comic book, and its fans loved it. ■

Editor in chief	Joe Quesada
Cover artist	Kaare Andrews
Writer	Bruce Jones
Penciler	John Romita Jr.
Inker	Tom Palmer
Colorist	Studio F
Letterers	Richard Starkings, Comicraft's Wes Abbott
Editor	Axel Alonso

Incredible Hulk #34
January 2002

> "Jones and Romita Jr. strip it all away—even the Hulk—leaving nothing but Bruce Banner, the mysteries that surround him, and the suspense that comes with a ticking human bomb. It's issue 34, but it remains one of the best No. 1 issues in modern comics."
>
> **Al Ewing**

In the early years of the new millennium, *Incredible Hulk* was still trying to find its feet after the departure of longtime writer Peter David in the late 1990s. *Incredible Hulk* #34 was the first issue for a new writer, and it proved to be the start of a new era for the character.

Bruce Jones had worked in comics at the start of his career before moving into advertising, novel writing, and television work. He was known for horror and science fiction, and had been one of the driving forces behind the independent *Twisted Tales* anthology title. After years away from the industry, Jones was contacted by Marvel editor in chief Axel Alonso to take over and revitalize *Incredible Hulk*. Jones' fresh perspective was intended to bring new life to the then 40-year-old character. *Incredible Hulk* #34 would also gain a formidable storytelling talent in John Romita Jr. A Marvel mainstay by this point, the artist had established his legend over more than two decades with key contributions to *Iron Man*, *Daredevil*, and *Amazing Spider-Man*. Romita Jr. and Jones would work together on *Incredible Hulk* for the entirety of the writer's debut six-issue arc, "Return of the Monster."

In many respects, the issue was groundbreaking, but its cover, by Kaare Andrews, was a striking homage to Jim Steranko's classic cover for *Incredible Hulk Special* (October 1968). Andrews would go on to create many great covers for the entire "Return of the Monster" run.

Jones and Romita Jr.'s first issue left readers in no doubt that they were taking the man-monster into new territory. There is less smash, more suspense—Banner is in hiding from the law after Hulk is blamed for the death of a young boy. In fact, Hulk doesn't appear at all in the issue, save for brief glimpses on a TV news report and in Banner's thoughts. The Jade Giant does feature "off panel," making short work of local drug dealers in the St. Louis neighborhood where Banner is laying low.

This kind of small-scale vigilantism is something Jones and Romita Jr. would return to repeatedly. It raised the question of whether Banner should "allow" the Hulk out in certain situations, even if there is a risk of a rampage. Readers were also shown how Banner tries to keep his emotions—and therefore the Hulk—in check with yoga and meditation. When he attempts to help a promising young man whose life is being ruined by a drug gang, Banner makes every effort to use his own powers of persuasion rather than resorting to the Hulk's brute strength.

Jones and Romita Jr. wanted to examine the duality of Banner and the Hulk, two identities that were separate yet part of the same being. *Incredible Hulk* #34 was almost entirely focused on Bruce Banner, and readers, like Banner, felt as if they were just passing through. The result signaled a new phase for the Green Goliath that played out more like a crime drama than a Super Hero adventure. ∎

Mind control
While on the run after a devastating Hulk rampage, Bruce Banner uses meditation, regulated by a metronome, to keep his anger—and his alter ego—under control. Jones and Romita Jr. put Banner front and center as they began their trailblazing run.

Mean streets
Artist John Romita Jr.'s gritty depiction of the neighborhood in which Bruce Banner is hiding out emphasizes the character's sense of isolation. It also provided him and writer Bruce Jones the opportunity to present Banner with the moral choice of when he feels it is right to unleash the Hulk.

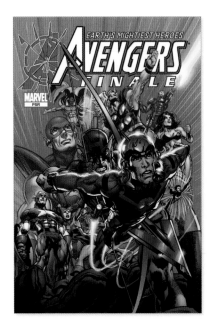

Avengers Finale #1
January 2005

❝This elegiac, deeply moving conclusion divided fans... but it remains a powerful episode in Avenger's history: a visual feast celebrating everything that made the heroic alliance so memorable and enjoyable.**❞**

Win Wiacek

Editor in chief	Joe Quesada
Cover artists	Neal Adams, Laura Martin
Writer	Brian Michael Bendis
Pencilers	George Pérez, Alex Maleev, Steve Epting, Lee Weeks, Michael Gaydos, Eric Powell, Darick Robertson, Mike Mayhew, David Mack, Gary Frank, Michael Avon Oeming, Jim Cheung, Steve McNiven
Inkers	Mike Perkins, Alex Maleev, Steve Epting, Lee Weeks, Michael Gaydos, Eric Powell, Darick Robertson, Mike Mayhew, David Mack, Gary Frank, Michael Avon Oeming, Mark Morales
Colorists	Brian Reber, Frank D'Armata, Morry Hollowell, Eric Powell, Andy Troy, Pete Pantazis, Justin Ponsor, David Mack
Letterers	Richard Starkings Albert Deschesne
Editors	Tom Brevoort, Molly Lazer, Andy Schmidt, Nicole Wiley

If the Fantastic Four's debut signaled the start of the Marvel Age, the coming of the Avengers confirmed the revolution was a success, establishing a bold new way to tell epic tales. One of the company's most consistently popular titles, the quintessential team book always combined intense human dramas and emotional conflicts with spectacular battles on Earth, across the universe, and throughout many realities. Beloved stars shone in action beside novel new characters, and, for years, Avengers Mansion was a refuge for heroes—and villains—some of whose own titles and careers had faltered or momentarily paused.

Since their formation in 1963, "Earth's Mightiest Heroes" have set the standard for glorious valor and a tradition of service through an ever-changing core team and the many expansion squads such as Avengers West Coast, Avengers Academy, Force Works, and the Secret Avengers. With such a glittering reputation, and a strong presence in games and on television, no one believed that Marvel would shatter the team and cancel the series, but that is exactly what happened in 2004. The beginning of the end developed through a series of interlinked story lines (also seen in *Thor*, *Iron Man*, *Spectacular Spider-Man*, *Fantastic Four*, and *Captain America*), which was designated as "Avengers Disassembled."

Driven insane by the loss of her children and her escalating though uncontrollable "Chaos Magic" powers,

veteran Avenger Wanda Maximoff— the Scarlet Witch—systematically and secretly reorders reality to bring about the worst day in the team's history. These subtle, catastrophic manipulations destabilize the lives of her closest friends and culminate in a synchronized wave of attacks by Kree warriors and a horde of Ultron robots. The end result is the death of Wanda's mystic mentor Agatha Harkness, Hawkeye, new Ant-Man Scott Lang, Jack of Hearts, and her former husband, the Vision.

Manipulated into being Wanda's weapon against the Avengers, She-Hulk loses control and her sanity, and in the aftermath of her rampage, the Mansion that has been the team's cherished home and sanctuary is reduced to smoking rubble. With every surviving Avenger assembled to tackle the overwhelming— but still unknown—hidden mastermind, the end comes relatively quietly as Sorcerer Supreme Doctor Stephen Strange materializes to reveal their enemy is the Scarlet Witch, before subsequently shutting down her mind. Her comatose form is then claimed by Magneto, presumed to be her father at the time, and spirited away to be cured by Professor Charles Xavier.

The end of the era was commemorated in the one-shot comic *Avengers: Finale* by Brian Michael Bendis and an army of artists united to celebrate the team's achievements and in anticipation of a radical fresh start in *New Avengers* and

Young Avengers. Thor went on a year-long publishing hiatus, and ancillary titles such as *Thunderbolts*, *Captain America*, and *Iron Man* were all rebooted.

In the mansion's ruins, veteran comrades and founding Avengers gather for a wake: one last supper together to recall past triumphs and tragedies, and honor the fallen. Almost bankrupt, Tony Stark reveals that he can no longer fund the team, but discovers that most of his friends have no appetite to be in one. Officially disbanding, the heartbroken heroes leave and find thousands of people gathered beyond the gates, also honoring the lost in a candlelit vigil.

This elegiac, deeply moving conclusion divided fans and provoked a degree of controversy, but it remains a powerful

episode in Avenger's history: a visual feast celebrating everything that made the heroic alliance so memorable and enjoyable. All the deaths were reversed over succeeding years, which most readers expected. However, the shock of so many deaths galvanized interest in the new titles and set the tone for a wave of similar reality-warping, apocalyptic themed events such as the "Children's Crusade," "House of M," "Secret Invasion," and "Dark Reign." Rebirth through destruction became standard policy for Super Hero comics, but this evocative tribute to iconic Avengers moments, captured by some of the most talented artists in the business, demonstrated Marvel's grateful thanks to generations of faithful readers. ∎

Final vigil
In any conflict, the hardest burden falls to those who remain behind. The bereaved survivors unite in a last tribute for the fallen, only to find those sacrifices and losses are acknowledged and shared by the people they fought and died for.

New Avengers #1
January 2005

❝It was a transgressive idea for Spider-Man and Wolverine to join the Avengers. But Bendis and Finch made it work... *New Avengers* became the most popular Marvel series of the era. And Spidey and Wolvie weren't hurt one bit by their association with the team.❞

Tom Brevoort

Editor in chief	Joe Quesada
Cover artists	David Finch, Danny Miki, Frank D'Armata
Writer	Brian Michael Bendis
Penciler	David Finch
Inker	Danny Miki
Colorist	Frank D'Armata
Letterers	Richard Starkings, Albert Deschesne
Editors	Tom Brevoort, Nicole Wiley, Molly Lazer, Andy Schmidt

Solitary Sentry
Writer Brian Michael Bendis was eager to use the Sentry in New Avengers. The troubled hero allowed Bendis to explore what would happen when enormous strength is combined with a fragile psyche, and the character would feature strongly in later issues of the title.

Writer Brian Michael Bendis had started his long run on the Avengers titles with a bang—literally. His "Avengers Disassembled" story in 2004 had blown Avengers Mansion to smithereens and seen the deaths of three team members and the traumatizing or severe wounding of several others. In the aftermath of this event, caused by the Scarlet Witch's mental breakdown, the Avengers essentially ceased to exist as a team. However, Bendis was a longstanding Avengers fan, and he had immediate plans to bring the team back, refreshed and different from what had gone before.

At a Marvel retreat, an event where creatives would discuss the current state of Marvel titles and map out potential story lines, Bendis and fellow writer Mark Millar had been exploring why the Avengers team was, at the time, lagging behind the X-Men in terms of popularity with fans. Bendis suggested that it would make sense to take Marvel's biggest heroes and put them on the team, giving readers the most bang for their buck. That meant Spider-Man and Wolverine.

The idea caused some consternation among the assembled Marvel creatives. Spider-Man and Wolverine had never been on the Avengers roster—Spidey was famously a loner and Wolverine was arguably much the same, his longtime membership of the X-Men notwithstanding.

However, Marvel editor in chief Joe Quesada and executive vice president Bill Jemas saw that the controversial idea was precisely what could make the series great, and they greenlighted Bendis as the new Avengers writer.

New Avengers #1 was the first step for this new, reimagined, and revitalized Avengers lineup. Although Wolverine was not yet on the scene, the opening issue sees Spider-Man swinging into action at the Raft "maximum-maximum security" jail to try to stop a mass breakout led by his old adversary Electro. Already on the scene at the island prison are Luke Cage, Jessica Drew (Spider-Woman, although later revealed as the Skrull Queen Veranke), Matt Murdock (Daredevil), Sentry, and Captain America.

Although the lineup would change frequently over the course of the *New Avengers* run, Bendis kept Luke Cage in the team for the entire series. Bendis had already written the character during his landmark *Alias* series and saw him as one of the key members of the newly configured group. The writer also insisted on using Spider-Woman, as she was one of his favorite Marvel heroes, and also included relatively new characters that he considered had been underused since their debuts, such as Sentry, Echo, and Hood. These fresh characters gave the creative teams new dynamics to explore and play

with, resulting in the book having a very different feel from previous Avengers titles. It was more convincing and realistic, with the characters bickering and bonding just as they might do in a family.

While Bendis dealt with the Avengers' present, bringing the new team together to deal with a problem that only they could, he was also establishing the groundwork for the future. He was playing a long game and planning another significant story arc about the Skrulls that would be called "Secret Invasion." When *New Avengers* #1 was published, "Secret Invasion" was still more than three years away, but Bendis was laying a trail of bread crumbs that would reward long-term readers with an "a-ha!" moment or two further down the line.

The cover of this issue showed exactly the direction that this new lineup would be taking. Art team David Finch, Danny

Miki, and Frank D'Armata did not proclaim the team with a fanfare of bright colors but rather showed them almost entirely in shadow, illuminated by red lightning. *New Avengers* would be a darker, grittier take on Earth's Mightiest Heroes. The interior art followed the same theme, with most of the action taking place on a dark and stormy night, or deep underground in the super-max prison. The art team cleverly used lead villain Electro's own bolts to augment the bursts of natural lightning and dramatically break through the gloom.

New Avengers #1 marked the start of a new era for the famous superteam, one in which its popularity would soar to unprecedented levels. Bendis' sharp storytelling made the Avengers' comic book adventures more real, more emotionally resonant, and unmissable. ∎

Welcome aboard

This panel from *New Avengers* #1 depicts the historic moment in which Spider-Man enters a new era as an Avenger. The dramatic, muscular art by David Finch, Danny Miki, and Frank D'Armata captures Avengers stalwart Captain America in all his power and charisma, lit only by lightning and the fires of a burning helicopter.

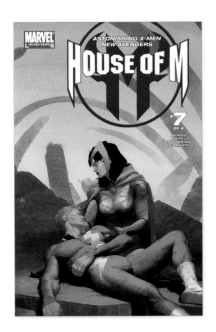

House of M #7
November 2005

"Three words that changed the course of the Marvel Universe... "No More Mutants," uttered by the Scarlet Witch as she grappled with her sanity in this modern classic, brought to life by Brian Bendis and lavishly illustrated by Olivier Coipel."

C. B. Cebulski

Editor in chief	Joe Quesada
Cover artist	Esad Ribic
Writer	Brian Michael Bendis
Penciler	Olivier Coipel
Inkers	John Dell, Scott Hanna, Tim Townsend
Colorists	Frank D'Armata, Paul Mounts
Letterer	Chris Eliopoulos
Editor	Tom Brevoort

"House of M" was an event that changed the comic book industry, sparking a new wave of crossovers that became the must-buy titles of every summer. Its genesis came when *New Avengers* writer Brian Michael Bendis was asked to take over the *Astonishing X-Men* title while Joss Whedon was working on another project. Bendis felt that the Scarlet Witch would be the perfect vehicle to tell a story that involved both superteams, since she was a mutant and an Avenger. She was also the linchpin in his seismic story of the previous year, "Avengers Disassembled," when her sanity had broken and caused her to destroy the Avengers. In the aftermath of that epic story, fellow writer Jeph Loeb asked Bendis what Magneto did when his daughter went crazy, and Bendis realized that "what Magneto did next" would be a promising narrative avenue to explore.

The result was the first crossover comics event since 1995's "Age of Apocalypse" that would affect the continuity of the entire Marvel Universe. In an innovative marketing strategy, Bendis promoted the event in the chat rooms and online forums that were the forerunners of social media, creating unprecedented hype for "House of M" before a single issue had been published. Later, the internet would also provide a space for fans to debate the central themes of the series.

Another pioneering aspect of "House of M" was its publishing model, using a main title book augmented by spin-off one-shots or miniseries. These were intended to add depth to the story for those who wanted to dive deeper into the event but were not necessary to understand the ongoing plot. This is now the standard model for major comic book events.

The Scarlet Witch, with her uncanny reality-altering powers and suffering from mental instability, presented a terrible dilemma for both the X-Men and the Avengers. "House of M" illustrated that dilemma for readers: the tension and potential conflict between two very high-powered factions, and the very persuasive arguments on both sides. While the X-Men and Avengers debated, Scarlet Witch's twin Quicksilver took action, rushing to her side and urging her to use her powers to alter the world for the better. The result was the House of Magnus—a mutant-dominated world ruled by Magneto and his family.

By the time the series reached *House of M #7*, some of Earth's heroes have realized that their world is not the true reality but a fiction created by the mind of Wanda Maximoff. They travel to Genosha to confront Magneto, whom they believe to be responsible for the deception, arriving in time to disrupt a glamorous gala full of dignitaries gathering to honor the House of Magnus.

No more mutants

During his time on Avengers, writer Brian Michael Bendis explored the magnitude of the Scarlet Witch's incredible power to remake reality, and the devastation she could cause if she ever went rogue. On this historic spread, artist Olivier Coipel closes right in as Wanda Maximoff utters the fateful words, before pulling out to show the nearby X-Men, reminding the reader exactly what "No more mutants" could mean.

Doctor Strange visits Scarlet Witch using the astral plane and discovers that it is not Magneto who is the architect of the House of Magnus, but Quicksilver, desperate to save his sister from being killed by either the Avengers or the X-Men for the greater good. Hawkeye, who had been killed by the Scarlet Witch in "Avengers Disassembled," but resurrected by her in House of M, tries to kill Wanda in his fury, but she erases him from existence. In response, Magneto angrily confronts Quicksilver and mortally wounds him. With her family fragmenting around her, a distraught Wanda remakes reality once more, uttering three words: "No more mutants."

This simple line of dialogue from Brian Michael Bendis would go down as one of the most famous in the history of comic books. With it, Scarlet Witch removed the powers of all but 198 of the world's mutants, changing the Marvel Universe dramatically. Bendis' script for "House of M" was beautifully complemented by the dreamy art of relative newcomer Olivier Coipel throughout the series, and *House of M* #7 remains a visual tour de force. It combined riveting, eye-popping action with emotionally resonant drama as Scarlet Witch struggled to hold a fractured mental landscape—and her own fragile psyche—together. The series is still considered one of the best comic book events of all time, while this issue, in particular, is a true milestone in Marvel history. ∎

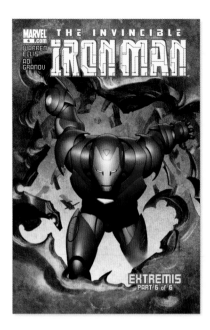

Editor in chief	Joe Quesada
Cover artist	Adi Granov
Writer	Warren Ellis
Penciler, inker, colorist	Adi Granov
Letterer	Randy Gentile
Editors	Andy Schmidt, Molly Lazer, Aubrey Sitterson, Tom Brevoort

Iron Man #6
April 2006

“Extremis was a compelling examination of the delicate symbiosis between Tony Stark and Iron Man… [and] its astute treatment of issues like the cost of progress and the role of machines in human achievement made it an instant classic… one of the finest Iron Man stories ever told.”

Melanie Scott

At the outset of the 21st century, Marvel editor in chief Joe Quesada was eager to reimagine the character of Iron Man to give him a new lease of life in the modern era. He enlisted the talents of feted British writer Warren Ellis, who was known for his enthusiastic embrace of dark futurism, and rising art superstar Adi Granov. Granov's passion for science fiction and his ultrarealistic style would prove the perfect foil for Ellis' sharp, stripped-down narrative exploring Tony Stark's relationship with Iron Man.

The result was the acclaimed “Extremis” miniseries, of which *Iron Man* #6 was the concluding part. Extremis was a nanovirus, created in an attempt to remake the Super-Soldier serum that had created Captain America. When its inventor Aldrich Killian caused it to be injected into a man named Mallen, the recipient became both very powerful and highly unstable. Iron Man set out to stop him but was defeated and his armor immobilized. Stark decided that the only way to beat Extremis was to use Extremis himself. He told his friend Maya Hansen, who had worked with Killian on the project, to inject him with the virus.

As Extremis took over his body, Stark went into a coma-like state. This gave the creators the chance to revisit Iron Man's origin story in the form of hallucinatory flashbacks. They reimagined his building of the Iron Man armor as having happened during the conflict in Afghanistan, not Vietnam. However, Professor Ho Yinsen, and his tragic death during Stark's escape from captivity, remained part of the story. Before writing “Extremis,” Ellis had read only the earliest *Iron Man* comic books, wanting to boil the character down to its essence rather than being laden with decades of continuity.

The upgrade that resulted from Extremis was effectively Tony Stark becoming one with his Iron Man armor. He could activate it on mental command and could sync up to a whole variety of devices, like phones, computers, and satellites. *Iron Man* #6 sees Stark arriving in Washington, DC, to confront Mallen as he attempts to assassinate the president. Equipped with Extremis, Iron Man is now more than a match for Mallen. Although he tries hard not to use lethal force, his deranged opponent leaves him no choice. With Mallen out of the picture, Stark has one more difficult task—to tell Hansen that he knows she has been complicit in the Extremis virus being let out into the public domain.

Inspiration in Extremis
Adi Granov's sensational artwork on "Extremis" not only found grace and beauty in a relentless down-and-dirty brawl between Iron Man and an Extremis-infected host but also served as inspiration for the Iron Man movies.

The legacy of the "Extremis" miniseries was felt not only in the comic book world but also in the Marvel Cinematic Universe that appeared just two years later. The book would be a key source for bringing Iron Man and Tony Stark to the big screen. Artist Adi Granov's work on "Extremis" was so definitive that he was brought onto the creative team for the *Iron Man* movie by director Jon Favreau. Granov's stunningly true-to-life, painted style made it easier for the filmmakers to envision his designs in a live-action milieu. The "Extremis" story's reworked origin also became the basis for Iron Man's on-screen beginnings. The studio executives returned to the miniseries for *Iron Man 3*, where the story line and the key characters of Aldrich Killian and Maya Hansen, created by Ellis and Granov, were critical to the plot.

At its heart, "Extremis" was a compelling examination of the delicate symbiosis between Tony Stark and Iron Man and how Stark could learn to live with himself after his early start in arms dealing. Its astute, provocative treatment of issues like the cost of progress and the role of machines in human achievement made it an instant classic, and one of the finest Iron Man stories ever told. ▪

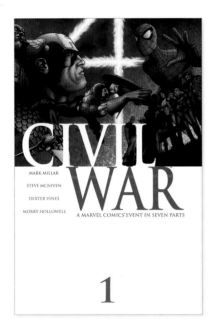

Civil War #1

July 2006

Editor in chief | Joe Quesada
Cover artists | Steve McNiven, Morry Hollowell
Writer | Mark Millar
Penciler | Steve McNiven
Inker | Dexter Vines
Colorist | Morry Hollowell
Letterer | Chris Eliopoulos
Editors | Molly Lazer, Aubrey Sitterson, Andy Schmidt, Tom Brevoort

◀ **Hitching a ride**
One of the most dramatic sequences in *Civil War* #1 comes when Captain America is forced to break out of a helicarrier in flight. Steve McNiven's pencils rise to the challenge with a series of eye-popping panels as Cap fights his way past S.H.I.E.L.D. and commandeers a jet plane— from the outside.

> 66 The movie version was different, but the groundwork for it was laid here—Iron Man vs. Captain America with different heroes lining up behind each of them and having a series of absolutely [ferocious] slugfests. 99

Peter David

Civil War #1 was the opening salvo of a summer event that would have far-reaching impact on Marvel Comics. It was hugely successful but also divisive by design, with its famous tagline asking readers "Whose side are you on?"

The encompassing "Civil War" event was the result of a Marvel creative retreat. The company wanted to build on the success of "House of M" in 2005 by launching another memorable crossover. Like "House of M," the new event would have multiple spin-offs tying it in to almost the entire Marvel Comics output. Ideas were pitched, but none seemed big enough to justify the billing until Mark Millar, with input from Brian Michael Bendis and Jeph Loeb, suggested repurposing an idea he'd been thinking about for a while. Up until that point, most of Millar's work for Marvel had been for the House of Ideas' Ultimates offshoot. He had been planning to write a book about the X-Men where the team would be split over the future of mutants, but instead this idea was tweaked so that the Avengers would be the central focus.

Millar remembered the Marvel comics he'd read as a child, where Hulk had battled another hero like Thor or Spider-Man, a manifestation of the playground debates over "who would win in a fight between..." that had existed as long as comic book heroes themselves. In order to get his heroes to the point where they would be willing to fight each other for a cause, Millar took inspiration from the existing political landscape. At the time, in the post-9/11 world, debates were

raging about legislation that some saw as restricting individual liberty to heighten public safety. This moral dilemma was the perfect vehicle to split the Avengers and the rest of the Marvel pantheon in two— were individual freedoms more important than national security?

The Marvel Universe needed an event that would bring this debate into sharp focus, and this would form the opening sequence of *Civil War* #1. Using another contemporary phenomenon, reality TV, Millar envisioned a disastrous attempt by inexperienced young Super Heroes to become more famous by catching a gang of villains live on air. The situation rapidly gets out of control, and one of the villains causes an explosion that kills hundreds of innocent civilians, including children at an elementary school. In the aftermath of this tragedy, the devastated families of the dead call for Super Heroes to be registered and trained, to be made official like any other branch of the emergency services. Many heroes, horrified by the loss of life, agree to abide by the strict terms of this Superhuman Registration Act. However, others believe it to be wholly unjust and offensive to criminalize those heroes who choose to remain anonymous while risking their lives every day to help people.

For the government and S.H.I.E.L.D., at the time led by Maria Hill, who is less well-disposed toward Super Heroes than her predecessor Nick Fury, this situation is untenable. All heroes had to sign up to the Act, or face imprisonment; there was no room for discussion. So the first duty for registered superhumans is to hunt and catch those among their colleagues who would not sign. The stage was set for a bitter, factional conflict that would change the Marvel Universe forever.

Leading the two opposing sides were Iron Man and Captain America. Both seemed to epitomize different aspects of the US, with Stark representing the forward-looking future and Rogers standing up for the values on which the nation's democracy had been founded. Writer Millar ensured that both sides had a convincing position—it was supposed to be a tough choice not only for the characters but the readers as well.

Civil War #1's classic status comes not only from the significance of its story line, but the superlative art on display. Penciller Steve McNiven was on virtuoso form as he depicted the devastating disaster that triggered civil war and the fallout that follows. Sumptuous detail adorns big action sequences and intense emotional beats alike. In the previous year, McNiven had been named one of Marvel's "Young Guns," a group of artists that the company believed were on the road to becoming superstars. The main *Civil War* series was McNiven's chance to prove himself to a wide mainstream audience, and he did not disappoint.

Mark Millar described *Civil War* as a "once-in-a-generation book," and its performance certainly bore that out. Sales figures soared, especially once the completed series was released as a collection, and fans were left shocked by the consequences of the schism between longtime comrades Iron Man and Captain America. A decade after it was published, *Civil War* spawned not only a comic book "sequel" but also an enormously successful big-screen adaptation. The event was credited with attracting a new generation of comic book fans as well as bringing older fans back to the fold. ∎

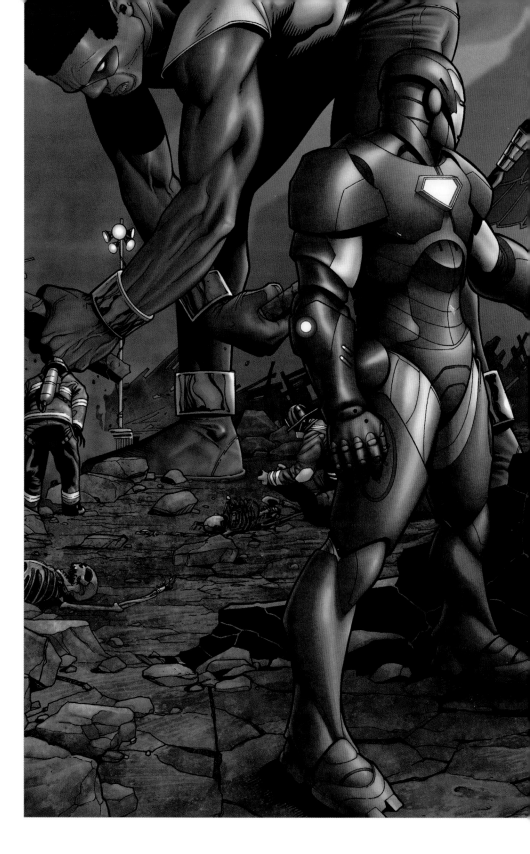

Fallout
After a team of impetuous young heroes causes a terrible humanitarian disaster, their more senior colleagues must deal with the cleanup. Steve McNiven's powerful double-page spread illustrates the dramatic schism that follows, as former allies Iron Man and Captain America find themselves on opposing sides of the argument over how to regulate Super Hero activity.

New Avengers Illuminati #1
February 2007

66A controversial read? Absolutely. A captivating read? Totally. In the face of certain doom, how far will desperate people go to ensure the survival of those they feel responsible for?99

Bill Rosemann

Editor in chief	Joe Quesada
Cover artists	Jim Cheung, Justin Ponsor
Writers	Brian Michael Bendis, Brian Reed
Penciler	Jim Cheung
Inker	Mark Morales
Colorist	Justin Ponsor
Letterer	Cory Petit
Editor	Tom Brevoort

Over the decades, the distinction between Marvel heroes and villains has grown ever more blurred. Following the breakup of the Avengers and the formation of a more hard-line New Avengers, writer Brian Bendis revealed a terrible truth about the best and brightest Super Heroes in a five-issue miniseries—*New Avengers Illuminati*—that redefined the notion of a "good guy." The story exposed a clandestine cabal secretly guiding the future of the world. However, these overlords were not Super Villains, but intellectual powerhouses regarded as Super Hero paragons, each representing a different faction of Earth's various empowered communities.

The Illuminati were first encountered in *New Avengers* #7 (July 2005) as Iron Man hunted for escaped superhuman Sentry. This led to a confrontational one-shot in May 2006 as the covert think tank was warned by Black Panther T'Challa that their arrogant actions would end in disaster after they resolved to exile the Hulk into space. T'Challa was right: their arbitrary actions resulted in horrific destruction after the Jade Giant returned in World War Hulk. The group's origins were finally explored in *New Avengers Illuminati* #1, which detailed its genesis and explored what might compel such independent, strong-willed geniuses—and sometime enemies—to work together. Writers Bendis and Brian Reed offered a far-reaching untold story that began in the wake of the Kree-Skrull War in *Avengers* #89–97 (June 1971–March 1972).

The intergalactic rivals nearly destroy humanity as Earth is caught in the crossfire, before the Avengers bring the war to a halt. Unbeknownst to any, in the aftermath, X-Men's Charles Xavier; Black Bolt of the Inhumans; Atlantean monarch Namor, the Sub-Mariner; Avenger Iron Man; mystic master Doctor Strange; and the Fantastic Four's Reed Richards brashly invade the Skrull throne world to threaten the recently defeated emperor, warning him off further attacks on Earth. Emperor Dorrek VII reacts with typical intransigence, and, in response, Black Bolt destroys his flagship. A savage confrontation ensues, before the Earth heroes are captured and intensively examined. Although they eventually escape, the damage has been done; the Skrulls will never rest until Earth is theirs. Moreover, now the aggrieved aliens have absolute knowledge of all types of Terran superhumanity and can confidently duplicate the powers of Earth's various defenders.

As well as laying the groundwork for the mega-event Secret Invasion, this grim and controversial tale confirmed that Earth's heroes had crossed a moral rubicon. It now seemed possible for Marvel's mightiest champions to make brutally tough decisions, kill when required, and even lie to each other in the service of their duties. It also acknowledged that Marvel's mainstream readership had grown up. ▪

Imperial imperative
When enraged and humiliated Emperor Dorrek orders the Skrulls' Secret Invasion, he has no idea that he will not lead it. Earth's fate will rest in the hands of his eventual successor— and religious extremist—Princess Veranke.

Brains trust
As Earth's wisest defenders make a bold entrance on the Skrull Throne world, it is clear these elite heroes and leaders feel they have the right—and the duty—to take charge and do whatever it takes to protect humanity from outside threats. Regrettably, for all concerned, the net result was always making a bad situation even worse.

The Eternals #7
March 2007

" Gaiman and Romita Jr.'s smart, stylish saga cemented the Eternals into mainstream Marvel continuity, laying the groundwork for a new series... It also rewrote Earth's evolution. **"**

Win Wiacek

Editor in chief	Joe Quesada
Cover artist	Rick Berry
Writer	Neil Gaiman
Penciler	John Romita Jr.
Inker	Danny Miki
Colorist	Matt Hollingsworth, Paul Mounts
Letterer	Todd Klein
Editor	Nick Lowe

Here be monsters
Gaiman and Romita Jr. take care to reveal that wicked acts are not dictated by a monstrous appearance. The beautiful Eternals are just as savage and remorseless as the Deviants who inspired humanity's primeval fear of devils.

When Jack Kirby's *The Eternals* debuted in 1976, it told how a human anthropologist and his daughter had discovered that Celestial Space Gods had visited Earth in ages past, transforming proto-hominids into three species: humans, monstrous Deviants, and super-beings called Eternals. Interacting with each other for millennia, the Deviants and Eternals informed human culture, populating its mythology as gods and demons, before fading into racial memory. These revelations would arise again as the Space Gods returned to check up on their experiment.

Largely unfolding outside mainstream Marvel comics during Kirby's tenure, the Eternals became a core concept explaining many mysteries of Earth's unnatural history under subsequent creators. They wove the ancient war between the Deviants and Eternals into continuity. One major story arc in *Thor* revealed Earth's actual god pantheons had united in prehistory to resist the Celestials. Another revealed that the Titans who spawned Thanos and the Uranians who sponsored Marvel Boy were both rebel factions of Eternals that fled Earth after civil war among the immortals.

In 2006, superstar creators Neil Gaiman and John Romita Jr. finally exposed the true nature and purpose of the Eternals in a miniseries that found them all amnesiac, depowered, and scattered across the Earth. Over seven spectacular issues, defiant lone survivor Ike Harris, aka Ikaris, hunts down and restores a handful of his brethren and divines the intended function of their subspecies. A million years ago, Deviants were designed as ever-changing beings:

raw, replete with unpredictable potential, and unleashed by the Celestials. Their anticipated excesses would be forever monitored and counteracted by an unchanging control group of Eternals—the stabilizing stewards of the planet.

That experiment takes a wild turn after one of those faithful stewards turns on his own kind for selfish reasons, triggering global chaos, renewed Deviant hostilities, and the waking of a "Dreaming Celestial" buried under California. Long ago, the Space Gods punished one of their own for an unknowable sin by burying the Celestial deep in the Earth. Now the sleeper wakes, threatening life on Earth and only a unique sacrifice from newly restored Eternal Makkari will stop it.

The cost of free will is demonstrated in the last issue, *The Eternals #7*, as "Journey's End" reveals the Celestial to humankind. This provokes Tony Stark into recruiting former Avenger and restored Eternal, Sersi, to deal with the emergency. Makkari and Ikaris counter the Deviant surge with help from ruthless comrades Ajak and Druig, while mighty Zuras takes control, calming the situation and dealing with the traitor Sprite. With stability restored, Zuras commands Ikaris and Makkari to locate the remaining lost Eternals.

Gaiman and Romita Jr.'s smart, stylish saga cemented the Eternals into mainstream Marvel continuity, laying the groundwork for a new series further examining their role. It also rewrote Earth's evolution in themes that coalesced more than a decade later in the Avengers of 1,000,000 BCE and explored in their own blockbuster movie. ▪

Captain America #25
April 2007

> "There have been so many Super Hero deaths (and resurrections), it's very hard to make such a story feel impactful anymore. But Brubaker and Epting [delivered] a gut-punch of a story where yet another civil war ends with the assassination of a beloved American leader."
>
> **Wil Moss**

Editor in chief	Joe Quesada
Cover artist	Steve Epting
Writer	Ed Brubaker
Penciler, inker	Steve Epting
Colorist	Frank D'Armata
Letterer	Joe Caramagna
Editors	Tom Brevoort, Molly Lazer, Aubrey Sitterson

Since his revival in 1964, Captain America had been deployed by a succession of writers and artists to hold up a mirror to the hopes, aspirations, and beliefs of the American people. Through turbulent, constantly changing times, the Star-Spangled man "out of time" has been portrayed as a vibrant and passionate symbol and advocate of American values: from the divisive era of the Vietnam War and political mistrust engendered by Watergate, to the terrorism-fueled anxieties of a post-9-11 world. In the discordant, partisan first decade of the 21st century, a major publishing event saw Super Heroes on opposing sides of a political issue that ruptured Marvel.

The first "Civil War" event split the Super Hero community like few other conflicts. Some heroes—led by Tony Stark/Iron Man and the Fantastic Four's Reed Richards—believed that the Superhuman Registration Act and the measures it enforced were acceptable and, indeed, necessary. Others—with the Sentinel of Liberty himself, Captain America, as their spokesman—feared mere bureaucracy could not protect their loved ones from villainous retaliation. The resisters, as they became known, were also concerned that registered superhumans could be drafted into the military under future administrations.

Steve Rogers refused to comply, and when disagreement turned into defiance of the new law and outright rebellion, the living legend led a band of fellow dissidents in a brutal and costly civil war against the government-backed heroes. The conflict ended in a savage clash between both camps on the streets of Manhattan. At the height of the battle, Rogers realized the damage the conflict was causing to the nation he loved and the people he had sworn to protect. He abruptly surrendered, allowing himself to be arrested and vilified in the media: a symbolic sacrifice. The Super Hero civil war was over but one final tragedy remained to shake the nation.

Crafted by writer Ed Brubaker and artist Steve Epting, the stellar creative team that had steered Cap's increasingly intense and elaborate story lines for the previous two years, *Captain America* #25 was an official epilogue to the "Civil War" event, signifying the beginning of even darker days to come. "The Death of the Dream: Part 1" revisits the long, valorous career of America's first Super-Soldier, from World War II to his resumed crusade against evil in modern times, with new allies, such as S.H.I.E.L.D. agent Sharon Carter, at his side. These flashbacks occur as—unmasked and shackled—Rogers is transported to his arraignment. Cap has no notion his friends are planning to free him but senses that something is not right. As the crowds harangue their once-adored champion, he spots a sniper zeroing in and pushes a guard out of harm's away

rather than save himself. As shots ring
out and panic ensues, Steve Rogers
falls to the courthouse steps. A second
shot at close range finishes the job and
Captain America dies.

With Agent Carter cradling Cap's
body, the scene dramatically shifts
to James Buchanan Barnes. Recently
rescued from years as the brainwashed
Soviet super-assassin Winter Soldier,
"Bucky" is barely adjusting to life
as a free agent. Spotting the shooter,
Bucky gives chase, aided by Cap's
former brother-in-arms the Falcon.
Together they capture the Red Skull's
assassin Crossbones but are unaware
of a greater time-bending scheme in
play that would eventually lead to the
subjugation of America. In the mortuary,
a heartbroken Sharon Carter hears a
posthypnotic trigger word and suddenly
remembers that she fired the kill shot.

Framing Captain America's shocking
murder in such a stark, unsentimental
fashion recalled the assassination of
American presidents and civil rights
activists. It was a bold and controversial
move, but it catapulted the comic book
to the top of the sales charts and into
many newspaper and TV media outlets.
It also kicked off a new era for the hero.
Bucky became a harder, darker Cap as
befitted a more dangerous, conflicted
nation, only to pass the shield back
to a revitalized Steve Rogers after his
triumphant and inevitable resurrection. ∎

Editor in chief	Joe Quesada
Cover artists	Joe Quesada, Danny Miki, Richard Isanove
Writers	J. Michael Straczynski, Joe Quesada
Penciler	Joe Quesada
Inkers	Danny Miki, Joe Quesada
Colorists	Richard Isanove, Dean White
Letterer	Chris Eliopoulos
Editors	Daniel Ketchum, Axel Alonso

Amazing Spider-Man #545
January 2008

> "It is perhaps the most controversial story of the modern era. But then-editor in chief Joe Quesada utterly believed that a married Spider-Man did the character a disservice... and he illustrated and helped co-plot a story that would break up the web-slinger's marriage forever."
>
> **Tom Brevoort**

Amazing Spider-Man #545 was the conclusion to the four-part "One More Day" story line, which saw a seismic shake-up of Spider-Man's comic books at Marvel. Following its release, it became one of the most talked-about arcs of the character's long history. Editor in chief at the time was Joe Quesada, who felt that Spider-Man needed to be reset to ensure the character's future for another few decades. A longtime Spidey fan, Quesada wanted to bring Peter Parker back to basics, and this involved some major changes to the continuity of the time. Chief among these was Peter's marriage to Mary Jane. Quesada did not like the idea of the characters getting a divorce, as he felt that their on-page love was too strong for this to ever happen. So another way needed to be found.

The plot structure of "One More Day" was years in the making and coalesced over several Marvel creative summits, with contributions by all the top writers at the company. However, the person who would actually write the comics was acclaimed filmmaker and comics writer J. Michael Straczynski, for whom "One More Day" would be the last story line in a memorable six-year run on Amazing Spider-Man. "One More Day" was a crossover event that included the other Spider-Man titles of the time,

Friendly Neighborhood Spider-Man and Sensational Spider-Man. Following the event's shattering finale, those titles would be stopped and only Amazing Spider-Man would continue, streamlining the character's narrative arc for a new generation of readers.

The terrible dilemma that was set up in the first issues of the event was Peter's struggle to find a way to save Aunt May, mortally wounded by a sniper's bullet intended for him. This in turn was something that had occurred as a result of the "Civil War" event in 2006, in which Spider-Man's secret identity had been revealed to the world, putting all Peter Parker's loved ones in jeopardy from crazed villains. Having seemingly exhausted all other avenues to save his aunt's life, by Amazing Spider-Man #545, Peter is left with one diabolical option. True to form, the demonic Mephisto has seized the chance to pounce on Spider-Man's vulnerability and offer him an appalling deal—to keep Aunt May alive in exchange for having Peter's marriage to Mary Jane expunged from reality.

The issue was almost wholly focused on Peter and MJ as they wrestled with the terrible decision, knowing what it meant for their love. The guilt over causing his uncle Ben's death years before was something that had haunted Peter ever

Deal with the demon
The demon Mephisto was the narrative catalyst to dissolve the marriage of Peter Parker and Mary Jane Watson, resetting the hero for a new era.

since, and the thought of the same thing
happening with Aunt May was unbearable.
For her part, MJ didn't want to feel
responsible for Aunt May's death by holding
onto the marriage. Eventually, the couple
agreed to the deal, but MJ added something
to the bargain—Mephisto also had to erase
the public knowledge of Spider-Man's
identity, making sure that his family and
friends were safe. This way, she reasoned,
at least Peter had a shot at happiness again,
even if the cost was their marriage.

"One More Day" was a huge editorial
gamble, so Joe Quesada felt he had to
put his money where his mouth was.
Not only did he take a story credit alongside
J. Michael Straczynski, but he also penciled
the covers and interiors for the entire event.
His dramatic, moving artwork for *Amazing
Spider-Man* #545 uses extensive shadow
to emphasize the darkness of the situation
that Peter and MJ found themselves in.
However, the ending gave a glimpse of what
lay ahead for Spider-Man, the pages being
bright and colorful as befitted a relaunch
entitled "Brand New Day." Readers soon
discovered that not only was Aunt May
hale and hearty again, but also that
Harry Osborn was not dead as had been
previously believed, but rather back from
a long stint in rehab. "Brand New Day"
would kick-start a new era for Spider-
Man as a more youth-oriented hero. ■

Editor in chief	Joe Quesada
Cover artist	Clint Langley
Writer	Dan Abnett, Andy Lanning
Penciler	Paul Pelletier
Inker	Rick Magyar
Colorist	Nathan Fairbairn
Letterer	VC's Joe Caramagna
Editor	Bill Rosemann

Guardians of the Galaxy #1
July 2008

"Abnett, Lanning, and Pelletier successfully import the *2000AD* sensibility to Marvel— a coherent science-fiction universe, weird characters who take themselves seriously, and most of all, a pace that never lets up."

Al Ewing

Sacred and profane
The first enemy faced by the newly formed Guardians of the Galaxy was the mysterious Universal Church of Truth. Artist Paul Pelletier went to town on the ecclesiastical theme, using it to create majestic, cathedral-like architecture.

In 2006, Marvel Comics had published the "Annihilation" event, comprising a central miniseries and several spin-off titles. It brought together in one story line many of Marvel's top-tier cosmic characters, including Thanos, Ronan the Accuser, the Skrulls, and the Silver Surfer. The Annihilation Wave was a devastating invasion force breaking into the universe from the Negative Zone. An eclectic band of heroes emerged from the survivors of the destruction to face the Annihilation Wave, led by Nova (Richard Rider) and including Star-Lord (Peter Quill), Gamora, Drax, Phyla-Vell, and Ronan. After Nova killed the villain Annihilus, an uneasy peace was agreed.

The following year saw a sequel, "Annihilation: Conquest," written by Dan Abnett and Andy Lanning and edited by Bill Rosemann. This story featured a fresh threat to the universe from the Phalanx, invading during the chaos following the Annihilation Wave. At the end, Star-Lord decided to form a team to proactively meet these kind of threats. Rosemann had been given editorial responsibilities for all Marvel's cosmic properties. He had liked what Abnett and Lanning had done on the *Nova* title and thought that it would be neatly complemented by the creation of a cosmic team. Looking through his Marvel handbook, he picked out a few

characters that he wanted to see added to the roster. These included Rocket Raccoon, created by Bill Mantlo and Keith Giffen and best known for a miniseries written by Mantlo and drawn by Mike Mignola, and Groot, a villain from the 1960s added on the suggestion of fellow editor Tom Brevoort. Marvel history would also contribute the name for the new team: Guardians of the Galaxy. The originals were created in the 1960s, although their adventures were set in the distant future, and they were later retrofitted as Guardians 3000 and situated in an alternate universe.

The Guardians of the Galaxy were envisioned as an eclectic, disparate team of underdogs, coming together almost by accident but held together by a spiky chemistry and an almost familial bond. Abnett and Lanning would write the new title at the same time as *Nova*. Although this was a lot of work, it enabled Marvel's cosmic creatives to keep their stories tight and working well together. Rosemann liked the way the two writers approached science fiction, keeping it realistic and grounded within its own boundaries.

Guardians of the Galaxy #1 was a visual triumph from artist Paul Pelletier, who dazzled with several full- and double-page splashes. The seasoned penciler's imagination knew no bounds

as he created atmospheric spaceship interiors and stunning starscapes, sprinkling the pages with humor and action in equal measure. The creative team also made excellent use of a jumbled chronology to bring readers into the heart of the drama, rather than beginning with a slow "assembling-the-team" setup.

Clever use of the characters as talking heads in debrief videos provide the backstory and introduce readers to the team and their first mission, against the sinister Universal Church of Truth. The secondary character Mantis, who was telepathic and could see the future, was also a useful storytelling device to tease readers with what was coming next.

As the story progressed, it became clear how and why the team, now comprising Star-Lord, Adam Warlock, Phyla-Vell, Gamora, Drax, and Rocket, came together and why they work so effectively with each other in a battle.

The issue established a new team for the modern era of cosmic comics, with a unique blend of characters and a special tone that hit just the right notes of drama and comedy. Such was the success of the book that it led directly to the acclaimed big-screen outing of the team with almost the same roster as in the comics. It is perhaps appropriate that the final panel of *Guardians of the Galaxy* #1 promises: "Next: Legacy." ■

Eclectic mix
The team goes into battle for the first time. On the face of it, the Guardians were an unusual combination, but the chemistry of the motley crew proved a hit with fans. *Guardians of the Galaxy* embraced the weird and wonderful while still maintaining a warm heart and a dry sense of humor.

Editor in chief	Joe Quesada
Cover artists	Gabriele Dell'otto, Leinil Francis Yu
Writer	Brian Michael Bendis
Penciler	Leinil Francis Yu
Inker	Mark Morales
Colorist	Laura Martin
Letterer	Chris Eliopoulos
Editor	Tom Brevoort

Spider-Skrull
Writer Brian Michael Bendis had been
building up to "Secret Invasion" for many
years in the pages of his other titles. Shocks
like Spider-Woman being revealed as the Skrull
Queen had long been part of Bendis' plans.

Secret Invasion #8
January 2009

"The conclusion to the controversial Skrull
invasion of Earth features the (temporary)
death of the Wasp, the disbanding of
S.H.I.E.L.D., the breakup of the Avengers, and
a cameo of Elvis revealing he was captured by
the Skrulls—which actually explains a lot."

Peter David

The "Secret Invasion" was Marvel
Comics' blockbusting summer event
for 2008. Written by Brian Michael
Bendis with pencils by Leinil Francis Yu,
the idea had percolated for more than
three years. Bendis' concept for the plot
had been further honed at Marvel's
famous creative retreats, and Bendis had
been dropping clues into the pages of the
titles he was writing over a long period.
When he began his tenure on *New
Avengers* in 2005, Bendis already knew
that the character of Spider-Woman in that
title was not all she appeared to be.

The premise behind "Secret Invasion"
was that alien shape-shifting Skrulls had
been infiltrating Earth's population after
the devastation caused to their home by
Annihilus in the Annihilation crossover
story line in 2006. Some of Marvel's
highest profile characters had been
replaced by Skrulls, unbeknownst to other
characters, or readers. The bombshell
was finally dropped in the pages of *New
Avengers* #31 (August 2007), also by
Bendis and Yu, when it was revealed on
her death that the assassin Elektra had
actually been a Skrull. The seeds of
paranoia and uncertainty were sown.
The Avengers and their allies had no
idea who might be an alien imposter,
especially as "Elektra's" convincing

disguise had even deceived Wolverine,
with his usually unerring sense of smell.

Although the Skrull policy of "divide
and rule" had early success in the pages
of *Secret Invasion*, the event title that
debuted in April 2008, by the time later
issues were published, Marvel's heroes—
and some of its villains—had united
against the common foe. *Secret Invasion*
#8 opens in the end stages of a huge
battle in New York City, as the heroes
discover that the Skrulls had turned
founding Avenger Wasp (Janet van Dyne)
into a deadly human biological weapon.
Wasp would be the shocking casualty
of this issue, as her old comrade Thor
is forced to turn Wasp's energy back
onto her, killing the hero.

While Wasp was a surprise departure,
there were also some equally unexpected
returns. When Iron Man located and
brought back to Earth the captive humans
who had been replaced by Skrulls,
Mockingbird (Bobbi Morse) was among
their number. She had died in the pages
of *Avengers West Coast* #100 (November
1993), so her appearance was a big shock,
especially for her husband, Hawkeye.

Touching moments like this were
captured by Yu with understated sharpness.
The diverse plot threads meant that the
artist had to be at the top of his craft to

create a variety of moods. Super-sized panels perfectly capture the tragedy of Wasp's demise and the routing of the Skrull invasion fleet in space, while wordless sequences evince telling character moments, such as Thor turning away from his former friend Iron Man, or dramatic ones like the ever-scheming Norman Osborn taking over Avengers Tower.

Osborn was the linchpin around which "Secret Invasion" would move into Marvel's next big story line—"Dark Reign." In *Secret Invasion* #8 Osborn shot and killed the Skrull Queen Veranke, who had been disguised as Spider-Woman.

As the moment was broadcast worldwide on live TV, Osborn became the unlikely hero of the battle against the Skrulls. S.H.I.E.L.D. was disbanded at the end of the issue and all its assets, including the Avengers Initiative, handed over to Osborn. This setup offered numerous intriguing storytelling opportunities across multiple Marvel Comics titles.

"Secret Invasion" was one of Marvel's most celebrated summer events, with the uncertainty over the identities of even the most long-established characters encapsulated in the series' famous tagline: "Who do you trust?" ∎

Biological weapon
One of the most vile deeds of the invading Skrulls was to turn longtime Avenger Wasp (Janet van Dyne) into a living weapon. Penciler Leinil Francis Yu uses a double-page spread to capture the terrifying moment when the Wasp loses control and risks taking down everyone around her.

ULTIMATE
DEATH OF SPIDER-MAN
BENDIS · BAGLEY · LANNING · PONSOR
MARVEL
ISSUE
160

SPIDER-MAN

Ultimate Spider-Man #160
August 2011

" Masterfully echoing the web-slinger's heroic 'I did it! I'm free!' sacrifice in *Amazing Spider-Man* #33, Bendis and Bagley deliver final redemption for Peter Parker. To quote Bendis via Uncle Ben: 'You did good, kid.' **"**

Bill Rosemann

Editor in chief	Axel Alonso
Cover artists	Mark Bagley, Justin Ponsor
Writer	Brian Michael Bendis
Penciler	Mark Bagley
Inkers	Andy Lanning, Andrew Hennessy
Colorist	Justin Ponsor
Letterer	Cory Petit
Editors	Mark Paniccia, Sana Amanat

◀ **Fallen hero**
The Ultimate line of comic books gave creators the opportunity to explore the unthinkable—the death of Spider-Man. The tragic event would mark the end of one era and the start of another, as new Spider-Man Miles Morales stepped up to the role.

The Ultimate imprint of Marvel Comics began in 2000. It was a way of starting afresh on Marvel's key characters in an alternate universe that would not affect mainstream continuity. It offered new readers a chance to get in at the start with modern takes on their best-loved Super Heroes, without the need to go back and rework decades of backstory. One of the flagship titles of this Ultimate Universe, and a smash hit beyond expectations, was *Ultimate Spider-Man*.

The first 111 issues of the comic were produced by writer Brian Michael Bendis and artist Mark Bagley, in a Marvel record for a creative pairing's time together on a title, exceeding even Stan Lee and Jack Kirby's extraordinary run on *Fantastic Four*. Bagley had a record all his own, too— he had spent six years prior to *Ultimate Spider-Man* on *Amazing Spider-Man*, making him, at the time, the longest-serving creator on the character.

Having departed to work on other titles, Bagley was nevertheless tempted back by Bendis to work on the five-part story arc revealingly titled "Death of Spider-Man." This story line would rock the Ultimate Universe and lead to a new era for the web-slinger in that reality—and eventually in the mainstream Marvel Universe, too.

While the mainstream Peter Parker had left high school, gone through college, and clearly matured into a Super Hero who could fight alongside the most powerful heroes on Earth, his Ultimate counterpart was different. Although his backstory was the familiar tale of powers gained through a spider bite and the tragic death of Uncle Ben, Peter Parker was still at high school throughout his *Ultimate Spider-Man* run. Writer Bendis felt that there was plenty of narrative potential in Spider-Man as a teenage hero, as he had been on his 1962 debut. A young hero still learning how to manage his powers, and at the same time juggling the problems that anyone still at school would be facing, was a character with whom readers would readily be able to empathize.

The first four issues of "Death of Spider-Man" had featured the hero fighting the Ultimate Six, that universe's equivalent of the Sinister Six. Under the leadership of Norman Osborn, whose Ultimate version could transform into a monstrous Green Goblin, the villains go after Spider-Man. By this point, though, they are one member down, since Doctor Octopus had refused to take part in the plan to kill Spider-Man, only to be slain by Osborn in a mad fury. The remaining villains head straight to Forest Hills, as they know Spider-Man's secret identity and where he lives. The web-slinger is already seriously wounded, having heroically taken a bullet meant for Captain America when the Ultimates—the equivalent of the mainstream Avengers— fought rogue agents of Nick Fury.

Despite his injury, Spidey tries his best to fight off this team-up of his worst foes and prevent them from hurting anyone he loved and destroying his neighborhood.

Incredibly, he prevails—with a little help from Aunt May and his girlfriend, Mary Jane—but *Ultimate Spider-Man* #160 saw the story line conclude exactly as had been promised. Having used every last ounce of his strength to defeat the demonic Osborn, Spider-Man lies on the ground dying from his bullet wound, and surrounded by family and friends. Although tears run down his face, Peter Parker is smiling. His last words are, "I did it." He had not saved Uncle Ben, but he had saved Aunt May, and many other people besides. His crime-fighting career, which had begun with the shameful act of letting a dangerous criminal go free, ended here with a selfless display of true heroism. Writer Bendis later commented that, while Peter Parker's death was tragic, his life was not.

Mark Bagley, a veteran Spider-Man artist, moved seamlessly between extremes in this issue, depicting phenomenal fights and blinding explosions with aplomb before moving to heartwrenchingly emotional scenes. Both he and Bendis had years of experience and affection for the character to bring to this story line, and it showed. The pair would also collaborate on the follow-up story "Ultimate Fallout," which showed the effect that the hero's passing had on the rest of the Ultimate Universe.

The death of Peter Parker left a vacancy in the Ultimate Universe that Marvel soon filled with a new character, Miles Morales. Morales would be the first character of African American heritage to take up the mantle of Spider-Man, in a new volume of *Ultimate Spider-Man* beginning in fall 2011. The creation of Bendis and artist Sara Pichelli, Miles would go on to become a popular Spider-Man in his own right and star of the hit 2018 animated movie *Spider-Man: Into the Spider-Verse*. Following the destruction of the Multiverse in 2015's "Secret Wars," Miles found himself in the reformed mainstream Marvel Universe, in the same reality in which the original Peter Parker lived. The long history of Spider-Man had entered a fresh and exciting phase. ■

Green demon
The Ultimate version of the Green Goblin was a terrifying giant demon, but a badly wounded Spider-Man summoned the last of his strength to protect his loved ones. Artist Mark Bagley showed his great skill and knowledge of the character to balance big, powerful action sequences with heartbreakingly tender moments in *Ultimate Spider-Man* #160.

Mutant revolutionaries
A dynamic full-page splash from artist Stuart Immonen shows rogue mutants clashing with the authorities in *All-New X-Men* #1. After his terrible actions while possessed by the Phoenix Force, Cyclops (Scott Summers) had split with the X-Men and teamed up with Emma Frost and Magneto.

All-New X-Men #1
January 2013

“ Bendis and Immonen presented an exciting new take on the ever-present danger for mutants. Bringing back the original X-men allowed a fresh perspective while remaining true to what X-fans love of X-books. ”

Dan Buckley

Editor in chief	Axel Alonso
Cover artists	Stuart Immonen, Wade von Grawbadger, Marte Gracia
Writer	Brian Michael Bendis
Penciler	Stuart Immonen
Inker	Wade von Grawbadger
Colorist	Marte Gracia
Letterer	Cory Petit
Editors	Nick Lowe, Jordan D. White

After eight years working on the *Avengers*, Brian Michael Bendis was eager for a new challenge. The epic crossover event "Avengers vs. X-Men" in 2012 seemed to provide the perfect jumping-off point for Bendis to move across to the *X-Men*. It also marked a new start for Marvel Comics, which planned to launch *All-New X-Men* as a key part of the Marvel NOW! rebrand. The X-Men titles were always something of a law unto themselves, allowing writers to explore story lines that would not work so well in other properties. One such was time travel. Bendis thought that it would be interesting if the original lineup of X-Men was able to see what had become of their future selves, especially in the fallout of Avengers vs. X-Men.

Cyclops (Scott Summers), possessed by the power of the Phoenix, had killed his mentor Professor X and gone rogue, roaming the globe for new mutants to recruit to his cause. Cyclops was one of the original 1960s team, and Bendis believed that it would have been unthinkable for his idealistic teen predecessor to imagine a reality in which he would have killed Xavier and incite a civil war between mutants

All-New X-Men #1 shows Beast admitting to himself that his mutation is killing him and resolving to do one last meaningful deed before his time came. That deed would be to return to the past and bring back the original Scott Summers to try to reason with his future self, hopefully avoiding the catastrophe of conflict between rival factions of mutants. When picking the right moment for Beast

to travel back to, Bendis was careful to choose one from the 1960s, rather than create an entirely new scene. He selected *X-Men* #8 (November 1964), in which Iceman and Beast return to the X-Men's mansion after being attacked by a mob of ordinary humans. Bendis admitted that one of the most exciting parts about being able to use the teenage X-Men as characters was that he could bring back Jean Grey as she had been in the days before she merged with Dark Phoenix. In the next issue, the young Jean would get a shock when she arrived at what she thought of Charles Xavier's school only to find that it was now posthumously named after her.

Stuart Immonen was chosen as the artist for *All-New X-Men* #1, having previously worked with Bendis on *Ultimate Spider-Man*. His sleek, vibrant style was perfect for the original teenage X-Men, who were not burdened with the emotional baggage of years of combat in a world that often hated them. The naïveté of the original team was also perfect for newcomers to the *X-Men* title, as the characters could act as ciphers for new readers to help them catch up on decades of history without having to read hundreds of back issues first.

All-New X-Men offered a unique opportunity for fans to see Marvel's glorious Silver Age past meet its grittier, morally ambiguous present. What would the original X-Men make of their future selves' decisions or, in some cases, their terrible fates? Simultaneously, the reader is also asked: what would our younger selves think about what we've become?

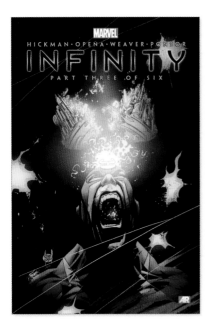

Infinity #3
November 2013

66With more than three dozen heroes, a dozen villains, half a dozen races, and the destruction of the Inhuman's Attilan home, there's enough in this issue to fill an entire limited series.99

Peter David

Editor in chief	Axel Alonso
Cover artist	Adam Kubert
Writer	Jonathan Hickman
Pencilers, inkers	Jerome Opeña, Dustin Weaver
Colorist	Justin Ponsor
Letterer	Chris Eliopoulis
Editors	Tom Brevoort, Lauren Sankovitch

Conscience of the king
As Thanos demands his tribute and revels in his presumed success, Black Bolt turns the tables and forever alters Earth's balance of power with one shouted act of proud defiance.

In the first decade of the 21st century, the Avengers experienced constant change. With the superteam frequently evolving and splitting off into smaller, specialist units, such as the Mighty, Uncanny, and USAvengers, those who were collectively regarded as Earth's Mightiest Heroes seemed to lurch from one cosmic crisis to another. This period of chaos ultimately culminated in the annihilation of the Multiverse and the birth of a revised eighth incarnation of Marvel reality.

While many of these catastrophes had metaphysical or mystic underpinnings, the most transformative and sweeping was prompted by simple paranoia and selfishness among humanity's unrelenting enemies. Written by Jonathan Hickman, the mega-event "Infinity" ran across numerous Marvel titles between August and November 2013. It comprised two war stories told in parallel on separate fronts.

One strand reveals how primordial race the Builders—who claim to have seeded life throughout the universe—try to eradicate every Earth in the Multiverse, as well as any planets failing to meet their expectations. Heading to Prime Earth in a mighty armada, the Builders decimate many civilizations en route, including Kree, Badoon, Skrulls, Spartax, and Shi'ar.

Infinity's other strand detailed the unanticipated consequences of the Avengers' response to the Builder threat. By sending their most powerful members to stop the armada before it reached Earth, they leave their homeworld virtually defenseless. With the Avengers off-planet

unifying former alien enemies against the Builders, Thanos opportunistically invades Earth. Ostensibly out for profit and revenge, he covertly probes Earth to locate and kill his lost son, Thane. The Mad Titan's armies and assassination cadre the Black Order run amok but are constantly thwarted by those Avengers who remained behind, unaffiliated Super Heroes, and stubborn, proud humans defending their world.

Hickman's vast, ambitious concept was illustrated by two art teams assigned to specific regions of the war, who made the otherwordly spectacle seem terrifyingly convincing and beautiful. The expansive saga's pivotal moment arrives in *Infinity #3*.

Jerome Opeña depicts the outer space segment "Kingdoms Fall," in which many former belligerents capitulate to the Builders. Ashamed of his warrior species' defeat, Kree warlord Ronan the Accuser allies with the Avengers. When the anti-Builder alliance almost fractures, Captain America rallies the panicking rulers of myriad worlds with a shrewd plan. Later, as Kree homeworld Hala officially surrenders, a suicide attack on the Builder fleet allows Avengers, Skrull, and Shi'ar Imperial Guard commandos to capture the invaders' World Killer dreadnoughts. Their counterattack liberates previously captive Avengers who take the battle to the Builders.

Victory comes after untried hero Kevin Connor unleashes the unstoppable cosmic force of the "Starbrand," which had previously sought out and possessed him. The Starbrand energy release vaporizes the Builder unit tasked with eliminating resistance. As the tide of conflict turns,

Star power
The Starbrand is a planetary defense
system fueled by the Superflow
separating and connecting parallel
universes. Bestowing infinite power,
it usually heralds global evolutionary
ascension. In Kevin Connor's case, the
system malfunctions, granting power
but not knowledge. After accidentally
vaporizing his entire college, Connor is
recruited by the Avengers and proves
his worth as a living doomsday
weapon against the Builders.

the Builder fleet cautiously divides, with
two units continuing toward Earth, while
a third remains to pacify the Kree system.
The Earthbound units are unaware that
Thanos' invasion of their target world
is being met with savage defiance.

Illustrated by Dustin Weaver, "What
Maximus Built" reveals how the Mad Titan
attacks Black Bolt in the floating city Attilan.
In response, the Inhuman king detonates
a massive bomb built by his brother,
Maximus. The explosion floods Earth
with the gene-warping Terrigen Mist—the
trigger for Inhuman transformation and
empowerment. This desperate tactic sparks
a whole new generation of super-warriors.
After Thanos' defeat, these Inhumans and
NuHumans would become a new breed
of Super Heroes. Young champions such
as Ms. Marvel, Kamala Khan, and grade-
school super-genius Moon Girl, along with
her constant companion Devil Dinosaur,
would take the Marvel Universe into fresh,
thrilling, culturally diverse directions.

In the aftermath of "Infinity," Earth
was radically transformed but still not safe.
Under the promotional title Marvel NOW!,
a company-wide reboot reformed the
overarching continuity: a major reshuffle
and rethink of characters and concepts,
with an eye to winning new readers.
Moreover, all the disparate story strands
across various comic books were slowly
building toward the next crisis, with new
Avengers titles forming the spine of an
approaching mega-epic. This would be
the collision of parallel Earths, which
decisively conclude in the reality-
shattering event "Time Runs Out."

Ms. Marvel #1
April 2014

❝Kamala Khan is many things: Muslim, South Asian, Jerseyite, but she has all the trimmings of a classic Marvel hero. A heartwarming, funny, new kind of a hero... a cultural phenomenon [who] I think is the future of Marvel.**❞**

Sana Amanat

Editor in chief	Axel Alonso
Cover artists	Sara Pichelli, Justin Ponsor
Writer	G. Willow Wilson
Penciler, inker	Adrian Alphona
Colorist	Ian Herring
Letterer	Joe Caramagna
Editors	Sana Amanat, Devin Lewis, Stephen Wacker

In April 2014, *Ms. Marvel* #1 saw a dramatic change of alter ego for the legacy Super Hero. Carol Danvers had left the Ms. Marvel identity behind to become Captain Marvel in 2012. The following year, Marvel announced big plans for a new era of *Ms. Marvel*. As part of its All-New Marvel NOW! relaunch, Ms. Marvel would now be Kamala Khan, a Muslim teenager from Jersey City. This made Ms. Marvel the first Marvel comic book to feature a Muslim in its title role.

Although she was inheriting Carol Danvers' Super Hero identity, Kamala Khan's powers were very different from those of her predecessor. They were acquired through Terrigenesis, the process that occurred when Terrigen Mists spread across the planet and activated dormant Inhuman genes in ordinary people, who then manifested superhuman abilities. In Kamala's case, she was able to change the size and shape of her body and had a rapid healing factor, although these were not revealed until later issues.

Ms. Marvel #1 was the first of a five-issue arc introducing Kamala Khan as Ms. Marvel. Unlike comic books of earlier eras, when a new hero would be in costume and defeating a bad guy by the end of their debut issue, the longer story line gave the creative team time and space to develop the character so that readers could really get to know her. It was not until the end of *Ms. Marvel* #1

that Kamala got her super-powers—the rest of the issue was about her day-to-day life as a Pakistani American teenager.

In many ways, Kamala Khan's story mirrored Peter Parker's decades before, in that they were both nerdy outsiders trying to do well at school and not disappoint their families. Like Peter, Kamala appealed to readers across the board with her universally recognizable problems: annoying siblings, strict parents, and butting up against the cool crowd at school. If that wasn't enough to make fans identify with Kamala, the creators added the lightly meta touch of her being a huge Super Hero geek, posting fan fiction online about the Avengers, with Carol Danvers being her idol.

Kamala Khan was created by editors Sana Amanat and Stephen Wacker, writer G. Willow Wilson, and artist Adrian Alphona. Amanat and Wilson are both Muslims originally from New Jersey, so Kamala's backstory was filled with the authentic details of lived experience. They made identity a major theme of *Ms. Marvel* #1, as Kamala found herself caught between two worlds. The 16-year-old wanted to fit in with the cool kids at her high school, but she did not want to reject her culture and her family. Like many second-generation immigrants, she wondered where she was supposed to fit in.

By issue's end, Kamala had another identity to puzzle over, as she emerges

Generation NOW!
Part of Kamala Khan's appeal is that she is extremely relatable. As a second-generation immigrant, she is not entirely of one group nor another, and this struggle with her identity only increases with her powers.

My heroes
As Kamala undergoes Terrigenesis and acquires superhuman powers, she sees a vision of her favorite Super Heroes. Writer G. Willow Wilson and artist Adrian Alphona created a splash page that was uniquely Kamala, merging traditional heroes with a flavor of the new Ms. Marvel's Pakistani heritage.

from her Terrigenesis cocoon as an old-style Ms. Marvel, complete with blonde hair and swimsuit-like costume. Later issues would see Kamala find her own Super Hero style, with an outfit based on a salwar kameez but still bearing the symbols of a legacy Ms. Marvel costume.

Artist Adrian Alphona's work on *Ms. Marvel* #1 plunged readers into Kamala's world. While the book did not yet feature any big fights with Super Villains, Alphona was able to concentrate on creating a cast of characters that, unusually for a Super Hero comic, were like regular people in a regular neighborhood. He had previous experience illustrating the world as seen from a teenager's perspective from his time working on the successful *Runaways* title. However, Alphona and colorist Ian Herring did bring a little more Super Hero pizzazz to the pages in two imaginary sequences: one illustrating Kamala's fanfic, and another showing a vision she has while she is undergoing Terrigenesis, where her favorite heroes appear, speaking Urdu.

Ms. Marvel was a hit, especially in the digital sales sector, and its first volume won a Hugo Award for Best Graphic Story. Since her debut, Kamala Khan has gone from strength to strength as she learns to use her powers and integrates more fully with the rest of the Marvel Universe. In 2016, she fulfilled the ultimate fangirl dream by joining the Avengers. ■

Original Sin #8

JASON AARON • MIKE DEODATO • FRANK MARTIN

ORIGINAL SIN #8 of 8

THE FINAL JUDGMENT!

AR MARVEL

Original Sin #8
November 2014

> “*Original Sin* #8 concludes a story that really *does* change things. You can't walk back Nick Fury's actions. Thor's life (and Jane Foster's) is significantly impacted. And the Watcher? Well, let's just say he's now finally upholding the "non-interference" part of his oath.”

Wil Moss

Editor in chief	Axel Alonso
Cover artist	Julian Totina Tedesco
Writer	Jason Aaron
Penciler, inker	Mike Deodato Jr.
Colorist	Frank Martin Jr.
Letterer	Chris Eliopoulos
Editors	Tom Brevoort, Wil Moss

THIS IS HIS CURSE.

The Unseen
Original Sin #8 concluded by introducing a new era for longtime Marvel stalwart Nick Fury. He would now be the Unseen, the replacement for the deceased Uatu the Watcher.

Published in 2014, "Original Sin" was a Marvel Comics event unlike any that had gone before. It began as a murder mystery before expanding into a boundary-pushing epic that had a huge cast of characters in the Marvel Universe questioning their deepest motives and inner conflicts. Writer Jason Aaron was well matched with artist Mike Deodato, the two pooling their considerable talents to produce a gritty yet cosmic tale with long-lasting repercussions for some of Marvel's oldest characters.

The story line gave center stage to some of Marvel's hitherto less trumpeted heroes. Tying in with the huge box-office successes of the Marvel Cinematic Universe, characters like Doctor Strange, Black Panther, Gamora, and the Winter Soldier led the investigation into the puzzle at the heart of "Original Sin": who had killed Uatu the Watcher?

Uatu had been a feature of Marvel since the earliest days of the Silver Age. He was a character who was extremely powerful but whose remit was only to observe the goings-on on Earth from his home on the Moon. He, like others of his kind, was not supposed to interfere with events as they unfolded, although in his long history he had been known to help Earth's protectors on more than one occasion. *Original Sin*'s opening issue featured the macabre sight of the Watcher's dead body, minus his eyes.

As the event unfolded, it became clear that everything the Watcher had ever seen was recorded in his eyes—the unknown murderer and possessor of those eyes had access to every secret deed of every person on Earth, including its heroes.

Jason Aaron used the revealing of important secrets, like the fact that another person had been bitten by a radioactive spider on the same day as Peter Parker and that Captain America's mind had been wiped by his so-called friends in the Illuminati, to examine the battle between the altruistic and the selfish that each hero had to face. Did they always pursue a course of action for the greater good, or were they sometimes following their own agenda?

As the investigation proceeded, the creators had fun with the unusual team-ups that *Original Sin* facilitated, including a "buddy cop" dynamic between Doctor Strange and the Punisher. But by *Original Sin* #8, the series focused on the key protagonists: Nick Fury, the grizzled World War II veteran and former S.H.I.E.L.D. director, and Uatu the Watcher. The issue revealed the terrible truth at the center of the mystery—Uatu had provoked Nick Fury into killing him. For many years, Fury had secretly been the "Man on the Wall," appointed to counter all threats to Earth by any means necessary. The seasoned soldier-spy had been chosen as someone who could make

The killer unmasked
Original Sin was a dark, atmospheric murder mystery worthy of Patricia Highsmith, and its concluding issue revealed the shocking answer to the question of who killed Uatu the Watcher.

the tough decisions, who would shoot to kill when the situation demanded it.

The issue concluded with Fury being reborn as the Unseen, a replacement for the deceased Watcher, condemned to witness events on Earth but never intervene. This cleared the decks for the character of Nick Fury Jr., modeled on his movie counterpart, to take over S.H.I.E.L.D. back on Earth. Meanwhile, the original Fury's successor as the Man on the Wall was revealed to be the Winter Soldier (Bucky Barnes), continuing the tradition of appointing a super-spy to the role.

Original Sin #8 had one last surprise in store. Thor was suddenly unable to lift his hammer, Mjölnir, meaning that he was no longer worthy to wield the power of Thor. This set up the new *Thor* series, also written by Aaron, in which Jane Foster would pick up the mantle as the first female Thor, while the original, now known as Odinson, would try to find his place in this new status quo.

Aaron and Deodato presented a dark, gripping twist on the summer event book. Deodato's dazzlingly detailed artwork across the full event was unfailingly consistent, while Frank Martin's clever use of color helped differentiate the extensive flashbacks from the present-day action. Indeed, the artist's photorealistic, moody style, honed through many years on various Avengers titles, was ideal for this significant slice of space noir. ■

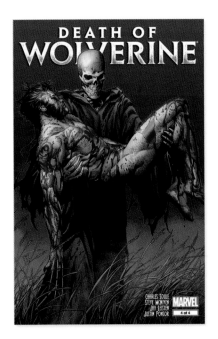

Death of Wolverine #4
December 2014

> "Steve McNiven's incredible linework breathes amazing visual life into the death of one of our most popular heroes, as Charles Soule's words pay fitting tribute to his heroic arc."
>
> **Jordan D. White**

Editor in chief	Axel Alonso
Cover artists	Steve McNiven, Jay Leisten, Justin Ponsor
Writer	Charles Soule
Penciler	Steve McNiven
Inker	Jay Leisten
Colorist	Justin Ponsor
Letterer	Chris Eliopoulos
Editor	Mike Marts

A life well lived
With his entire extended life of violence flashing before his eyes, Logan finds peace in his final moments by focusing on the good he has done and the decent people with whom he has shared his life.

Since the first glimpse in *Incredible Hulk* #180 (October 1974), James Howlett, aka Wolverine, has been a Super Hero, spy, teacher, soldier, assassin, husband, and fugitive, whose gritty exploits had made him one of Marvel's highest profile stars. Ultimately, the man beneath the legend would began to fade, worn down by personal tragedy, ceaseless conflict, and the loss of close comrades.

His final reckoning would come not long after Logan surrendered his unique healing factor to stop a rampaging sentient virus from the Microverse in the publishing event "Killable." In his own title, Wolverine tried to adapt to his loss of powers by dealing with unfinished business and hunting down old enemies Sabretooth and the Hand in a fast-paced run of issues with the tagline "3 Months to Die." The end came in the weekly miniseries *Death of Wolverine*.

Writer Charles Soule and artists Steve McNiven and Jay Leisten portrayed a contemplative Logan seeking peace and solitude but dragged back into battle as a mystery mastermind orchestrates the murder of Adamantium-using heroes, placing a huge bounty on Logan's head. Choosing to die on his own terms, Wolverine tracks down his remaining foes, clashing with ex-wife Viper and former mentor/malign spirit Ogun, who reveals that Logan's shadowy nemesis is none other than Abraham Cornelius, the deranged scientist who first bonded Adamantium to the hero's bones.

Death of Wolverine #4 sees a depowered but resolute Logan in Paradise Valley, Nevada, invading Cornelius' base, hell-bent on preventing the horrors of Weapon X being repeated. Cornelius has resumed his experiments, attempting to transform hapless victims into cyborg slave-soldiers using Adamantium harvested from prior users. On discovering Logan no longer has his healing powers, Cornelius activates a prototype soldier to kill him while trying to infuse Adamantium in his test subjects. To save them and end the madness, Logan doses the subjects with an unproven regeneration serum and intercepts the liquid metal with his own body. Inundated in molten Adamantium, Logan chases a fatally wounded Cornelius. As the lunatic scientist dies, Wolverine greets his final sunset, a warrior finally at rest, and a man who has proven he is not a beast.

The *Death of Wolverine* gave readers a necessary break from the often over-exposed mutant, spawning several spin-off series such as *The Logan Legacy*, *Life After Logan*, and *Wolverines*, starring old foes Mystique, his evil son, Daken, Sabretooth, and the survivors of Cornelius' experiments. Logan's clone Laura Kinney became the All-New Wolverine, fiercely upholding his name and legacy—until his inevitable return. Deeply moving, beautifully illustrated, and powerfully satisfying, the *Death of Wolverine* is a felicitous, elegiac coda to one of Marvel Comics' unlikeliest yet best-loved heroes. ■

Dying of the light
In a moving finale, Logan's life comes full circle as he faces his past and thwarts the plans of the ruthless scientist who made him an indestructible, metal-boned killer. Steve McNiven, Jay Leisten, and colorist Justin Ponsor's gorgeous art references Logan's origins as Weapon X, recapturing the unflinching intensity of Barry Windsor-Smith's inceptive saga in *Marvel Comics Presents* #72–84 (January–July 1991).

Unbeatable
Squirrel Girl #4
June 2015

"In the 1990s, Squirrel Girl was considered a bit ridiculous. Ryan North and Erica Henderson [turned] her into a worthy protagonist who could be taken seriously, and was surrounded by a diverse cast of friends, allies, and antagonists."

Tom Brevoort

Editor in chief	Axel Alonso
Cover artists	Erica Henderson, Rico Renzi
Writer	Ryan North
Penciler, inker	Erica Henderson
Colorist	Rico Renzi
Letterer	Clayton Cowles
Editor	Wil Moss

Although Squirrel Girl was often dismissed as a joke character, her lineage demanded that she be respected—she was created in 1991 by the team of writer Will Murray and the legendary artist Steve Ditko. In her debut comic book, *Marvel Super-Heroes* #8 (December 1991), Squirrel Girl, aka Doreen Green, started as she meant to go on by defeating Doctor Doom. After this, she made sporadic appearances until July 2005, when she was made a regular in the Great Lakes Avengers team by writer Dan Slott. Squirrel Girl defied expectations once more when her continued popularity led her to be chosen by Brian Michael Bendis for inclusion in the *New Avengers* books, as nanny to Luke Cage and Jessica Jones' daughter, Danielle.

The character's upward trajectory prompted Marvel Comics to commission a regular Squirrel Girl title. Editor in chief Axel Alonso was also eager to diversify Marvel Comics, allowing greater freedom in how a Marvel comic could look. Wil Moss was appointed editor of the new title, named *Unbeatable Squirrel Girl* in reference to the hero's almost unmatched record against big-league villains like Thanos and Fin Fang Foom. Moss recruited writer Ryan North and artist Erica Henderson to be the creative team, which proved to be an inspired choice. The two would form a productive

working partnership and a close friendship, which made their collaboration on the Squirrel Girl series a natural success.

North and Henderson filled the pages of *Unbeatable Squirrel Girl* with humor yet still managed to make Doreen Green extremely real and relatable. The book's cartoonish style set it apart from nearly every other comic in the Marvel stable. It was filled with in-jokes yet was accessible to first-time comic readers. A useful narrative tool in *Unbeatable Squirrel Girl* was the set of "Deadpool's Guide to Super Villains" cards. This inventive in-story device not only helps Squirrel Girl learn about the villains she faces, but they were also perfect for filling in new readers on the backstory and powers of someone like Kraven the Hunter, the antagonist of the first issue. However, unlike Deadpool's adventures, Squirrel Girl did not break the fourth wall, something North and Henderson felt would lessen the character's impact.

The conclusion of *Unbeatable Squirrel Girl* #1 (March 2015) left readers with an irresistible cliff-hanger. A confrontation between Squirrel Girl and the planet-eating Galactus was imminent, putting her moniker as "The Unbeatable" to the test once more. What finally happened when the two met is revealed in *Unbeatable Squirrel Girl* #4. After "borrowing" some of Iron Man's tech to launch into space,

Nuts about nuts
Squirrel Girl earned her "Unbeatable" nickname the hard way, seeing off numerous A-list villains. Writer Ryan North wanted to keep the character true to herself, and so her method of confronting these bad guys was usually to talk things through.

Artist Erica Henderson had no
shortage of humorous situations
to explore with her pencils for
The Unbeatable Squirrel Girl.
However, despite the quirky
nature of the hero's adventures,
they all took place in the main
Marvel Universe—the Galactus
she "defeated" by feeding him
nuts was the real deal.

Squirrel Girl confronts Galactus. Initially
trying to beat him up, reasoning that if she
had already beaten Thanos then it was
worth a try (a fact that amused Galactus
enormously), she finally decides to just
talk to him. This offbeat method of dealing
with tricky situations was a hallmark of
Squirrel Girl and one that served her well
throughout her Super Hero career. She
could listen and be empathetic—asking
questions before throwing punches.

Squirrel Girl, shocked that Galactus
had never eaten nuts, locates a planet
that is uninhabited but well stocked
with nuts for him to eat, in exchange
for him sparing Earth. The fearsome
world-devourer—and Squirrel Girl and
Tippy-Toe (Doreen's squirrel pal)—
gorged on the planet's bounty and then
returned to Earth's Moon to rest after
their feast. Here, Squirrel Girl manages
something that no other hero had—she
connects with Galactus on a personal
level and the two part as friends.

Unlike many Super Heroes, Squirrel
Girl's powers did not cause her angst—
she reveled in them. This gave her stories
a joyous tone, offering something very
different from most mainstream comics.
Unbeatable Squirrel Girl was a breath
of fresh air and a surprise hit, going on
to win an Eisner Award. Once again,
what had looked like a creative gamble
by Marvel Comics had paid off. ■

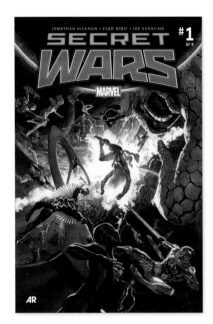

JONATHAN HICKMAN • ESAD RIBIC • IVE SVORCINA

SECRET WARS

MARVEL

#1 OF 8

AR

Editor in chief	Axel Alonso
Cover artist	Alex Ross
Writer	Jonathan Hickman
Penciler, inker	Esad Ribic
Colorist	Ive Svorcina
Letterer	Chris Eliopoulos
Editors	Tom Brevoort, Wil Moss, Jon Moisan, Alanna Smith

◄ **End of the world**
Artist Esad Ribic created many dramatic scenes for *Secret Wars* #1 as the heroes of the 616 universe tried to fight off the incursion of the 1610 Ultimate Universe. Although Earth's champions gave everything they had to the battle, it turned out to be the end of the Marvel Universe as readers knew it.

Secret Wars #1
July 2015

“Hickman and Ribic delivered on multiple fronts: it was epic and personal; wholly original and the ultimate homage to the 1980s *Secret Wars*... One of my favorite moments in 2010 was Hickman pitching his 4–5 year Avengers plan that would culminate with *Secret Wars*. My mind and every mind in that room was blown!”

Dan Buckley

“Secret Wars” was a crossover event more ambitious than any Marvel Comics had published before. It carried the entire Marvel legacy on its shoulders, forming the end of multiple eras and preparing the ground for nothing short of a brand new Marvel Universe. The very first clue that “Secret Wars” would be a crucial part of Marvel history was its name. “Secret Wars” had also been the title for one of the first Marvel Comics events in 1984–85. In both titles, old and new, an exciting lineup of Marvel heroes and villains would be brought to a place called Battleworld, but how they got there and what happened next was very different in the 2015 iteration.

While “Secret Wars” was playing out, Marvel put all its other titles on hold, an unprecedented move that signalled the importance of the event. The continuity of all Marvel Comics titles was replaced with dozens of miniseries about the various encounters and conflicts taking place on Battleworld, a patchwork planet that arch-villain Doctor Doom had managed to pull together from fragments of the dying Multiverse. True to character, Doom would end up installing himself as “god-emperor” of Battleworld.

The sheer scale of “Secret Wars” meant that the creative team for the core series needed to be carefully chosen. The writer was Jonathan Hickman, who had been crafting the run-up to the event in the *Avengers* and *New Avengers* titles, in an extended story line called “Time Runs Out.” In those books, certain heroes had become aware that the Multiverse was shrinking, with universes disappearing until only two remained—the core 616 universe and the “Ultimate” 1610 universe. Hickman had been thinking about the idea behind “Secret Wars” for years and finally had the chance to make it a reality when he took over from Brian Michael Bendis on the *Avengers* titles.

Prior to working on *Avengers* and *New Avengers*, Hickman had spent four years writing *Fantastic Four*, so it was no surprise that, when “Secret Wars” began, the Fantastic Four and their longtime nemesis Doctor Doom would play pivotal roles. They had also been the characters who launched the Marvel Silver Age revolution back in 1961, so it was entirely fitting that they were front and center when that universe officially ended.

Complementing Hickman's flair for complex, epic storytelling would be artist Esad Ribic. Ribic showed that he was a natural at everything the main *Secret Wars* series would require: explosive battle scenes, universe-ending drama, otherworldly tech, and the extreme emotions of individuals caught up in unimaginable catastrophe. Colorist Ive Svorcina employed a largely pastel palette to conjure a dreamy aesthetic without losing any of the impact. Another treat for fans of high-quality comic book art came in the form of beautiful painted covers by Alex Ross.

Secret Wars #1 is an apocalyptic opener to the series, with a truly downbeat, heart-wrenching conclusion. It features the moments when the two remaining universes in existence are about to collide, with the heroes in each believing that if they could destroy the other universe first, there was a chance they would survive. However, behind the explosive battle scenes there are desperate plans being enacted. The Ultimate Reed Richards, an evil genius from the 1610 universe, tries to launch a doomsday weapon against the 616 universe. Meanwhile, his 616 counterpart has finally acknowledged the futility of battle and is coordinating a "life raft" to save as many people as possible, who could try to remake reality after the incursion. Although the 616 Richards manages to rescue some heroes on his life raft, he loses those closest to him—his family and the rest of the Fantastic Four—in one of the most devastating moments of the issue. Never before had such a vast assembly of heroes so spectacularly failed to "save the day."

However, arguably the most moving page of *Secret Wars* #1 was not a high-octane battle scene, mega-weapon deployment, or exploding cityscape, but one that was plain white, bearing only the legends: "The Marvel Universe 1961–2015" and "The Ultimate Universe 2000–2015." The effect was like a memorial or tombstone and starkly emphasized to readers just what had been lost. How the story would continue on Battleworld and beyond was for later issues of *Secret Wars* to tell.

The first issue of *Secret Wars* was a smash hit with readers and critics alike, selling an estimated 550,000 copies. It was especially rewarding to those readers who had been patiently following the build-up in the "Time Runs Out" story line in *Avengers* and *New Avengers*. The years of carefully crafted storytelling from Jonathan Hickman had paid off, and a brave new dawn awaited that would usher in a new era of Marvel Comics. ▪

Personal tragedy
Among the large-scale disaster of *Secret Wars* #1, there was also a crushing loss for the Fantastic Four's Reed Richards. Despite his meticulous planning, he lost his wife, Susan, the rest of his family, and his teammates when their rescue craft broke up.

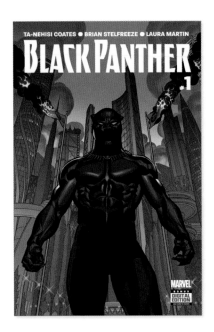

Editor in chief	Axel Alonso
Cover artist	Brian Stelfreeze
Writer	Ta-Nehisi Coates
Penciler, inker	Brian Stelfreeze
Colorist	Laura Martin
Letterer	Joe Sabino
Editors	Wil Moss, Chris Robinson, Tom Brevoort

Black Panther #1
June 2016

❝The enthusiasm and ambition of the creators are palpable... [as] the world of Black Panther is infused with new ideas, new designs, and new directions. The start of a truly character-defining run.**❞**

Wil Moss

Since his inception in July 1966, Black Panther has always been one of Marvel's most politically attuned Super Heroes: one whose exploits often mirrored real-world concerns. As leader of Wakanda, a fictional African nation hidden for centuries, King T'Challa has confronted head-on American White Supremacy (*Jungle Action* #19–24, January–November 1976), South African Apartheid (*Marvel Comics Presents* #13–37, February 1988–December 1989), and economic imperialism and Serbian nationalism (*Black Panther: The Man Without Fear,* February 2011), all inspired by actual events.

In 2016, as Black Panther was becoming a global cinema sensation, his comic book stories resumed with a new series and creative team. Crafted by author, journalist, and lifelong comics fan Ta-Nehisi Coates working with legendary comics artist Brian Stelfreeze, the result was a radically fresh look and feel for Wakanda, a proud and independent nation that had never suffered from European expansionism.

Having Marvel's preeminent black Super Hero written by the MacArthur Genius and National Book Award winner Ta-Nehisi Coates (*Between the World and Me*) granted the series significant literary and political heft, generating huge interest outside comic book circles. Coates lived up to expectations, devising a compelling reevaluation of all aspects of what was already a utopian black culture. For *Black Panther*'s opening story arc, the creative team took its inspiration from Steven Hahn's *A Nation Under Our Feet: Black Political Struggles in the Rural South from Slavery to the Great Migration*—a Pulitzer Prize-winning epic history of African Americans' battle for equality and a political voice. The book's insights into black America's hard-won independence and political nationhood act as a telling counterpoint to Coates and Stelfreeze's new take on Wakanda. In "Black Panther: A Nation Under our Feet," the creators shape the future of an African nation that has never known privation or conquest, and enjoys the highest standards of living, education, and health care on planet Earth.

The series built on years of turmoil, as Wakanda recovered from a succession of calamities. T'Challa had abdicated, becoming King of the Dead, while sister Shuri ruled the country as a new Black Panther, facing global catastrophe, economic collapse, and consecutive invasions from Namor's Atlanteans and Thanos' Black Legion, which decimated Wakanda. When Shuri sacrificed her life defending the nation, T'Challa regretfully returned to resume the throne.

"A Nation Under Our Feet" opens with the overburdened king hoping to reassure his emotionally conflicted people. When violence erupts during a Vibranium miners strike, T'Challa's senses a hidden enemy intensifying popular disquiet. In the ensuing clash with the miners, he fails to catch the unseen instigator. Discontent, dissent, and rebellion escalate everywhere. Elite Dora Milaje Aneka is sentenced to death for overstepping her authority when she punishes a local chieftain who has been exploiting women. And beyond Wakanda's

Royal blood
King T'Challa constantly struggles to manage external threats and internal religious and political pressures. As dissent grows, another national crisis begins with Vibranium miners: a hurled stone, a bloodied brow, and a chilling accusation.

Under pressure

A king cannot always pick his battles. While T'Challa is desperately seeking a way to revive his sister, the needs of his divided people pull him one way, the demands of his coruling mother take him in another, and the machinations of insurgents armed with compelling philosophies and deadly powers drag him down yet another path.

borders, super-powered rebels calling themselves "The People" wait for their moment, dreaming of a new nation born of violent change and ancient sorcery.

Aneka is liberated by comrade-in-arms and lover, Ayo. Fleeing the city, they join women escaping bandits and abusive chieftains, and become leaders of an emancipated third faction in Wakanda's civil war. T'Challa becomes too distracted to deal with the crisis, lost in a desperate plan to resurrect his sister. As the saga unfolds, Queen Shuri's spirit returns from the Plane of Wakandan Memory, fortified by the entire history and mythology of her people. Her new powers and knowledge will help save her embattled people from rebels, invaders, and super-powered American corporate raiders. The result forces Wakanda to evolve, creating a new role for the ruling family, who now govern by popular consent through debate and democratic decision-making, not divinely sponsored regal diktat.

The new series was a hit, securing Coates' ongoing tenure on the title, which would go on to explore Wakanda's fraught mythic origins and shift the action to outer space. It also spawned equally daring spin-offs that would expand the Panther's world, such as *Black Panther and the Crew* and *World of Wakanda*, and led to Coates turning his attention to America's national symbol. In 2018, he began writing the new *Captain America* series, challenging concepts of patriotism and national identity, while also taking Black Panther into unchartered territory. ■

THE VISION
KING | WALTA | BELLAIRE
MARVEL 012

Vision #12
December 2016

❝The last issue of a deservedly acclaimed limited series ingeniously features the Vision as the creator and head of an idealized robotic nuclear family.❞

Peter David

Editor in chief	Axel Alonso
Cover artist	Michael Del Mundo
Writer	Tom King
Penciler, inker	Gabriel Hernandez Walta
Colorist	Jordie Bellaire
Letterer	Clayton Cowles
Editors	Wil Moss, Charles Beachum, Tom Brevoort

Family ties
As Viv tries to comprehend the futility of human genetics, scripter Tom King goes on to imply that her artificial family was not dissimilar to many natural ones: dysfunctional, broken, and separated, but still devoted to all within it.

Marvel Comics has always had great success in creating misunderstood outcasts and beings somehow set apart from common humanity. Many are antiheroes like the Hulk or Namor, the Sub-Mariner, or unrepentant vigilantes like the Punisher, or benign but feared nonconformists like Silver Surfer. But of all the heroes at the fringes of society, only one is a synthetic machine-creature who desires nothing more than to be an ordinary human.

The Vision debuted in *Avengers* #57 (October 1968): a humanoid weapon devised by killer robot Ultron, who overrode his programming to become a noble and valiant hero. Decades before artificial intelligence became headline news in the real world, Vision was a symbol of computers attempting to integrate with mankind. Incorporating the heritage (and component parts) of vintage Super Heroes the Original Human Torch, android Jim Hammond, and Wonder Man, Simon Williams, Vision became a trusted and valued Avenger. He found friends and even settled down into marriage with Wanda Maximoff, the Scarlet Witch, only to have those he most admired and from whom he craved acceptance eventually turn on him.

He has undergone numerous radical reboots, being forcibly returned to "factory settings" as a ghostly white Vision drained of color and character, rebuilt with new personality engrams, and simply destroyed several times. He was even briefly reformed as a teenager but could never find true satisfaction or happiness. Ultimately, Vision achieved a semblance of the life he always wanted by building it himself.

In the 2015 miniseries *Vision*, the ever-determined synthezoid constructed his own idealized vision of the American Dream: life, liberty, and the pursuit of happiness. Acquiring a suburban home in Cherrydale, Virginia, he furnished it with a wife, two kids, and a dog: painstakingly, personally handmade and programmed to grow into independent beings in his own image. At last, he had the existence he yearned for—it was the most tragic mistake of his life.

In writer Tom King and artist Gabriel Hernandez Walta's potent, poignant exploration of humanity, *Vision* follows the perfect wife, Virginia, awkward twin teens, Vin and Viv, and faithful robo-mutt Sparky as they strive to fit into society as regular citizens. Vision's dream is never given a chance to succeed, as the mechanical clan are constantly confronted by their artificial origins, as seen through the suspicions of the community they are trying to join. Compounding the problem is the Vision himself. As an Avenger, his career includes many villains and even friends trying to keep tabs on him. When an old enemy, the Grim Reaper,

Do androids dream?
Illustrator Gabriel Hernandez Walta
beautifully captures the isolation and
suppressed inner turmoil of the
supposedly emotionless Vision
through quiet, understated staging.
At the threshold of a new life,
the artificial Avenger sees his hopes
and dreams slip away. The humanity
he has always doubted he possessed
is confirmed in grief, resignation,
and, ultimately, hope.

attacks the household while the Vision
is away, he almost destroys Viv before
Virginia kills him. Hiding the body, she
conceals her actions from her husband
and subsequently begins to devolve
into electronic neurosis.

The family's descent into existential
chaos is sealed when a neighbor who
witnessed the event tries to blackmail
Virginia. This leads to the death of one
of Viv's classmates, forcing the Avengers
to plant a spy—Victor Mancha—in the
Vision household. Another product of
Ultron's deranged tinkering, Mancha
accidentally kills Vin, and the outraged,
distraught Vision battles and defeats the
entire assembled Avengers as they try
stop him from killing his "brother." He is
thwarted only by the increasingly erratic
Virginia, who murders Mancha first.

In *Vision #12*, King and Hernandez
Walta bring the family saga to a thought-
provoking, affecting, and suspenseful
conclusion as the surviving android
intelligences realize just how human they
have become. With the epic battle
concluded, Virginia confesses to every
crime her family committed, falsifying
records, and memories to exonerate her
husband before ending her own life in
a final, loving act of devotion. When Viv
leaves—to join teen hero alliance the
Champions—her father wistfully retires
to their home to begin work on his latest
secret project: Virginia Mark II. ▪

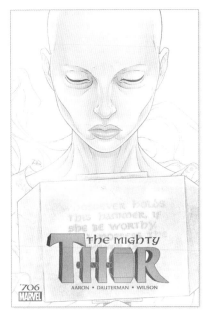

Editor in chief	C. B. Cebulski
Cover artist	Russell Dauterman
Writer	Jason Aaron
Penciler, inker	Russell Dauterman
Colorist	Matthew Wilson
Letterer	Joe Sabino
Editors	Wil Moss, Sarah Brunstad, Tom Brevoort

Mighty Thor #706
June 2018

> 66 Jane Foster proves herself worthy as the mighty Goddess of Thunder... The story is a poignant tribute to her as her battle with cancer ends, and she's forced to put down the hammer for good. A moving and unforgettable close to an epic story line. 99

Sana Amanat

By summer 2018, writer Jason Aaron had already been working on Thor titles for more than six years. His time with the character had seen some seismic changes, including the rendering of the original Thor as "unworthy," no longer able to pick up the mystical weapon Mjölnir. However, there must always be a Thor, and so the hammer searched for someone worthy to wield it. This led to another of Aaron's game-changing plotlines—Jane Foster becoming the Mighty Thor. Although this caused consternation among some readers, the story played into the themes that Aaron had been exploring throughout his run, of how worthiness could be defined and how it could be lost or earned.

Jane Foster's first issue as Thor came in *Thor* #1 (December 2014), as part of the Avengers NOW! initiative, which continued a process of introducing a range of more diverse characters to continuity to appeal to a broader range of readers. Jane was already suffering from breast cancer, and, as her time as a hero progressed, it was revealed that wielding Mjölnir was reversing the effects of her chemotherapy treatment and therefore killing her. By the time of *Mighty Thor* #705 (May 2018), Jane had been told that one more outing as Thor would destroy her mortal form. However,

with the monstrous Mangog threatening all of Asgard, Jane made the heroic decision to sacrifice herself to save others. This act exemplified why a frail human had been chosen in the first place as worthy of possessing the power of Thor.

Mighty Thor #706 opens with Jane Foster lying lifeless, having hurled the Mangog—and Mjölnir— into the Sun. Her soul is at the gates of Valhalla, having more than earned the right to spend eternity in the warriors' paradise, when she is confronted by Odin. The All-Father had initially been angry that a human woman could have taken what he considered to be his son's birthright, but he acknowledges that Jane has sacrificed herself to save everything he held dear. As Jane hesitates at the gates, not feeling ready to go to her death, the two realize that the original Thor, then known as Odinson, is trying to harness the power released after the destruction of Mjölnir to revive Jane's human form. Odin returns to the mortal plane to help his son, and with their combined power, Jane Foster is returned to life. She decides to focus on getting well, urging Odinson to assume the role of the Thunder God once more, even without Mjölnir.

The issue was a highly emotional end to the story of Jane Foster as Thor. Both writer Aaron and illustrator Russell

Worthy warrior
After her death, Jane Foster finds herself at the gates of Valhalla with All-Father Odin. It was proof, if any were needed, that she had been a worthy Thor.

The hero's journey

Returned to life by Thor and Odin, Jane Foster no longer had the power of Thor and now needed to focus all her energies on her fight against cancer. The poignancy of the contrast between the frail human and the Goddess of Thunder helped make *Mighty Thor* a critical success and a favorite with creators and fans alike.

Dauterman commented that they had never felt so attached to a character, or worked with one that connected them so strongly to readers. Jane's battle with cancer had struck a chord with many, and her ascension to becoming Thor had made headlines around the world.

Dauterman's art on *Mighty Thor* was distinct from what had gone before, as if to underscore that this was a different version of the hero and therefore a new era. His pencils were intricately detailed and given added impact by Matthew Wilson's sumptuous color palette. The entire creative team used the Jane Foster-as-Thor era to really extend the boundaries of the character and bring the realms of gods, mythical monsters, and dark villains to breathtaking life. Of all Marvel characters, Thor offers perhaps the broadest scope for storytelling, and this was maximized throughout Jane Foster's time as the Asgardian champion.

Mighty Thor was also a critical success, netting Eisner Awards for writer Aaron and colorist Wilson. *Mighty Thor* #706 was a fitting, elegiac end to a near four-year arc for a long-standing character that had reached a new cohort of readers. It has also inspired the upcoming Marvel Cinematic Universe sequel *Thor: Love and Thunder*, with actress Natalie Portman's Jane Foster set to wield Mjölnir. ∎

Avengers #6
October 2018

"Cosmic craziness comes to Earth as Jason Aaron and Ed McGuiness try to top Stan Lee and Jack Kirby in an Avengers adventure the likes of which we've never seen before, as Loki unites the heavens and hell against Earth's Mightiest Heroes.**"**

C. B. Cebulski

Editor in chief	C. B. Cebulski
Cover artists	Ed McGuinness, Mark Morales, Justin Ponsor
Writer	Jason Aaron
Pencilers	Ed McGuinness, Paco Medina
Inkers	Mark Morales, Juan Vlasco
Colorist	David Curiel
Letterer	Cory Petit
Editors	Tom Brevoort, Alanna Smith

Secret Avenger
Loki's role in Avenger history began when he accidentally caused the team to form. Recent revisions have made him more complex, and with each Machiavellian turn, it is harder to see whether he is a force for good or evil.

Throughout its numerous incarnations, the Avengers has an incomparable record as the go-to title for epic events. In many ways, it is the natural successor to Stan Lee and Jack Kirby's stellar run on the Fantastic Four, which defined the Marvel Universe. The Avengers are now the take-charge team whenever the continuity undergoes one of its frequent reality realignments. Earth's Mightiest Heroes are almost always on hand whenever things get seriously difficult and are themselves generally reshaped and reformed through each crisis. A prime example of this came in 2018 when a squad of retired veterans and a spooky new kid on the block assembled to save the world—once again.

It begins with a dismaying chain of events: deep beneath Africa, Black Panther T'Challa and mystic master Doctor Strange discover the corpse of a four-billion-year-old Celestial infested with horrific alien bugs. The heroes' presence awakens the voracious monsters, later identified as the Horde, which start burrowing toward the surface and eventually spread across the entire world. In Los Angeles, demonically possessed street racer Robbie Reyes transforms into the Ghost Rider and is magically drawn toward rampaging She-Hulk Jennifer Walters in Manhattan as she smashes Horde bugs. In a nearby bar, former Avengers Steve Rogers and Thor try to convince fellow founder Tony Stark to get the gang back together. They make no headway until a dying, Horde-infested, 2,000-foot tall Celestial smashes into the Manhattan shoreline, despite every effort of Captain Marvel (Carol Danvers) to prevent the calamity. It is only one of hundreds of dead and dying star gods impacting all over Earth. It transpires that Celestials have been locked in a civil war since reality began, and the Horde were devised eons ago as their ultimate weapon. As a group of Celestials—the Final Host—appear, accompanied by the Avengers' old foe Loki, Stark reluctantly concedes it's time for Avengers to assemble again.

The six-part saga opened a new era, as the god of mischief reveals that in 1,000,000 BCE Asgardian warrior Odin led another team of Avengers—comprising the first Iron Fist and Black Panther, Sorcerer Supreme Agamotto, a Mammoth-riding spectral Ghost Rider, primal Hulk-ish warrior Starbrand, and cosmic entity Lady Phoenix—against the First Host. The Celestial star gods were on Earth only because the prehistoric Avengers had rashly executed a mad Celestial endangering the primitive planet.

Loki then shares a shocking truth. Billions of years earlier, as the world was forming from cosmic rubble, a Celestial named the Progenitor—fatally infested with Horde bugs—perished on Earth. Its escaping bodily fluids contaminated Earth's protomatter, warping the biosphere

Celestial Avengers Assemble

Above all else, the Avengers are
designed for epic adventures.
Their real power rests, not in their
members' individual skills or gifts,
but in the ability to combine radically
different personalities and power sets
into a unified force that always gets
the job done—even if that means
accepting Celestials into their ranks.

and creating conditions that made the
planet a crucible for incredible life forms,
including gods, mutants, Inhumans,
and an infinitely adaptable mankind.
Due to the Progenitor's corrupting
essence, the Earth and all its inhabitants
were an anathema to and different from
the rest of the universe, having become
a "Planet of Pathogens."

Combining cosmic spectacle,
blockbuster action, and history-altering
revelation, writer Jason Aaron and art
team Ed McGuinness, Paco Medina,
Mark Morales, and Juan Vlasco united
to deliver a cathartic final act as the
heroes use Loki's jibes and gloating
disclosure to divine a solution to the
alien invasion. United with last Celestial,
Eson the Searcher, the heroes eradicate
the Horde and drive off the Final Host,
again saving the world and reinvigorating
the Avengers for the future.

In the aftermath in *Avengers* #6, the
superteam get a new HQ inside a dead
Celestial at the North Pole, a new leader
in Black Panther, and are repositioned to
lead a reinvigorated Marvel Universe to
greater glories and against deadlier threats.
The altered cosmology at last explained
in credible terms just why Earth and its
occupants are so unique in the cosmos.
It rationalized the existence and role of
different strands of superhumanity, while
also opening up new vistas—at least
one million years' worth—of hitherto
untapped Super Hero story lines. ▪

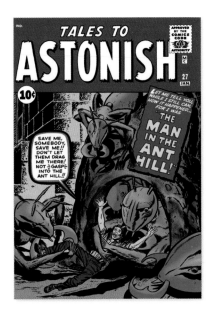

Cover artist: Carl Burgos **Writers:** Hank Chapman (Torch), Don Rico (Captain America), Bill Everett (Sub-Mariner) **Pencilers/Inkers:** Russ Heath, Carl Burgos (Torch), John Romita Sr., Mort Lawrence (Captain America), Bill Everett (Sub-Mariner) **Editor:** Stan Lee

Cover artists: Jack Kirby, Dick Ayers **Writers:** Stan Lee, Larry Lieber **Penciler:** Jack Kirby **Inker:** Dick Ayers **Editor:** Stan Lee

Cover artists: Jack Kirby, Don Heck **Writers:** Stan Lee, Larry Lieber **Penciler/Inker:** Don Heck **Editor:** Stan Lee

Young Men #24
December 1953

Super Hero comics dominated during World War II but waned once hostilities ceased. After the Korean War, Marvel Comics (then Atlas Comics) briefly revived their "Big Three" in a climate of anti-communist paranoia. In *Young Men #24*, Human Torch, Captain America, and Namor, the Sub-Mariner, starred in short solo exploits, maintaining their presence on the newsstands. The Torch—ambushed by Soviet-backed gangsters in 1949—was resurrected from a desert grave by nuclear tests, making him Marvel's first atomic age hero, while Cap and Bucky came out of retirement when Red Skull attacked the UN. Namor made his appearance when called on to solve a missing-ships mystery and battle alien robots.

Further tales followed in *Young Men* and *Men's Adventures*, and Captain America and Sub-Mariner's own titles would be restarted, before the heroes retired again in 1955. ∎

Tales to Astonish #27
January 1962

Henry Pym, aka Ant-Man, is the first crossover hero to migrate from the Atlas Era to the Marvel Age. He graduated from a stand-alone story in the anthology title *Tales to Astonish #27*—released the same month as *Fantastic Four #2*—to gain stardom in Stan Lee and Jack Kirby's Super Hero revolution.

"The Man in the Ant Hill!" sees maverick citizen-scientist Hank Pym create shrinking potions and discover peril, wonder, and even companionship among the lowliest creatures on, and under, the Earth. Rapidly retooled as a costumed crusader, Pym debuted again later that year in *Tales to Astonish #35* (September 1962). "The Return of the Ant-Man" finds Soviet agents holding Pym hostage in his own laboratory. Using his shrinking serum and cybernetic devices he had built to communicate with ants, Pym defeats the spies and resolves to use his powers for the good of humankind. ∎

Tales of Suspense #39
March 1963

Released at the beginning of 1963, *Tales of Suspense #39* was the latest in a run of hit comic books introducing a new star to the Marvel firmament. The star in this case was Tony Stark and his alter ego, the invincible Iron Man. The story, plotted by Stan Lee and scripted by his brother, Larry Lieber, established the origin of the character. The locations may have been updated for topical relevance in later issues of the character's own title and for the big screen, but the essentials remain Iron Man lore.

Captured by a band of terrorists, a near fatally wounded Tony Stark creates an armored suit to preserve his life and escape, aided by imprisoned genius Professor Ho Yinsen. Jack Kirby created the look of Iron Man, while interior artist Don Heck based Tony Stark on dashing movie star Errol Flynn. Stan Lee's real-life model for Stark was bon vivant, technologist, and high-flying business magnate Howard Hughes.

Cover artists: Jack Kirby, George Roussos
Writer: Stan Lee **Penciler:** Jack Kirby
Inker: Steve Ditko **Editor:** Stan Lee

Fantastic Four #13
April 1963

In the early 1960s, nearly every successive Marvel Comics Super Hero release was a winner, but *Fantastic Four* #13 was a standout even by these standards. "The Red Ghost and His Incredible Super Apes!" was ostensibly a riotous Cold War thriller pitting the year-old team against a Soviet scientist in the race to reach the Moon. But it also discloses more about the mutating cosmic rays that created the Fantastic Four (FF) and now empowers a new foe. The villain is Soviet scientist Ivan Kragoff who, with his trio of trained apes, replicates the FF's origin accident, deliberately exposing himself and his soon-to-be Super Apes to an even higher dose of the deadly radiation.

An action-packed romp notable for Steve Ditko's moody inking over Jack Kirby's pencils, Stan Lee's story makes another major revelation. It depicts a mysterious and ancient oxygen-rich city on Luna and introduces the omnipotent Watchers, silently surveilling humanity for millennia: an invaluable plot device of numerous future adventures. ∎

Cover artists: Jack Kirby, Dick Ayers
Writer: Stan Lee **Penciler/Inker:** Steve
Ditko **Editor:** Stan Lee

Strange Tales #110
July 1963

Although his full origin would not be revealed until *Strange Tales* #115 (December 1963), this issue saw the debut of Doctor Strange, his mystic teacher, the Ancient One, and Strange's (unnamed) assistant Wong. Doctor Strange was the creation of the great Steve Ditko, whose offbeat, psychedelic style was perfect for both the character and the tenor of the times. "Dr. Strange: Master of Black Magic," sees Strange's astral form enter a man's troubled dreams, where he first encounters and battles the demonic Nightmare, a future, recurring foe. With the help of the Ancient One, Strange defeats his enemy and returns to his corporeal form.

In *Strange Tales* #110, Doctor Strange was a mere five-page backup to the headlining Human Torch, but by the end of the decade, *Strange Tales* would be renamed *Doctor Strange*. The character proved to be a big hit with Marvel's increasing college-age readership, giving them something very different to regular Super Hero titles. ∎

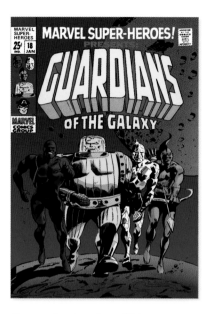

Cover artist: Gene Colan **Writer:** Arnold
Drake **Penciler:** Gene Colan **Inker:** Mike
Esposito **Editor:** Stan Lee

Marvel Super-Heroes #18
January 1969

While lauded for reinventing Super Heroes for the modern era, Marvel always maintained strong connections with other popular genres, such as science fiction and war stories. In 1968, as America was undergoing sweeping social change, and with the Vietnam War on TV screens every night, writer Arnold Drake created a uniquely topical band of champions for *Marvel Super-Heroes* #18. "Guardians of the Galaxy!: Earth Shall Overcome!" introduced Vance Astro—last survivor of 20th-century Earth—united in 3007 CE with Centauran Yondu and genetically modified humans Charlie-27 and Martinex in a guerrilla war against alien Badoons who had conquered mankind.

Despite an intriguing story line and dynamic, experimental artwork from Gene Colan and Mike Esposito, the freedom fighters were a rare Marvel misfire. However, their mid-1970s revival saw the "Future Avengers" become a key part of Marvel continuity and the inspiration for today's hugely successful star-spanning incarnation. ∎

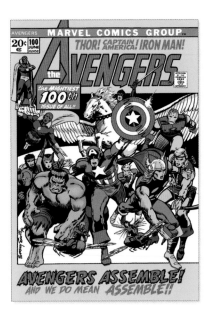

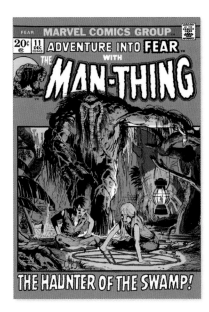

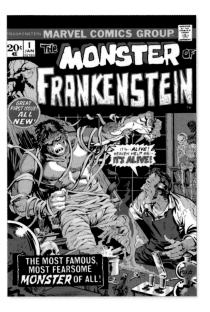

Cover artist: Barry Windsor-Smith
Writer: Roy Thomas **Penciler:** Barry
Windsor-Smith **Inkers:** Barry Windsor-Smith,
Joe Sinnott, Syd Shores **Editor:** Stan Lee

Cover artist: Neal Adams **Writer:** Steve
Gerber **Penciler:** Rich Buckler **Inker:** Jim
Mooney **Editor:** Roy Thomas

Cover artist: Mike Ploog **Writers:** Mary
Shelley, Gary Friedrich **Penciler/Inker:**
Mike Ploog **Editor:** Roy Thomas

Avengers #100
June 1972

Adventure into Fear #11
December 1972

Monster of Frankenstein #1
January 1973

Under Roy Thomas, *Avengers* was a watchword for innovation and sheer quality. After completing the pioneering Kree-Skrull War saga, *Avengers* #98 (April 1972) saw Thomas and soon-to-be superstar illustrator Barry Windsor-Smith begin another momentous extended epic. The saga kicks off when an amnesiac Hercules ominously proclaims humanity's doom while mythological monsters orchestrate atomic Armageddon on Earth.

Inked by Smith, Joe Sinnott, and Syd Shores, the anniversary issue *Avengers* #100 "Whatever Gods There Be!" threw down the gauntlet to all, as every living Avenger, including the rampaging Hulk, the Black Knight (Dane Whitman), and disgraced criminal the Swordsman, join forces to invade heavenly Olympus and confront old foe Enchantress and War God Ares to save the world in spectacular style. Captivating, beautiful, and action-packed, the tale remains the epitome of Earth's Mightiest Heroes at their finest. ▪

Man-Thing, a being created when Professor Ted Sallis is transformed into a swamp creature in the Everglades, was created in the black-and-white anthology magazine *Savage Tales* #1 (May 1971) by Stan Lee, Roy Thomas, Gerry Conway, and Gray Morrow. Sallis has perfected a Super-Soldier serum when thugs raid his lab to steal the formula from him. To keep it from them, the fleeing scientist desperately injects himself with the serum but crashes his car into the swamp—only to rise as a muck-encrusted monster who wreaks brutal revenge on his attackers.

Adventure into Fear #11 would see a new era dawn for the character as future star scribe Steve Gerber took the helm in his first writing job for Marvel Comics. Gerber's run would become a cult classic, and, in this first issue, he laid down the signature tagline of the character: "Whatever knows fear burns at the Man-Thing's touch!" The book also saw the beginnings of Man-Thing's swamp home becoming a pivotal Marvel location: the Nexus of All Realities. ▪

The last "classic monster" to be incorporated into the Marvel Universe in his own title in the 1970s, "Mary Shelley's Frankenstein!" proudly debuted as a close adaptation and continuance rather than being simply based on the source material. Illustrated by new sensation Mike Ploog, and set in 1898, it introduces Robert Walton IV, great-grandson of the sea captain who rescued scientist Victor Frankenstein in Shelley's novel. His handed-down account of "the Modern Prometheus" is prompted by his own crew uncovering a massive figure in a block of Arctic ice and—under his orders—bringing it aboard his own foredoomed icebreaker.

This atmospheric retelling is so close to the original tale that Shelley is credited as cowriter. It is a gripping yarn that broadens Marvel's storytelling style with dark elegance and high impact. The monster, and subsequent clones, would become embedded in mainstream Marvel continuity, appearing alongside Spider-Man, the Avengers, and even S.H.I.E.L.D.'s Howling Commandos. ▪

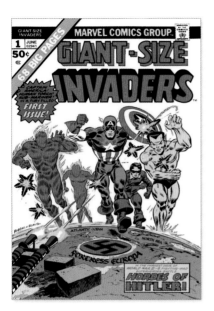

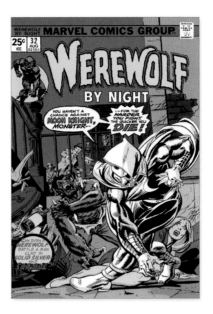

Cover artists: Frank Robbins, John Romita Sr.
Writer: Roy Thomas **Penciler:** Frank Robbins
Inker: Vince Colletta **Editor:** Roy Thomas

Giant-Size Invaders #1
June 1975

In 1975, a resurgence of interest in Super Heroes coincided with a general wave of nostalgia, resulting in a concept that finally married modern Marvel to its Timely Comics antecedents.

In *Giant-Size Invaders* #1, "The Coming of the Invaders!," Roy Thomas adroitly retrofitted Timely's "Big Three"—Captain America; the Human Torch (Jim Hammond); and Namor, the Sub-Mariner—into a formal fighting unit battling the Axis powers in a blistering, fast-paced tale illustrated by acclaimed veteran cartoonist Frank Robbins. After individually thwarting Nazi Super-Soldier Master Man, and attempts to assassinate Winston Churchill, they unite—at the British leader's insistence—to take the war to the enemy as "The Invaders."

The issue's stunning success prompted the rapid release of a regular title, adding new Golden Age heroes to Marvel's firmament. The Invaders would return over the decades with contemporary lineups, all paying homage to the original's WWII pedigree. ∎

Cover artists: Gil Kane, Al Milgrom **Writer:** Doug Moench **Penciler:** Don Perlin **Inker:** Howie Perlin **Editor:** Len Wein

Werewolf by Night #32
August 1975

Heralding a wave of supernatural stars, Jack Russell and his accursed alter ego debuted in *Marvel Spotlight* #2 (February 1972), the first Marvel horror hero in his own series. Three years later, *Werewolf by Night* #32 signaled the end of the trend as the dramatic debut of Moon Knight steered the lycanthrope's adventures toward more super-heroic territory.

In "The Stalker called Moon Knight," Marc Spector is a mercenary hired by capitalist cabal "the Committee," who are out to exploit the werewolf. Spector, aka Moon Knight, prepares for battle with silver-coated armor and weaponry and, with the aid of his partner Jean-Paul "Frenchie" Duchamp, captures Russell and his equally-afflicted sister, Lissa. Spector ultimately turns on his paymasters and frees his captives. After a return engagement with Jack Russell, Moon Knight would become a breakout star of 1980s Marvel, and his further stories a byword for intense psychological drama and darkly mature Super Hero storytelling. ∎

Cover artists: Dave Cockrum, Danny Crespi
Writer: Chris Claremont **Penciler:** Dave Cockrum **Inker:** Frank Chiaramonte
Editor: Archie Goodwin

X-Men #101
October 1976

The "All-New, All-Different X-Men" sparked a comics revolution. Chris Claremont and Dave Cockrum sought to create strong, believable women and spectacularly succeeded by reinventing diffident Jean Grey as the most powerful—and flawed—hero in the Marvel Universe.

X-Men #101 is equal parts miracle and mystery. "Like a Phoenix, from the Ashes!" sees Grey explode from a crashed space shuttle after piloting it through a deadly solar storm to save her comrades. In the process, she is transformed into a blazing paragon of energy exclaiming she is the Phoenix—"Fire and Life Incarnate!"

Grey's journey to this moment begins after her teammates are dispatched to Europe to battle villains Black Tom and the Juggernaut. Her intervention and miraculous survival will later be explained as intercession by a cosmic avatar. But at this crucial point, all readers knew was that this selfless hero had been reborn as a being of godlike power and unimaginable potential. ∎

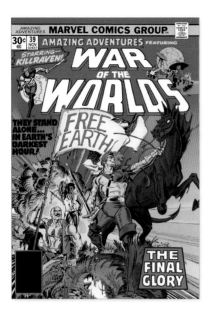

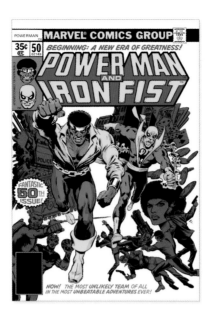

Cover artist: P. Craig Russell **Writer:** Don McGregor **Penciler/Inker:** P. Craig Russell **Editor:** Archie Goodwin

Cover artist: Dave Cockrum **Writer:** Chris Claremont **Penciler:** John Byrne **Inkers:** Dave Cockrum, Dan Green **Editor:** Archie Goodwin

Cover artists: Gene Colan, Tom Palmer **Writer:** Marv Wolfman **Penciler:** Gene Colan **Inker:** Tom Palmer **Editors:** Marv Wolfman, Jim Shooter

Amazing Adventures #39
November 1976

Power Man and Iron Fist #50
April 1978

Tomb of Dracula #70
August 1979

When the 1960s Super Hero boom started to stall a decade later, Marvel diversified into other genres, including perennial favorite science fiction. In May 1973, it created a cult comic classic that broadly reinterpreted H. G. Wells' *War of the Worlds*, pitting rebel leader Killraven against entrenched, man-eating Martian invaders. After several creators worked on the title, the series gelled from *Amazing Adventures* #27 (November 1974), with writer Don McGregor and artist P. Craig Russell examining contemporary American society in crisis with powerful, heartfelt story lines, strong characterization, and simply gorgeous artwork.

Amazing Adventures #39, the last issue, found Killraven's "Freemen" pursuing a winged mutant foe, only to discover she is simply a mother defending very strange children. In a series infamous for uncompromising violence, this vision of peace through compromise provided a potent note of optimism on which to end the saga. ■

Although this issue was the first titled *Power Man and Iron Fist*, it retained the numbering of the preceding *Power Man* title. It officially brought together Luke Cage (Power Man) and Danny Rand (Iron Fist) as an unlikely crime-fighting pairing, a shrewd move by Marvel Comics intended to raise the profile of both characters and tap into the continued popularity of Blaxploitation and martial arts action movies. It proved to be an inspired team-up, and the duo's close association would thrive well into the new millennium, even making the jump across to the small screen.

Power Man and Iron Fist #50 was written by legendary *X-Men* scribe Chris Claremont, laying the foundation for the odd-couple partnership that would later be known as Heroes for Hire. The issue, which sees our heroes prevent villains from ruining a party in Cage's honor, also features the timely arrival of regular guest stars, Daughters of the Dragon Colleen Wing and Misty Knight. ■

The 1970s horror boom spawned many supernatural heroes. In Marvel's *Tomb of Dracula*, it was an unrepentant, soulless monster who captivated readers with his deadly depredations and machinations. Over seven blood-chilling years, Dracula battled vampire hunters, Marvel Super Heroes, and eldritch combatants such as Blade the Vampire Slayer, before dramatically concluding in the extra-length thriller "Lords of the Undead!" Finally ousted as king of Earth's undead, Dracula destroys his vampiric usurper, Torgo, only to fall to dying human archenemy Quincy Harker, who executes Vlad Dracul in his own castle.

An era of horror heroes ended, fittingly written by Marv Wolfman and rendered by Gene Colan and Tom Palmer, whose indelible, much-praised run on the title remains an exemplar of the genre. Dracula soon regenerated in a mature-age magazine iteration, before returning to mainstream Marvel continuity in the 21st century. ■

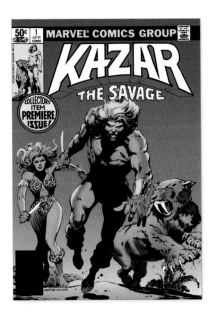

Cover artist: Brent Anderson **Writer:** Bruce Jones **Penciler:** Brent Anderson **Inker:** Carlos Garzon **Editor:** Louise Jones

Ka-Zar the Savage #1
April 1981

Debuting in comic strip form in *Marvel Comics* #1 (October 1939), Ka-Zar, or a namesake of his, was reintroduced into the Marvel Universe in *X-Men* #10 (March 1965) as a "Tarzan-like" jungle-reared hero and lord of the Savage Land.

In April 1981, Ka-Zar was brilliantly reimagined in "A New Dawn… A New World!," the first installment of a series that was thrilling, witty, and sophisticated. Now a cultured man and bored with all things primitive, Lord Kevin Plunder leaves his longtime mate Shanna to search for his missing sabretooth companion Zabu. In the course of his quest, Ka-Zar (and intrigued readers) learns that the primeval Savage Land is only part of a larger region stocked with many alien races and creatures. Exploring this "Pangea," he embarks on incredible explorations, romantically strays, and battles bizarre beings before ultimately discovering that his Antarctic Eden is an ancient Atlantean/alien theme park! ∎

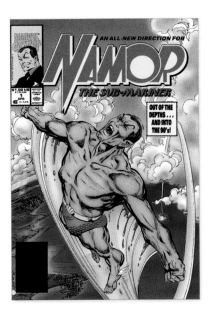

Cover artist: John Byrne **Writer/Penciler:** John Byrne **Inker:** Bob Wiacek **Editor:** Terry Kavanagh

Namor, the Sub-Mariner #1
April 1990

After decades as a dangerously unpredictable antihero and, at times, outright villain, Marvel's oldest super-being gets a radical revamp. Saved from himself by oceanographers Caleb and Carrie Alexander during a mindless attack on Pacific islanders, Namor learns his lifelong mood swings are caused by a blood imbalance. With the condition corrected, he becomes coldly rational and dedicates himself to acquiring vast riches to further his new goal: saving Earth from ecological collapse and mankind from mass suicide.

In "Purpose!," John Byrne brilliantly recaps Namor's origins, confirms his importance to Marvel history, cleverly channels the rampage that resurrected Captain America, sets the character's new direction, and introduces the Atlantean monarch's new archenemies in billionaires Desmond and Phoebe Marrs. Moreover, from the next issue, Namor is proudly redesignated as "Marvel's first and mightiest mutant." ∎

Cover artists: Michael Zeck, John Beatty **Writer:** Jim Shooter **Penciler:** Michael Zeck **Inker:** John Beatty **Editor:** Tom DeFalco

Marvel Super Heroes Secret Wars #1
May 1984

The first in a 12-issue miniseries, *Marvel Super Heroes Secret Wars* #1 was a milestone in the history of Marvel Comics and the comic book industry. It was the first time a story line unfolded across ten A-list titles, culminating in a series that sold more copies than any other comic in the previous 25 years. Its huge success also provided a model for subsequent crossover events.

Initially conceived to tie in with a range of toys, *Secret Wars* changed how comic creators thought about story lines forever. Written by editor in chief Jim Shooter, the first issue sees nearly all of Marvel's high-profile heroes and villains spirited away from their own titles by the all-powerful Beyonder to a patchwork planet called Battleworld. Here, they engage in a battle of strength and wits to win the Beyonder's cosmic game and return to their own world. The concept was reprised in a sequel the following year, and informed 2015's *Secret Wars*, which rebooted the Marvel Universe. ∎

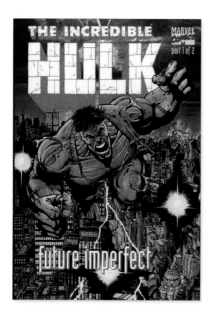

Cover artist: George Pérez **Writer:** Peter David **Penciler/Inker:** : George Pérez **Editor:** Bobbie Chase

Incredible Hulk: Future Imperfect #1
December 1992

*I*ncredible Hulk: Future Imperfect was a historic two-part story set in an alternate future dystopia. Written by celebrated Hulk scribe Peter David, whose 12-year run on *Incredible Hulk* greatly expanded the character's appeal, the stand-alone saga boasted epic, meticulous artwork by the great George Pérez. The story also debuted Maestro, a twisted version of Hulk who has Bruce Banner's intelligence but also all of the Jade Giant's more malevolent qualities.

In a world ravaged by war, Maestro's prodigious strength has enabled him to become a tyrannical ruler—one who can be stopped only by the Hulk himself. *Incredible Hulk: Future Imperfect #1* shows readers this terrifying future, which includes a shrine of memorabilia from dead heroes and villains collected by a now ancient Rick Jones. The issue concludes as Maestro and Hulk meet for the first time, ahead of an almighty battle in the second part that ends at the start of Hulk's story. ∎

Cover artist: Pete Woods **Writer:** Joe Kelly **Penciler:** Pete Woods **Inkers:** Nathan Massengill (1997), Al Milgrom, Joe Sinnott (1960s) **Editor:** Bob Harras

Deadpool #11
December 1997

*U*ndying assassin Wade "Deadpool" Wilson debuted as a wisecracking but deadly serious villain in *New Mutants* #98 (February 1991). He developed into the utterly absurd, fourth-wall busting sociopath of page and screen only after Joe Kelly began scripting his ongoing adventures. The pivotal moment occurs in *Deadpool* #11's "With Great Power Comes Great Coincidence," when the rationality-challenged antihero and his hostage-cum-sidekick Blind Al are accidentally catapulted back to April 1967 and hilariously inject themselves into the classic adventure from *Amazing Spider-Man* #47!

Constantly mistaken for Spidey— and Al for Aunt May!—Deadpool battles Kraven the Hunter while desperately, and uncharacteristically, trying to prevent continuity from unraveling in a surreal romp that defines the character and sets the scene for years of madcap mayhem. ∎

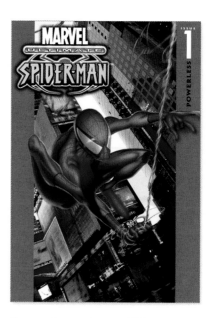

Cover artist: Joe Quesada **Writers:** Brian Michael Bendis, Bill Jemas **Penciler:** Mark Bagley **Inker:** Art Thibert **Editor:** Ralph Macchio

Ultimate Spider-Man #1
October 2000

*T*he first comic book released as part of the Ultimates initiative, *Ultimate Spider-Man #1* is now regarded as a modern classic. The Ultimate label was devised as a way to revitalize the most popular characters for a new millennium, making them accessible to a younger generation of readers who could jump on board without having to catch up on decades of continuity. In *Ultimate Spider-Man #1*, writer Brian Michael Bendis and artists Mark Bagley and Art Thibert retell the web-slinger's classic origin, shifting the fateful moment to Osborn Industries, where Peter Parker is accidentally bitten by an experimental radioactive spider. The issue also reveals that Peter's birth parents had died in a plane crash.

The Ultimate Universe proved to be a huge hit with fans, and these updated incarnations of Marvel's best-loved characters would become the go-to resource for the filmmakers of the Marvel Cinematic Universe. ∎

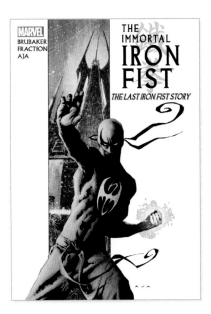

Cover artist: David Aja **Writers:** Ed Brubaker, Matt Fraction **Pencilers:** David Aja, Travel Foreman **Inkers:** David Aja, Derek Fridolfs **Editor:** Warren Simons

Cover artists: Chris Bachalo, Tim Townsend **Writer:** Jason Aaron **Penciler:** Chris Bachalo **Inkers:** Tim Townsend, Al Vey, Mark Irwin **Editors:** Nick Lowe, Charles Beacham

Cover artist: Amy Reeder **Writer:** Brandon Montclare, Amy Reeder **Penciler/Inker:** Natacha Bustos **Editor:** Mark Paniccia, Emily Shaw

Immortal Iron Fist #1
January 2007

Doctor Strange #1
January 2016

Moon Girl and Devil Dinosaur #1
January 2016

Marvel assembled a top creative team for Immortal Iron Fist, a title that expanded on the mythology of the character and revealed that Danny Rand was one of many people to have held the power of the Iron Fist.

Immortal Iron Fist #1 featured the first appearance of previous Iron Fist Orson Randall, who had held the role in the early part of the 20th century before being traumatized by his experience in World War I. As Danny Rand is relentlessly attacked by a Hydra legion in Manhattan, a Bangkok-based Randall makes his reluctant entrance at the end of the issue as a target of the fearsome martial artist Davos, a recurring foe of Rand's.

The series was nominated for an Eisner Award for Best New Series, with writer Ed Brubaker's work earning him a Best Writer win. Gritty, stylish artwork from David Aja and Travel Foreman also helped make *Immortal Iron Fist* a modern classic and establish the character as a Marvel mainstay. ▪

Following on from the "Secret Wars" event and also in the buildup to the title character's first solo movie, *Doctor Strange* #1 was the first in a relaunch of the Sorcerer Supreme's adventures. Written by award-winning scribe Jason Aaron with evocative, "otherworldly" pencils from Chris Bachalo, the book was part of Marvel's "All-New All-Different" initiative and confronted the good Doctor with a wholly unique and traumatizing dilemma.

"The Way of the Weird" sees Doctor Strange dealing on a daily basis with bizarre demons and otherdimensional phenomena that ordinary people just could not see. Strange discovered that the increase in weird, mystical activity might actually be a result of his continual use of magic and that there was always a cost for what he did. The series would later see Strange struggling to defeat the Empirikul, a technologically superior alien adversary determined to wipe magic from the face of the universe. ▪

Making her impressive debut in *Moon Girl and Devil Dinosaur* #1, Moon Girl may have been a brand-new character, but the title had plenty of Marvel legacy behind it. In 1978, Jack Kirby created the original Devil Dinosaur and his companion Moon Boy, whose fantastical adventures took place on a primeval alternate Earth. Editor Mark Paniccia was a fan of the Devil Dinosaur character and was looking for a way to use him in a modern context, and so Moon Girl was born.

An elementary school super-genius, Lunella Lafayette is trying to solve the world's problems with her extraordinary inventions when she inadvertently transports a ferocious Tyrannosaurus rex to her own time. After a tricky introduction, the two become BFFs in remarkably short order. Writers Brandon Montclare and Amy Reeder, with artist Natacha Bustos, get the style and tone spot-on for this delightful, heartwarming, all-ages title featuring an unlikely but irresistible team-up. ▪

Index

Page numbers in **bold** refer to main comic entries